Craft

Craft

techniques & projects

DK

LONDON, NEW YORK, MUNICH, MELBOURNE, and DELHI

Senior Editors Corinne Masciocchi, Hilary Mandleberg
Senior Art Editors Jane Ewart, Glenda Fisher
Project Art Editor Hannah Moore
Senior Production Editor Jennifer Murray
Senior Production Controller Seyhan Esen
Photographer Ruth Jenkinson
Photographic Assistant Carly Churchill
Creative Technical Support Sonia Charbonnier
Managing Editor Penny Smith
Managing Art Editor Marianne Markham
Publishers Mary Ling, Peggy Vance
Art Director Jane Bull

DK INDIA
Project Editor Charis Bhagianathan
Art Editor Prashant Kumar
Assistant Editor Swati Mittal
Assistant Art Editors Vikas Sachdeva,
Zaurin Thoidingjam, Anamica Roy
Managing Editor Glenda Fernandes
Managing Art Editor Navidita Thapa
DTP Manager Sunil Sharma
Senior DTP Designers Dheeraj Arora, Jagtar Singh
DTP Designers Sourabh Challariya, Anurag Trivedi

First published in Great Britain in 2012 by
Dorling Kindersley Limited
80 Strand
London WC2R 0RL

Penguin Group (UK)
4 6 8 10 9 7 5 3
008-181458-Oct/2012

A CIP catalogue record is available from the British Library

ISBN 978 1 4093 8390 1

Printed and bound in China by Hung Hing

Discover more at **www.dk.com**

Contents

Introduction

WHETHER YOU ARE A BEGINNER OR A SEASONED CRAFTSPERSON, THERE IS ALWAYS

SOMETHING NEW TO LEARN. THIS EXTENSIVE CRAFT COLLECTION PROVIDES A

VALUABLE REFERENCE FOR A WIDE RANGE OF TECHNIQUES AND IT'S THE PERFECT WAY

TO SAMPLE NEW CRAFTS. WHETHER YOU HAVE A PENCHANT FOR PAPER AND PAINT,

FABRIC AND THREAD, WOOD, WAX, OR WIRE, THERE'LL BE SOMETHING IN THIS BOOK TO

INSPIRE AND INSTRUCT YOU ON YOUR CRAFTING JOURNEY.

Crafting allows you to explore your creative side and it can be very addictive. Once you see how easy and satisfying it can be to make things yourself, you'll want to do it again and again. There is a wholesome satisfaction in making something from scratch, whether it's for yourself or for a loved one. The creative process can be just as fulfilling as the finished result – though it does help if the thing you have made is something to be proud of.

With this in mind, the techniques outlined in this book have been carefully written and illustrated in order to help build your skills and your confidence – and there is a dazzling array of inspirational projects, each broken down into manageable steps to help you produce perfect results. To help you find the crafts to suit you, the book is divided into six chapters. With clear illustrations throughout and each project explained step-by-step, you'll be guided through every stage, so you can feel confident in attempting an unfamiliar craft and acquiring a new skill.

None of the projects requires any particular expertise, most can be done without having to spend money on specialist tools or equipment, and all of them can be done at home using everyday resources. The projects have been devised by a team of talented and experienced craftspeople, and each project has been tried and tested to ensure a great outcome.

To make sure you get the best results, get organized. It's a good idea to read through your chosen project thoroughly before you begin, then make sure you gather all the tools and materials you will need. Some projects can be messy, so it's advisable not to wear your best clothes but to cover up with an old shirt or overalls. The same applies to your work surfaces: use old newspapers or plastic sheeting to cover the work table as certain concoctions – paints, dyes, and melted wax among others – might stain or damage surfaces they come into contact with.

Take your time, follow the instructions carefully, and before you know it you'll have created something to be proud of: something to grace your home, perhaps, something to wear, or something to give away as a present. Best of all is the enjoyment of making and the satisfaction of developing new skills or unearthing hidden talents. Embrace your creativity!

Textile crafts

Textile crafts

Fabric is a wonderful way to add colour, texture, and interest to your home and your wardrobe. Textile crafts embrace a wide range of diverse disciplines, from dyeing and decorating to stitching, weaving, and felting, so there are plenty of methods here to inspire you.

This chapter shows you simple ways to make decorative and practical items using fabric for your home – as well as one-off items of clothing. There are a number of ways to decorate and manipulate fabric and fibres without using specialist equipment or expensive materials and, once you've familiarized yourself with the techniques, there's plenty of scope to apply your own creativity. Discover how exciting it can be to dunk fabric into a dye bath and see it emerge, transformed into a kaleidoscope of colour. Find out how you can apply fabric paints in a variety of ways to a number of different items, such as a plain cook's apron or tea towel. A length of fabric can be decorated with eye-catching motifs then, with some simple stitching – no complicated sewing skills are required – made into a shoe bag, cushion cover, or sarong.

Patchwork and appliqué are popular crafts and you need only the most basic sewing skills – and a sewing machine – to make an heirloom bedspread or a cosy throw. A dazzling choice of fabrics is available to buy in the shops or online – though if you're already a seasoned stitcher, you will no doubt have suitable scraps of fabrics lurking in a drawer or work basket, destined to be joined together to make a pretty patchwork. While you have your sewing machine at the ready, try your hand at ribbon weaving, or if you prefer hand-sewing, embellish a plain cardigan with beads.

The pages on wet felting, needle felting, and upholstery provide an introduction to crafts that you might have thought were too complex to attempt, but the illustrated techniques and step-by-step projects demystify the processes involved, allowing you to try out these crafts for yourself.

Textile crafts TOOLS AND MATERIALS

Crafting with textiles allows you to really put your creativity to the test: immerse yourself in the colours, textures, and patterns that textiles have to offer. You'll probably already have most of the tools and materials listed here. A sewing machine comes in handy for larger projects, but is not a must.

Dip-dyeing and tie-dyeing

Measuring jug This is essential for measuring both dry ingredients such as salt, and wet ingredients like water. A glass jug is less likely to become stained with dye than a plastic one.

Plastic container A medium-size or large plastic tub is useful for immersing fabric in dye solution and is a better option than using the kitchen sink, which might become stained.

Dyes Cold water dyes are suitable for dyeing natural fabrics such as cotton, linen, and silk. Mix the powder according to the instructions on the packet.

Fabrics Choose 100% cotton, linen, or silk. Wash in hot soapy water and rinse before dyeing to remove any dressing.

Rubber bands and string Both of these are useful for tying fabric prior to dyeing to create patterned effects.

Fabric marbling

Cotton fabric White cotton absorbs dye best. Aim for 100% cotton and avoid poly-cotton mixes as the dyes will not adhere to them successfully.

Marbling dyes These dyes come in a variety of colours with a pipette or dropper for easy application. Use two or three colours at a time for best results.

Marbling combs and stylus These tools are used on the floating dye to achieve a variety of marbled effects. If you can't get hold of a marbling comb, use an ordinary wide-toothed comb instead.

Marbling size Usually sold as a powder, it is added to water to create a jelly-like base on which to drop marbling dyes, so that they float on the surface.

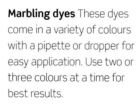

Plastic tray This needs to be wide enough to accommodate the fabric when it is laid out flat.

Fabric painting

Fabric paint pens Use these to outline edges and define shapes once the main design is complete.

Dressmaker's carbon paper Allows you to transfer designs on your chosen fabric. If the lines are too faint, go over them with a pencil.

Fabric paints These are available in a wide range of colours that can be mixed to create your own shades.

Artist's paintbrushes You'll need good-quality paintbrushes in a range of sizes to add colour and detail to designs.

Block printing

Fabric paints Specially formulated fabric paints come in small jars. Colours are intermixable and can usually be "fixed" onto fabric by pressing with a hot iron – check the instructions on the garment's label.

Wooden blocks These provide a firm base for homemade printing blocks. Children's wooden building bricks are ideal.

Potatoes The cut surface of a potato provides an excellent surface for printing. Large potatoes are best, as they are easy to cut and hold.

Craft foam This foam rubber, available in small sheets, can be cut with scissors or a craft knife and is used to create block printing shapes.

Silk painting

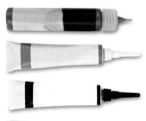

Iron-fixed outliner (gutta) This comes in a squeezy bottle or metal tube in black, clear, and a range of metallic colours. You can also buy fine nibs to draw thinner lines.

Silk fabric This can be bought in a range of weights and a variety of sizes. With ready-rolled hems, the fabric can be used as a scarf. Ponge 5 is a popular weight.

Iron-fixed silk paints All colours can be mixed using cyan, magenta, yellow, and black. Ready-mixed colours are also available.

Frame and pins Used to keep the fabric taut while painting, frames come in a variety of shapes and sizes. Use multiple-pronged pins to secure the fabric to the frame.

Vanishing fabric marker pen This is used for tracing designs on silk. The ink is usually purple and fades in sunlight.

Salt You can use any type of salt, from table salt to rock salt, to create textures on damp silk.

Silkscreening

Masking tape This is used to mask off the area between the edge of the filler and the frame before you start silkscreen printing.

Old toothbrush Helps remove drawing fluid from the mesh of the frame.

Drawing fluid This special ink is used for "drawing" the design onto the mesh of the frame.

Silkscreen printing frame with mesh The frame should be large enough to contain the image, with some room to spare around it. Some frames are hinged but you don't need a hinged frame when printing on fabric.

Screen filler This specialist product is applied once the drawing fluid is dry to mask out the areas you do not wish to print.

Fine paintbrushes You'll need a selection of good-quality fine paintbrushes.

Squeegee Use a squeegee or plastic spreader to apply the screen filler and silkscreening inks to the mesh.

Fabric screen printing inks These are special paints for silkscreen printing on fabric.

Fabric stencilling

Cardboard A piece of cardboard is useful to protect the work surface and absorb excess paint.

Stencil brushes These short, stubby brushes are used specifically for stencilling. Make sure you have a selection of sizes.

Freezer paper This special paper is coated with plastic on one side and is used for creating stencils. Make sure you buy freezer paper and not wax paper, which is coated on both sides.

Fabric paints These are special paints for use on fabric. Use them as they come or mix to achieve the desired colour.

Batik

Cold batik wax This is a water-based wax that can be used cold and is suitable for beginners. Stir well before using.

Wax-Out liquid This emulsifying liquid is diluted with warm water and used to remove wax from the completed piece of batik.

Tjanting This has a metal reservoir with a spout affixed to a wooden handle and is used to apply lines of wax. They come in various sizes.

Brushes You'll need several brushes. Chinese calligraphy brushes make great wax brushes. A foam brush, or a sponge, is useful for applying wax to larger areas of fabric.

Patchwork

Patchwork ruler This wide see-through ruler has precise markings for measuring strips, squares, and other geometric shapes. It is used in conjunction with a rotary cutter.

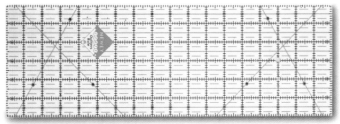

Waddings Waddings are usually either wool, cotton, or polyester. Wool and cotton shrink, so wash them before using.

Cutting shears Used for cutting large pieces of fabric, the length of the blade can vary from 20 to 30cm (8 to 12in).

Rotary cutter This tool has a circular blade that rotates as the cutter is pushed or pulled across the fabric. It can be used freehand but is designed to be used against the edge of a patchwork ruler.

Appliqué

Bonding web This web of special glue on a paper backing is ironed onto the back of appliqué fabric to enable the appliqué to be bonded in place.

Decorations Buttons, beads, and sequins are just some of the decorations you can use to embellish any appliqué project. If using beads or other decorations on washable items, make sure they are colourfast.

Bead embroidery

Embroidery hoop This is used to keep fabric taut while working embroidery or other forms of needlework. Embroidery hoops are made of wood, plastic, or metal.

Water-soluble pen A water-soluble pen looks like an ordinary felt-tip pen but the ink disappears when sprayed or dabbed with water. It is useful for tracing or marking designs on fabric.

Water spray This is useful for removing traces of water-soluble pen.

Ribbon weaving

Interfacing This can be woven or non-woven, iron-on, or sew-in. Available in white, black, or grey. Choose a colour to match your project.

Ribbons Available in various widths and colours, ribbons can be made from sheer fabric to heavy velvet. Wire-edged ribbons allow the ribbon to hold a shape.

Baking paper Lay a sheet of silicone baking paper on the adhesive side of iron-on interfacing before ironing to protect the iron and ironing board from damage.

Felting

Bamboo blind Holds fleece fibres while they are being rubbed, creating added friction and aiding the felting process.

Wool top Carded merino wool top or roving has a fine crimp and felts easily. It can be bought as a carded rope of fleece fibre that has been washed and dyed, and is ready for use.

Foam block You'll need a fairly deep block of foam sponge when dry needle-felting to work the fleece fibres on.

Netting Wrap fleece fibres in a piece of curtain netting to keep the felt in place when rubbing.

Soap solution dispenser A recycled plastic soup or milk carton with small holes punched into the lid will enable you to sprinkle water onto fibres without drenching them.

Felting needles These long, sharp, barbed needles compress and mould a mass of dry fleece fibres into 3D shapes by poking the fibres into each other so that they tangle together. Use a multi-needle tool to work over a large area; for smaller projects, use a single-needle tool.

Soap and soap solution A small handful of pure soap flakes dissolved in hot water makes a solution for dampening fleece. Olive oil soap brushed over felt aids the felting process and is low lather, but any soap will do.

Bubble wrap Can be used as a template instead of heavy-duty plastic sheeting, or to lay fleece fibres on instead of netting. It's also useful to lay on top of wetted fleece fibres, to help spread moisture evenly and release air.

Hand carders Use carders to blend fibres and straighten out unruly tufts of fleece. They come as a pair. The edge nearest the handle is called the "heel" and the opposite edge is the "toe".

Plastic sheeting or foam carpet underlay Use either material to create templates that prevent layers of wool from bonding to each other (see pp.72–73 for more information). Cut the template about 20% larger than the size of the finished piece to allow for shrinkage.

Upholstery

Wooden mallet and ripping chisel Used for stripping out old upholstery tacks and materials.

Tack lifter and staple lifter Used for lifting and removing tacks and staples.

Black and white or jute webbing When woven together, webbing forms a firm foundation for a seat.

Improved tacks These have larger heads than fine tacks and are used to fix the webbing and loosely woven materials, such as hessian and scrim.

Fine tacks Have small, finer heads and are used when fitting the calico, bottoming cloth, and top fabric.

Magnetic tack hammer This small-headed hammer has a magnetic end, which is ideal for picking up tacks.

Hessian Use medium-weight hessian for covering webbing and springs.

Medium twine or nylon twine Used to hold the stuffing in place.

Needles 30cm (12in) double-ended bayonet needle for stitching edges.

25cm (10in) round-point needle for buttoning.

12.5cm (5in) curved spring needle for stitching in springs and stitching through webbing.

Selection of smaller curved needles for stitching.

Web strainer A tool used to tension the webbing firmly enough to take your weight.

Regulator Used for moving the hair fillings into position.

Curled animal hair or coir fibre Used as a first stuffing.

Cotton or wool felt Used as a second stuffing.

Scrim Use 9oz weight for covering loose fillings ready for stitching.

Skin wadding A finer second stuffing that helps to stop animal hair working through the top fabrics.

Calico or fire-retardant interliner/barrier cloth Used to enclose the stuffings and to form the finished shape.

Top fabric Must comply with UK Fire Regulations, depending on the age of the chair frame being used.

Bottoming cloth Used as a dust cover to neaten and enclose all tacks and raw edges.

Dip-dyeing TECHNIQUES

The most straightforward dip-dyeing techniques involve natural fabrics – cotton, linen, and silk – with dyes that can be mixed using hot tap water. Dyeing fabrics produces attractive results, so try your hand at dyeing household linens such as sheets and pillowcases, or clothing such as T-shirts and socks. For best results when using new fabrics, wash first to remove the "dressing" in the fabric as this will prevent the dye from penetrating the fibres.

Preparing the dye bath

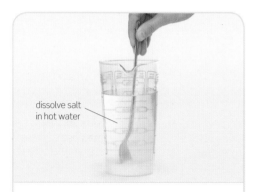

dissolve salt in hot water

dissolve dye in water

1 Always read the dye manufacturer's instructions. For dyes that require the addition of salt, dissolve the salt in very hot tap water.

2 Dissolve the sachet of dye powder in the specified amount of water, stirring until dissolved. For large amounts of fabric, you may need more than one sachet.

3 Combine the salt solution and the dye in a large plastic tub. Top up with enough water to cover the fabric, following the instructions on the packet.

Dyeing fabric

1 If the item is new, wash it to remove all traces of dressing, otherwise, just wet it. Place the damp item in the prepared dye solution, making sure it is completely submerged.

2 Move the fabric in the dye from time to time. It's best to use a metal or plastic spoon, or an old wooden spoon, as the wood will become permanently stained with dye.

3 After the specified time, remove the item from the dye bath, handling it with rubber gloves to prevent your hands from staining. Rinse thoroughly in cold water, then wash with hot water and detergent.

Dip-dyeing

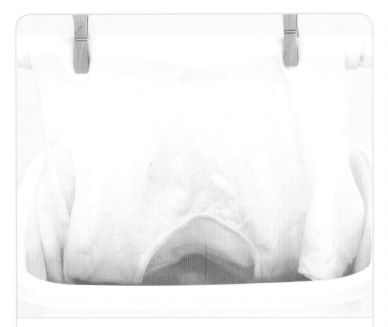

1 Instead of dyeing an item one colour all over, submerge only part of it in the dye. Suspend the item by rolling it around a stick, such as a bamboo pole, and hold it in place with pegs. Rest the pole on the rim of the tub. If you allow the fabric to drape over the side of the tub, the dye will seep up into the damp fabric.

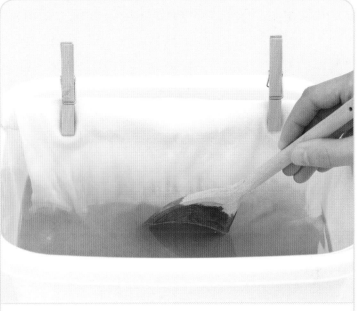

2 Stir the dye from time to time, carefully moving the fabric as you do so to ensure an even result. After the specified time, rinse in cold water until the water runs clear.

3 If you wish, you can mix up a second colour and dip the undyed portion in this dye. Again, suspend the item over the dye bath, keeping the part you do not wish to dye clear of the sides of the tub.

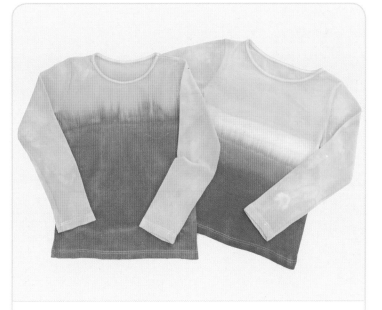

4 By carefully choosing colour combinations, you can create some interesting effects. Here, yellow and red dyes have been used. On one T-shirt the dyes have been allowed to overlap slightly, while on the other, an undyed band between the two has been left.

Dip-dyed café curtain PROJECT

With just one sachet of dye you can create subtle colour effects – perfect for a café curtain. If you're dyeing an existing curtain with a dye suitable for natural fabrics, check the fibre content of your curtain before embarking on the dyeing process. Alternatively, you can make your own curtain from cotton muslin. Make sure you stitch it with 100% cotton thread so that both the fabric and the thread take up the colour.

YOU WILL NEED

- cotton curtain
- fabric detergent
- bamboo, wooden, or plastic pole
- measuring jug
- salt, if needed (check instructions on dye packet)
- cold-water fabric dye
- plastic tub or other suitable container
- rubber gloves
- metal, plastic, or old wooden spoon

1 Wash the curtain and leave it damp. Slip a pole into the casing at the top of the curtain.

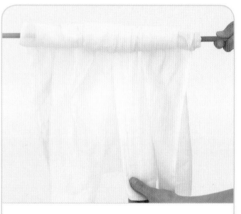

2 Roll the fabric around the pole, leaving the bottom section – about a quarter of the total length of the curtain – free.

3 Prepare the dye according to the manufacturer's instructions and pour it in the tub. Wearing rubber gloves, submerge the bottom section of the curtain in the dye bath for 20 minutes, resting the pole across the rim of the tub. Stir the dye gently from time to time to ensure even coverage.

4 After 20 minutes, unroll another length of the curtain so that about one-third is submerged in the dye. Soak for a further 20 minutes, then unroll a little more, so that about three-quarters of the curtain is in the dye. Soak for a further 20 minutes.

5 Remove the curtain from the dye and remove the pole. Rinse the curtain thoroughly in cold water, then wash in hot water and detergent, following the manufacturer's instructions. Iron before hanging.

Tie-dyeing TECHNIQUES

Tie-dyeing is an easy method of creating colourful patterns on clothing and home furnishings. For best results, use pure cotton fabrics and cold-water dyes. There are some tried-and-tested techniques of folding and tying the fabric to produce patterns such as circles and stripes. If you decide to use more than one colour, dye the lighter colour first.

Choosing items to dye

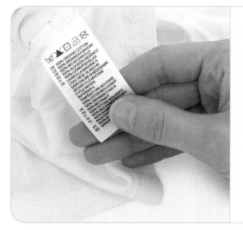

Check the label on the garment: for cold-water dyeing, choose items that are 100% cotton, linen, or silk. Wash the fabric first in hot water and detergent to remove the dressing.

Preparing the dye bath

Mix the dye according to the manufacturer's instructions and pour it into a container large enough to hold the fabric being dyed.

Creating a striped effect

1 To create a striped pattern, place the fabric on a flat work surface. Starting at one edge, pleat the fabric into concertina folds.

2 Bind the pleated fabric tightly using lengths of string. Bind at intervals along the concertina folds.

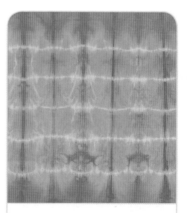

3 Submerge the fabric in the dye (in this case, deep pink) for the recommended time, stirring occasionally and keeping the fabric submerged. Remove from the dye, rinse in cold water until the water runs clear, then remove the strings.

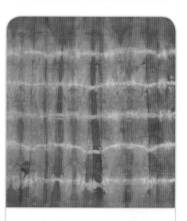

4 If you wish, you can pleat and bind the fabric again, and dye it a second colour. In this case blue was used, creating purple patches where the blue dye has overdyed the pink stripes.

Creating large and small circle motifs

marble

1 For a large circle motif, place a marble in the centre of the fabric and bind around the base with string to hold it in place. Pull the fabric into a cone shape with the marble at its tip, then bind at intervals.

2 For smaller circle motifs, tie single marbles tightly into the fabric using lengths of string. Submerge the fabric in the dye bath for the recommended time.

3 Remove the fabric from the dye and rinse thoroughly in cold water, then remove the strings and marbles. When the fabric is opened out, you will see the large and small circle motifs.

Creating a multicoloured swirl effect

1 Place the fabric on a flat work surface, pinch the centre, and twist it in a circular motion to form a spiral.

2 Secure the twisted fabric tightly with two rubber bands crossing in the centre and dividing the fabric into four sections.

3 Mix up dye in two or more colours – here, four different colours have been used. Instead of submerging the fabric in the dye, use a paintbrush to apply a different colour to each section. Apply the dye liberally and push it into the folds. Wear rubber gloves to avoid staining your fingers.

4 Place the dyed fabric in a plastic bag, seal, and leave for 24 hours (or according to the manufacturer's instructions), then rinse thoroughly in cold water and remove the rubber bands to reveal a colourful swirl pattern.

Tie-dyed T-shirt PROJECT

Choose a T-shirt that is 100% cotton. (Note that if the thread used to stitch the garment is made from synthetic fibres, it will not absorb the dye and will retain its original colour.) Wash the T-shirt before dyeing and leave it damp. The T-shirt shown here has been dyed using pink and purple; you could choose your own combination of colours, bearing in mind that, where colours overlap, they'll produce a third colour. For example, yellow and blue overlapping will make green.

YOU WILL NEED
- plain white cotton T-shirt
- string
- scissors
- measuring jug
- cold-water fabric dyes in pink and purple
- plastic tub or other suitable container
- rubber gloves
- metal, plastic, or old wooden spoon
- detergent

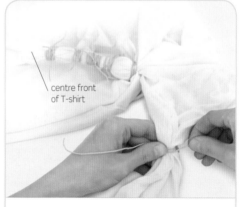

centre front of T-shirt

1 Find the centre front of the T-shirt and pull it up to form a cone shape. Starting at the tip of the cone, bind it at intervals with lengths of string. Bind the top of each sleeve in the same way.

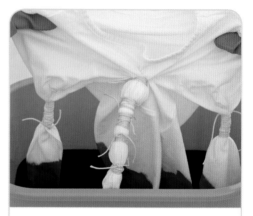

2 Prepare the pink dye and pour it into the tub, adding enough cold water to completely cover the garment. Wearing rubber gloves, submerge the T-shirt in the dye bath. Stir from time to time.

3 After 1 hour (or the recommended time), remove the T-shirt from the dye and rinse it in cold water until the water runs clear. Remove the strings. Discard the pink dye.

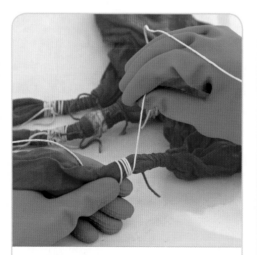

4 Repeat Step 1 to bind the front and the top of each sleeve again. Where the new strings are tied, the underlying colour will remain, so tie some strings around the white areas and some around the pink areas.

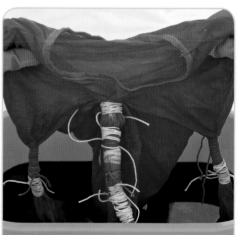

5 Prepare the purple dye and pour it into the tub, adding enough cold water to completely cover the garment. Submerge the T-shirt in the dye bath. After 1 hour, remove and rinse thoroughly in cold water.

6 Remove the strings and wash the T-shirt in hot water and detergent to fix the dye.

Fabric marbling TECHNIQUES

Fabric marbling requires patience and can get messy, so always make sure your work surfaces are properly protected. You'll need to experiment with various tools and colours before you settle on a pattern you like. Fabric marbling is similar to paper marbling, so if you enjoy this craft, turn to pp.102–05.

Preparing the bath

Follow the manufacturer's instructions to make a marbling bath. Dissolve 1 teaspoon of "size" in 1 litre (1¾pt) cold water in a large plastic tub and stir well. For best results, leave to set overnight or for at least two hours before using.

Skimming the surface of the bath

As the bath has been left to settle, you'll need to break the tension on the surface. Do this by skimming the surface with newspaper scrunched into a ball. You'll also need to do this every time you apply fresh dyes.

Adding colour and creating patterns

1 Add a few drops of marbling dye on the surface of the bath so that it is completely covered with dye, then skim the surface with newspaper.

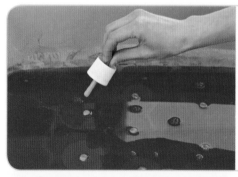

2 Add more drops of the first colour again to cover the surface, then dot a second colour onto the surface in a regular or random arrangement.

3 To create swirls, draw a marbling comb across the surface, from one edge of the tray to the other, pulling the dyes to create a wavy marbled effect.

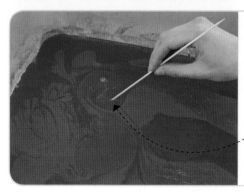

4 Use a stylus, the end of a paintbrush, or other pointed implement to manipulate the colours and create individual swirls.

Experimenting with patterns

The bath solution improves the more you use it, so view your first few attempts as experiments. Always pre-wash the cotton fabric to make it more absorbent and practise with remnants of fabric, adding more dyes, skimming, and then printing to get an understanding of the patterns that can be created. Always wear rubber gloves to protect your hands from staining.

Marbling the fabric

1 Once you're happy with the marbled effect, lay the fabric onto the surface in one go, patting it gently to ensure there are no creases. Do not move the fabric as this will spoil the pattern.

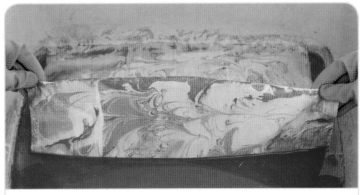

2 Holding on to two corners, lift the fabric up swiftly, holding it over the tub to allow excess water and ink to drip off.

Fixing the colour

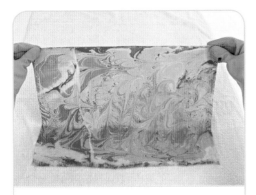

1 Leave the fabric to dry face up flat on a towel. Don't hang it up or wash it at this stage as the colours may run.

2 When the fabric is dry, it will be stiff due to the residue from the bath. Rinse under cold running water, then hang up to dry.

3 To fix the colour, iron the fabric on a medium setting. The fabric can now be washed.

Marbled napkins PROJECT

The unpredictability of marbling is what makes it such a fun craft. Each time you manipulate the dyes, new patterns emerge. If you don't like the pattern, simply skim off the dyes with newspaper and start again. If you like what you see, you can capture it on fabric forever. This introduction to fabric marbling shows you how to create a set of swirling marbled napkins.

YOU WILL NEED

- large shallow plastic tub
- measuring jug
- teaspoon
- marbling size
- newspaper
- blue and green marbling dyes
- marbling comb
- stylus or similar pointed implement
- rubber gloves
- 4 pre-washed white cotton napkins
- old towel
- iron

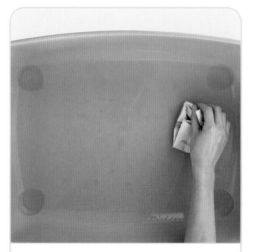

1 Make a marbling bath by dissolving 1 teaspoon of size in 1 litre (1¾pt) cold water in a tub. Leave to set overnight or for at least two hours. Skim the surface with a ball of newspaper to break the tension.

2 Dot a few drops of blue dye evenly across the surface of the bath. Skim the surface with newspaper before adding more blue dye. Then add a few drops of green dye in between the blue blocks of colour.

3 Draw a marbling comb across the surface of the bath, using a swift movement. If you want a more complex pattern, repeat the movement or use the stylus to create more swirls.

4 Wearing rubber gloves to protect your hands, carefully lower a napkin onto the surface of the bath. Pat it down gently then swiftly remove it. Repeat for the other napkins, skimming the bath and adding more dye each time.

5 Leave the napkins to dry face up flat on a towel, then rinse under cold running water. Hang up to dry, then iron on a medium setting to fix the dyes.

Fabric painting TECHNIQUES

Fabric paints are a permanent way to colour fabrics. They dry quite hard when applied but soften once the fabric has been washed. They can be mixed to create new shades or used straight from the pot, but it's best not to dilute them as you would water-based paints, as this reduces the pigmentation.

Preparing the fabric

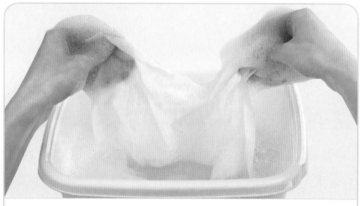

1 Always pre-wash the fabric to make it more absorbent. Rinse and hang up to dry.

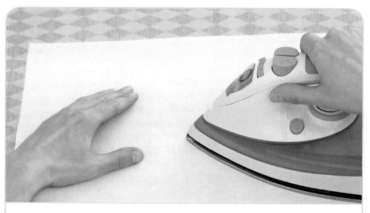

2 Once the fabric is dry, iron it to remove any creases. The surface of the fabric should be as smooth as possible, almost like a sheet of paper.

Transferring a template

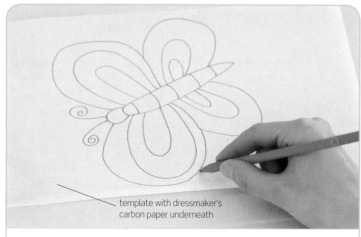

template with dressmaker's carbon paper underneath

1 Lay a sheet of dressmaker's carbon paper face down on the fabric and secure the template on top. Use a sharp pencil to trace over the template, then remove the carbon paper.

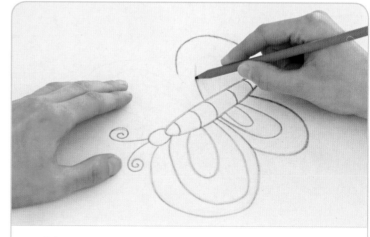

2 If the lines on the fabric are too faint, go over them again with a pencil.

Applying paint

sheet of paper

1 If you're painting onto a double layer of fabric (such as a bag for instance), place a sheet of paper inside the bag to prevent the paint seeping through to the layer underneath.

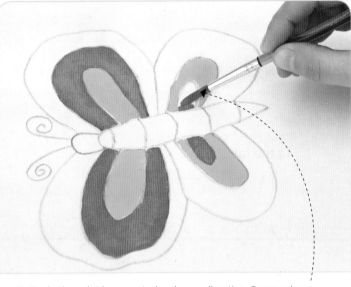

2 Apply the paint in even strokes in one direction. Some colours, especially lighter colours, may require more than one coat. Allow each coat to dry before applying a second.

3 Once the main design is complete and dry, add details with a fine paintbrush or draw on outlines with a fabric paint pen.

Fixing the colour

Leave the paint to dry for 24 hours. Place the fabric face down and iron on a high setting to fix the colours. The fabric can now be washed.

Shoe bag PROJECT

Shoe bags are great for when you're travelling or if you like to store your footwear away neatly. Customize a plain bag by painting on a shoe-themed motif, or draw designs that look like your own shoes, making them easy to identify. Use a mix of fabric paint and fabric paint pens – you can be as intricate as you like or stick to designing with block colours.

YOU WILL NEED

For the drawstring bag

- 1m x 69cm (40 x 27in) pre-washed white cotton
- cutting shears
- dressmaking pins
- sewing machine
- white thread
- 150cm (60in) ribbon
- iron

For the motif

- dressmaker's carbon paper
- pencil
- sheet of paper
- fabric paints
- paintbrushes
- fabric paint pen

1 To make the bag, fold the fabric over by 5cm (2in) along one long side. Pin and tack. Using a straight stitch on the sewing machine, sew along the edge of the fold to create the ribbon casing.

2 Fold the fabric in half lengthways with the casing on the outside. Sew the bottom and side edges using a straight stitch, stopping at the casing. Feed the ribbon through the casing then turn the bag to the right side.

3 Transfer the template on p.302 onto one side of the bag, following **transferring a template** on p.30. Make sure the design is centred.

4 Slip a sheet of paper inside the bag to protect the bottom layer. To prevent the colours merging, allow each colour to dry before painting the next. Add a second coat of paint if required.

5 Use the fabric paint pen to outline the shoe and draw on the swirls. Leave to dry for 24 hours.

6 Place the bag face down and iron on a high setting to fix the colours.

Block printing TECHNIQUES

Block printing was first practised in the Far East, centuries ago. Wooden blocks were carved with designs, coated with inks, and used to print onto fabric. Using a printing block allows you to make simple repeat patterns on fabric quickly and easily with the minimum of mess. You don't need any special materials to make a block: craft foam and a piece of wood, or even a potato can be used to create simple, eye-catching designs.

Making a foam block

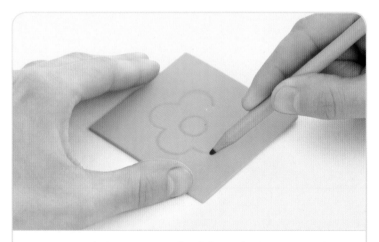

1 Draw your design on a scrap of craft foam. Simple, symmetrical shapes are the most effective and easiest as you don't have to worry about the fact that, when printed, your design comes out reversed.

2 Cut out the shape, using scissors. For a flower centre, as here, also cut away the centre of the flower using a craft knife over a cutting mat.

3 Apply an all-purpose glue to one side of the foam shape and stick the shape to a wooden block, such as a child's building brick.

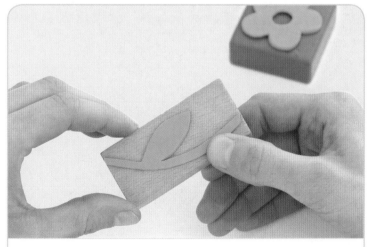

4 For a more complex motif that is to be printed in different colours, make separate printing blocks for each element – here, the second element is a one-piece leaf and stem.

Printing

1 Apply fabric paint to the entire surface of the motif. If the paint is fairly liquid, use a paintbrush; for thicker, stiffer paint, use a roller. To make sure you're happy with the design, test it on a scrap of fabric before printing a larger piece.

2 To make a print, place the paint-coated motif in position on the fabric and press down firmly, taking care not to move the printing block, or the image will be blurred.

3 Add further prints in different colours, as required, to complete the motif.

4 Allow the paint to dry completely, then fix the dye with a hot iron according to the manufacturer's instructions. Place a clean cloth over the fabric to prevent scorching.

Making a potato stamp

1 Slice a potato neatly in half, making sure the cut surface is level and smooth. Draw the shape onto one half using a felt-tip pen.

2 Cut around the outline of the shape using the tip of a sharp knife, then cut away excess potato around the shape.

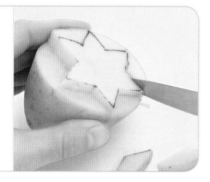

3 To add intricate detail to your design, use a knife or lino-cutting tool to gouge out small pieces of potato within the shape.

4 Wipe the surface of the potato with kitchen paper to remove any excess moisture, then apply fabric paint. Press the paint-coated surface firmly onto the fabric, hold for a few seconds, then remove.

Block-printed apron PROJECT

Decorate a plain apron with simple printed motifs, such as these stylized fish and citrus slices, to make a lovely gift for a cook. You can buy a plain apron or make one yourself from unbleached calico. Check the instructions on your fabric paints before you embark on the project: some paints work best on natural fabrics such as cotton or linen. You will probably be advised to wash and iron the fabric before applying the paints.

YOU WILL NEED

- paper
- pencil
- scissors
- craft knife
- cutting mat
- craft foam sheets
- all-purpose glue
- small wooden blocks
- fabric paints in blue, yellow, green, and white
- medium-size paintbrush
- cotton or linen apron
- clean cloth
- iron

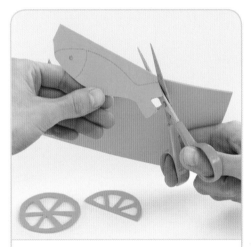

1 Trace the templates on p.303 onto paper, or draw your own. Cut out the shapes then place them on a piece of craft foam and draw around the outlines. Cut out each foam shape using scissors or a craft knife.

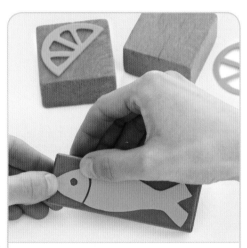

2 Glue each foam shape to a wooden block. For the fish, leave a gap between the body and the head.

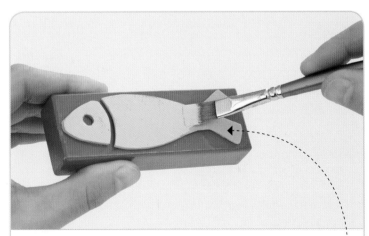

3 Apply fabric paint to the motif using a paintbrush. Most commercial fabric paints are intermixable: if, for example, the blue paint is too strong, you may wish to add a little white to make a paler shade.

4 To print a motif, place the paint-covered block in position on the apron, then press down to make your print. Reapply paint to the block before making second and subsequent prints.

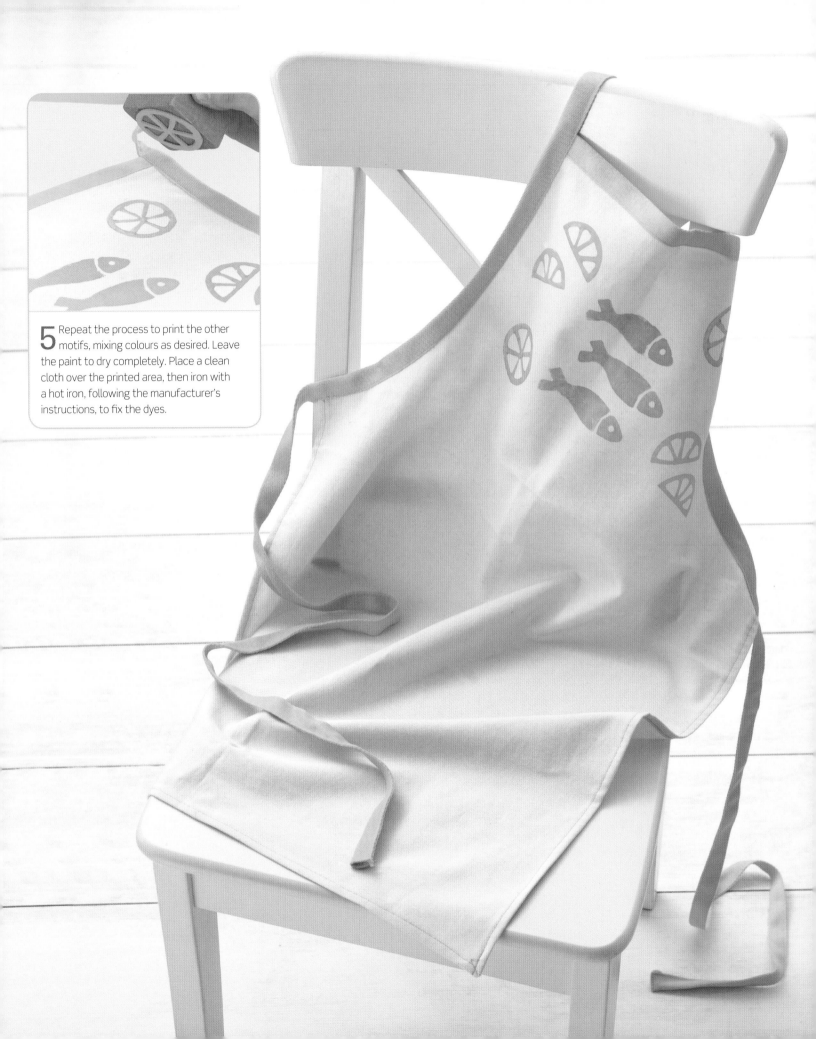

5 Repeat the process to print the other motifs, mixing colours as desired. Leave the paint to dry completely. Place a clean cloth over the printed area, then iron with a hot iron, following the manufacturer's instructions, to fix the dyes.

Silk painting TECHNIQUES

Silk painting is the traditional art of painting on silk. You stretch silk on a frame and use gutta (a resist) to draw a design before painting it with silk paint. You can also dye the whole piece of silk by dipping it into a bath of diluted paint. While the silk is wet, you can add a beautiful mottled effect by sprinkling it with salt crystals and leaving it to dry naturally.

Creating a mottled background colour

1 Mix the background colour in a bowl by adding a few drops of silk paint to water until you achieve the desired colour. Test the colour on a piece of paper to check how it will look.

2 Wearing rubber gloves, dip the silk into the bowl, moving it around so that the colour is evenly distributed. Leave to soak for a couple of minutes.

3 Remove the silk and gently squeeze out the excess paint. Spread the silk on a plastic sheet, then scrunch it up at intervals across its surface. Add a light sprinkling of salt crystals.

4 Leave the silk to dry naturally overnight. When it is completely dry, brush off the salt crystals; these will have produced a mottled effect. Fix the colour (see below).

Fixing the colour

1 Protect your ironing board with an old piece of cotton fabric and place the silk flat on top. Iron the silk for about three minutes per 30cm (12in) square on a medium heat to fix the colour.

2 Rinse the silk in a bowl of warm water to remove any loose colour and salt, then wash by hand using a non-biological detergent. Pat dry, then iron while damp for the best finish.

Stretching the silk

1 Starting in one corner and using three-pronged pins, pin the silk right side up to all four corners of the frame, ensuring the silk is taut and straight.

2 Pulling the silk taut again, pin halfway along each side, then pin quarters and eighths. You'll need a pin every 5 to 7.5cm (2 to 3in).

3 If using an embroidery hoop, place the silk between the hoops, with the inner hoop underneath. Press the outer hoop down and tighten it to pull the silk taut.

Painting a design

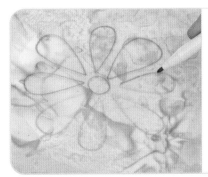

1 With the silk on the frame, draw your design onto it, using a vanishing pen. If you're working from a template, secure it underneath the silk using masking tape. Hold up to a window or over a light box and trace the design.

2 Remove the template and, using a coloured gutta outliner, draw over the traced design. Press the tube gently until a bead of outliner forms at the end of the nib, wipe on kitchen paper, and begin drawing. These lines will enhance your design.

3 Check that there are no gaps in the outlines, as the lines must contain the paint completely. Check by holding the silk up to the light. Touch up if necessary. Leave to dry naturally for about two hours, or use a hairdryer.

4 Using silk paint and a paintbrush, paint the design in your choice of colours. Dip the brush in a little paint and complete one area before moving on to the next. Set aside to dry naturally, or use a hairdryer, then remove the silk from the frame. Iron on the reverse to set the paint and gutta, following the manufacturer's instructions, then wash in warm water with a touch of detergent. Iron on the reverse while damp.

Butterfly scarf PROJECT

This gorgeous butterfly scarf would make a beautiful present for someone special. Create the patterned background first before outlining and painting the motifs using the traditional gutta method. If you wish, you can add extra swirls of silver to decorate your scarf, or change the size and placement of the butterflies to make your very own creation.

YOU WILL NEED

- rubber gloves
- bowl
- iron-fixed silk paints in yellow, blue, turquoise, pink, and purple
- 40 x 150cm (16 x 60in) plain white 100% silk scarf with rolled hems, Ponge 5 (lightweight), or similar
- plastic sheet
- salt crystals
- iron
- non-biological detergent
- paper
- pencil
- embroidery hoop
- masking tape
- vanishing fabric marker pen
- iron-fixed silver gutta outliner
- fine paintbrush (size 6 or similar)

1 Wearing rubber gloves, add one part yellow silk paint to 50 parts water in a small bowl. Add the silk and soak for a couple of minutes. Remove the silk, squeeze it gently, and spread it out roughly on a plastic sheet. Sprinkle over a small handful of salt to create a mottled background. Leave to dry then brush off the salt.

2 Iron the silk to fix the colour, then rinse in warm water to remove any loose colour and salt. Wash by hand then pat dry. Iron while damp to smooth out any creases.

3 Trace the template on p.303 onto a piece of paper, then see p.303 for where to place the butterflies. Secure the silk in the embroidery hoop. Tape the template to the underside of the silk and trace over the lines of the first butterfly with the vanishing marker pen.

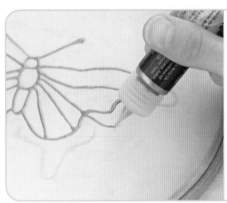

4 Remove the template and go over the lines with the silver outliner. Wait for the lines to dry and check they are solid.

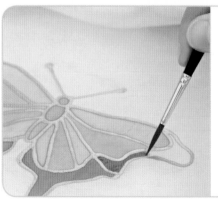

5 Paint within the outlines, using one colour at a time. Paint each section completely before moving on to the next. Repeat Steps 3, 4, and 5 until you have traced and painted all six butterflies onto the silk.

6 Once all the butterflies have been painted and the silk is dry, remove it from the frame. Iron it on the reverse to set the paint and the gutta, following the manufacturer's instructions. Wash in warm soapy water. Iron on the reverse while damp.

Silkscreening TECHNIQUES

If you want to print the same image lots of times, either on separate pieces of fabric or on the same piece of fabric, silkscreen printing is ideal. Some silkscreen printing techniques are quite complicated and time-consuming, but this version, using special drawing fluid and screen filler, is a great way to start. You can use it to create reasonably detailed images with a hand-printed feel which you can repeat time and time again.

Applying the image to the screen

Decide on the image you want to use. Here we are using a simple fish shape. Use a pencil to trace the image onto the mesh of the frame. To protect the work surface, place a jar lid underneath each corner of the frame to raise it by about 2cm (¾in), then go over the lines of your tracing using a fine paintbrush and drawing fluid. Leave to dry.

Applying the screen filler

1 Screen filler masks out the areas you do not want to print. Mix the filler until smooth and spoon it onto the mesh. Using a squeegee, apply a thin, even coat of filler over the screen. Do this in one go – if you try to reapply the filler, you may rub off some of the dried drawing fluid.

2 Leave the filler to dry in a horizontal position, making sure that the frame is still raised and that nothing touches the mesh while the filler is drying.

3 Once the filler is dry, spray cold water on both sides of the mesh using a shower head or hose fitted to a tap to remove the dried drawing fluid. If any stubborn bits remain, rub gently with an old toothbrush. Leave the filler to dry.

4 Mask any gaps between the edges of the filler and the frame with masking tape on the underside of the frame to avoid unwanted printing ink getting on your fabric.

Printing your fabric

padding cloth

fabric

1 Prepare the work surface by padding it with some cloth such as a smoothly folded old sheet; this will ensure there is good contact between the mesh of the frame and the fabric to be printed. Secure the fabric to the padding cloth using masking tape.

screen filler

printing ink

2 Place the frame in position on the fabric and hold it firmly. Pour about the same quantity of printing ink onto the mesh as the amount of screen filler used.

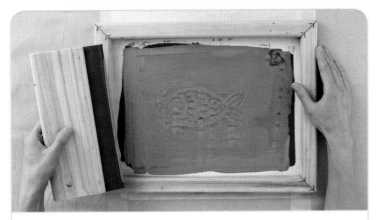

3 Hold the squeegee at a 45° angle and, using reasonable pressure, move it across the image from right to left in one smooth stroke. The image should be well coated with ink. Now pull the squeegee back over the image in the opposite direction.

4 Lift the frame immediately to reveal the silk-screened image. When the ink is dry, detach the printed fabric from the work surface. Place a pressing cloth over the image and, with the iron fairly hot, iron on each side for 3 to 4 minutes to fix the image and make it colourfast.

Silkscreened sarong PROJECT

This spotted cotton fabric has been printed with a classic pattern of a bird perched on a branch in a subtle shade of charcoal grey – a colour produced by mixing standard black and white silkscreen printing inks. The beauty of silkscreen printing is that once your image has been created, you can use it many times over with very little extra effort. To make the sarong longer and give it added appeal, we stitched a colourful border to the two short edges but you could leave it plain.

YOU WILL NEED

- pencil
- silkscreen printing frame
- 4 jar lids
- drawing fluid
- fine paintbrush
- screen filler
- squeegee
- old toothbrush
- masking tape
- scissors
- black and white screen printing inks
- water-soluble pen
- ruler
- 1 x 1.5m (1 x 1.6yd) washed and ironed pale grey polka dot woven cotton fabric
- cloth such as an old sheet
- iron and pressing cloth
- washing up liquid
- nylon scrubbing brush

1 Trace the bird template on p.304 onto the mesh. Raise the frame to protect the work surface. Go over the lines with drawing fluid, filling in the areas shown in grey on the template. Leave the fluid to dry.

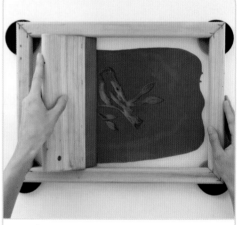

2 Apply the screen filler then, once dry, mask the gaps between the edges of the filler and the frame, as explained in **applying the screen filler** on pp.42–43.

3 Mix the black and white inks to make a dark grey, remembering that the final colour will look slightly darker once it has dried.

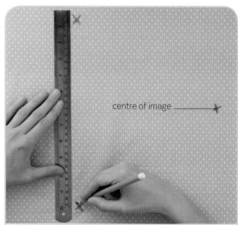

4 Using the water-soluble pen, mark the centre of each image, using the picture of the finished sarong as a guide. Each centre should be about 30cm (12in) from the centre of each of the images surrounding it.

centre of image

5 Print and fix the images as explained in **printing your fabric** on p.43, securing each section you are painting to the padded surface as you go. You'll need to work fairly quickly to make sure that the paint doesn't dry on the mesh and spoil your work. Keep the fabric flat while it is drying so that the wet images do not smudge. Clean your equipment as soon as possible.

Fabric stencilling TECHNIQUES

Stencilling is a really quick and easy way to produce your own bold and quirky designs on fabric and textile items. If you're just starting out, it's sensible to choose a plain, light-coloured fabric and a simple, one-colour design. Once you've learned the basics, you may want to experiment with printing on patterned or darker fabrics, using more intricate images, or building up your image in different layers and using two or more colours.

Cutting and applying a stencil

1 Select the image you want to use for your stencil. For this example, we are using a simple computer-drawn flower head and circle. Cut out a piece of freezer paper that is large enough to leave about 2.5cm (1in) all around the design to make sure that you do not get any paint on the fabric when you come to brush it on.

freezer paper

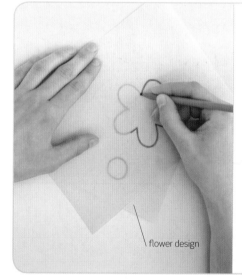

2 Place the freezer paper over the design so that the matt (non-glossy) side is uppermost. Trace the design onto the freezer paper using a pencil.

flower design

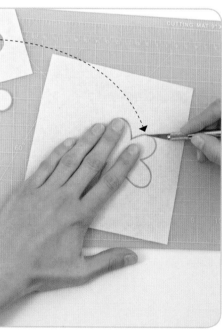

3 Cut out the design carefully, using a craft knife and cutting mat. For the main flower stencil, it is the area surrounding the actual flower head that will form the stencil, so keep this part intact. For the flower centre, you'll need to keep the cut-out circle intact.

4 Position the main stencil and the flower centre onto pressed fabric, making sure the glossy side of the paper is facing downwards. With the iron in the dry mode and on a medium setting, press the stencil onto the fabric, taking particular care to make sure that the edges are well stuck down.

Applying fabric paint

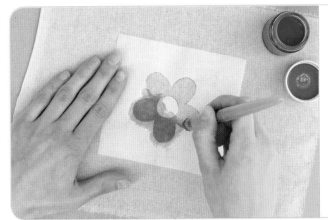

1 Place a sheet of cardboard underneath the fabric. Using a stencil brush, dab the paint over the stencil. Use a small amount of paint at a time and take particular care round the edges. Leave the image to dry thoroughly. If necessary, apply a second coat of paint.

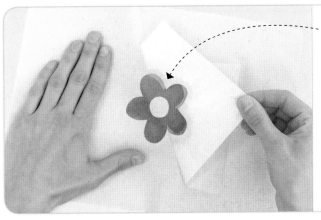

2 Once the image is dry, peel the two pieces of freezer paper away. They should not leave any sticky residue.

Ironing to fix paint

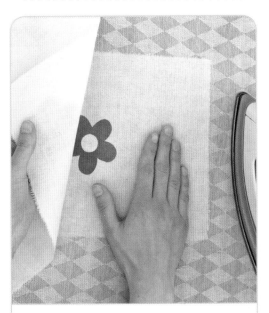

Check the instructions that come with your fabric paints on how to fix the paint. You will normally need to place a pressing cloth over the image and, with the iron set in the dry mode and on the maximum heat for the fabric, iron over the image for one to two minutes.

Masking for second colour and painting

1 To stencil the flower centre in a second colour, cut the flower centre from a piece of freezer paper, leaving a generous frame all round. Position the paper over the flower, aligning the centres.

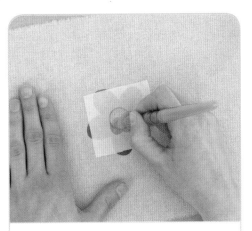

2 Place a sheet of cardboard underneath the fabric and, using the stencil brush, dab the paint over the stencil and leave to dry.

3 Peel away the freezer paper to reveal the finished image and fix the paint, following **ironing to fix paint**, above.

Stencilled tea towel PROJECT

This pure white linen tea towel has become home to six cheerful cups and saucers stencilled in bold shades of red and blue. The basic shape is the same for each teacup but each features different colours and decorations. Choose one of each design as we have done here, or put together your own unique combination. The teacups use only three colours – red, white, and blue – which are mixed to create different shades.

YOU WILL NEED

- 26 x 48cm (10¼ x 19in) piece of freezer paper
- ruler
- scissors
- craft knife
- cutting mat
- hole punch (either single or double-hole)
- plain white cotton tea towel
- fabric paints in bright blue, bright red, and white
- palette
- stencil brushes
- iron and pressing cloth

1 Cut out six cup and saucer stencils from freezer paper using the templates on p.304. Cut out one flower head and one flower centre stencil. Then cut out five stars, one border, four stripes, and one heart (keeping the heart surround as well). Using the hole punch, punch out 15 small freezer paper spots. Arrange the cup and saucer stencils in two even columns on the front of the tea towel and iron them in position. Iron on the stars, spots, flower head, border, stripes, and heart.

2 Use a palette to mix the fabric paints. Using a clean brush for each colour, dab on mid-blue paint to the star cup, bright red to the polka dot cup, bright blue to the flower cup, pale blue to the border cup, and creamy red to the striped and heart cups. Leave the paint to dry.

3 Peel off all the freezer paper. The star and polka dot designs are now complete. The other designs need further stencilling to add the second colours.

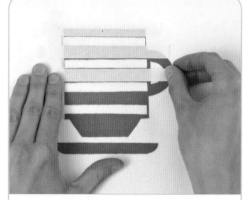

4 Place the flower centre stencil in the centre of the flower. For the border and striped designs, use strips of freezer paper to mask off all the areas where you do not want any paint. For the heart design, use the freezer paper from the cut-out heart to mask off the area around the heart.

5 Dab red paint on the flower centre and on the border of the teacup with a border. Dab very pale blue paint on the stripes of the striped teacup. Dab pale pink paint on the heart. Leave to dry, then remove the freezer paper and iron to fix the designs.

Batik TECHNIQUES

Batik is the art of painting fabric using a wax resist. Apply the wax using a paintbrush or tjanting, then paint over the fabric – the waxed areas will repel the paint and retain their base colour. You can use this technique to build up multiple layers of colour and to produce fabulous "crackle" effects. This technique can also be done using a wax pot and hot wax.

Stretching the fabric

Using three-pronged pins, pin all four corners of the fabric to a frame, ensuring the fabric is straight and taut. Next, pin halfway along each side, then pin at regular intervals so that there is a pin every 5 to 7.5cm (2 to 3in).

2 Using a fine paintbrush, paint cold wax over the traced lines: these lines will remain white on the finished piece. Leave to dry naturally for about 20 minutes, or for speed, use a hairdryer on a cool setting.

5 To add further detail, paint a line of cold wax around the inside of the petals. These lines will act as a barrier, keeping the next colour confined to the edges of the petals. Here a tjanting has been used, but you could also use a fine paintbrush.

Painting the design

1 Fix the template under the fabric and trace the design onto the fabric using a vanishing fabric marker pen.

3 Use a medium paintbrush to paint the flower centre and petals with iron-fixed silk paint, right up to the wax lines. Allow the paint to dry.

4 Paint the background using a sponge brush dipped in paint. Paint up to the edges of the flower but not over it. Allow to dry.

6 Once the wax has dried, paint between the two wax lines in the petal colour. The second coat will give a darker colour.

Adding crackle

1 Dip a small sponge into cold wax and brush it over the entire surface of the piece. Leave to dry for 20 minutes.

2 Remove the fabric from the frame and scrunch it to crackle the wax. The more you crumple the fabric, the more pronounced the crackle effect will be.

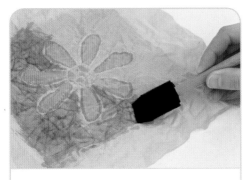

3 Spread the fabric out, face up, on a surface protected with plastic sheeting. Leaving some creases in place, paint over the background using a sponge brush.

4 Wait a few seconds for the colour to sink into the fabric. Darker lines showing on the reverse of the fabric indicate that the crackle effect is working. When you are satisfied with the effect, you can halt the process using a hairdryer on a cool setting.

Setting the paint

Once the fabric is dry, sandwich it between layers of newspaper and iron for three minutes per 30cm (12in) square, keeping the iron moving. This will set the paints and absorb some of the wax. Repeat with clean newspaper until most of the wax has been absorbed.

Removing residual dye and wax

1 Rinse the fabric in cold water to remove the residual dye and more of the wax. Stir 1 tablespoon of Wax-Out liquid into 2 litres (3½pts) warm (30 to 40°C/86 to 104°F) water. Soak the fabric for 10 minutes, stirring gently (or follow the manufacturer's instructions) to remove the remaining wax.

2 Remove the fabric from the Wax-Out solution and wash it gently in hot water with a little detergent. Iron on the reverse while damp.

Cushion cover PROJECT

Batik is a fun way to make a beautiful cushion cover. This project makes one cushion cover with an organic branch and leaf design. Start with plain white cotton and use wax and paints to build up the design in layers. You may wish to paint the back of the cushion to match the front before sewing the back and front together. Make the cover in an envelope-style, or stitch on a zip or buttons.

YOU WILL NEED

- 2 x 45cm (18in) squares of white 100% cotton fabric
- scissors
- 45cm (18in) square wooden frame
- three-pronged pins
- vanishing fabric marker pen
- fine and medium paintbrushes
- cold batik wax
- iron-fixed silk paints in yellow, light green, and dark green
- palette
- water pot
- sponge brush
- plastic sheeting
- small sponge
- Wax-Out liquid
- newspaper
- iron
- detergent

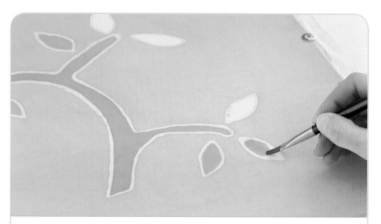

1 Stretch and pin one square of fabric to the frame. Using the vanishing fabric marker pen, trace the outline of the template on p.305 on the centre of the fabric. With a fine paintbrush, paint cold wax over the traced lines. Leave to dry for about 20 minutes. Paint the background yellow using a sponge brush, then paint the branch and leaves using light green paint. Leave to dry for 20 minutes.

2 With the template as a guide, paint the lines on the branch and the veins on the leaves. Use cold wax and a fine paintbrush. Leave to dry for 20 minutes.

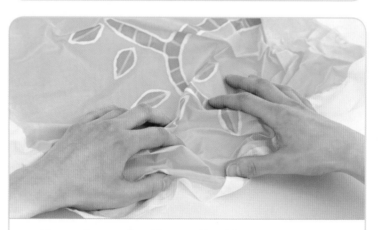

4 Dip a small sponge in cold wax and brush it over the entire piece so that it is covered in a layer of wax. Leave to dry for 20 minutes. Remove the fabric from the frame and scrunch it to crackle the wax. Protect the work surface with plastic sheeting then spread the fabric out, face up. Paint over the yellow background in the dark green, using a sponge brush. Wait a few seconds for the colour to sink into the fabric. When you are satisfied with the effect, use a hairdryer on a cool setting to halt the process.

3 Using the dark green, paint alternate stripes on the branch and on half of each leaf. Leave to dry for 20 minutes.

5 Once the fabric is dry, follow **setting the paint** on p.51. Then rinse the fabric in cold water to remove all traces of dye before soaking in a solution of Wax-Out liquid for 10 minutes. Wash gently in hot soapy water then iron on the reverse while damp. If you wish, you can paint the second square of fabric (the back of the cushion cover) in yellow, then add crackle by using a layer of cold wax and the dark green paint.

Patchwork TECHNIQUES

The secret to successful patchwork is accurate cutting then matching seams carefully before stitching them together. If the seams don't quite match up, try stretching the shorter edge slightly before sewing to ensure accuracy. One of the most important tools for patchwork is an iron; use it on the steam setting when pressing cotton to keep the seams flat and crisp.

Cutting patchwork fabric

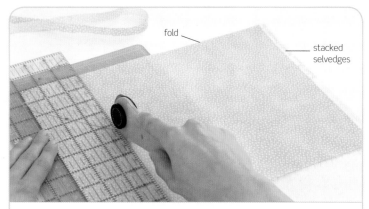

fold

stacked selvedges

1 Fold a piece of fabric selvedge to selvedge. Press with a steam iron, then place the folded fabric on a cutting mat. Trim the left edge straight, then align a patchwork ruler on the fold so that its right edge is 8cm (3¼in) from the trimmed edge. Cut along the ruler to make a strip. Move the ruler along to cut more strips the same width.

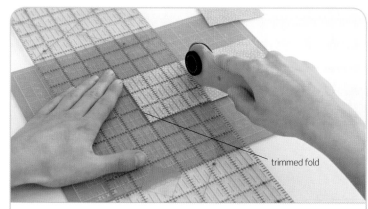

trimmed fold

2 Turn the double-layer strip and cut along the fold to make two strips. Using the lines on the ruler as a guide, cut the strips into 8cm (3¼in) squares. If you don't have a rotary cutter, draw pencil lines to mark squares and cut along the lines with dressmaking shears.

Sewing patchwork pieces

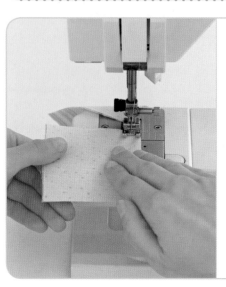

Place two squares with right sides together under the presser foot. Line up the edge of the fabric with the presser foot. Adjust the needle position if necessary to make the seam allowance exactly 6mm (¼in). Stitch the seam. For speed, you can stitch a row of squares one after the other, leaving a small thread gap between them.

Making a complete row

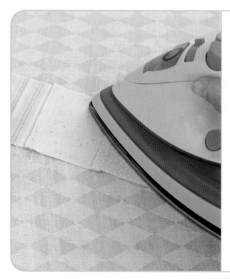

Cut the pairs of squares apart, then stitch one end of a pair to the end of another pair. Repeat to make a complete row, then press all seam allowances in the same direction. Press seams in alternate rows the opposite way to reduce bulk when sewing rows together.

Joining rows

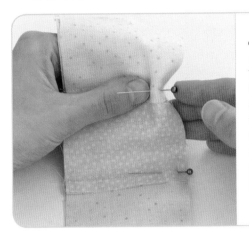

1 Place two rows of squares right sides together. To reduce bulk, ensure the seam allowances in each row face in the opposite directions. Pin together using glass-headed pins and match the seams exactly.

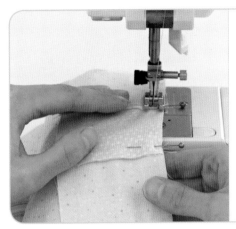

2 Using the edge of the presser foot as a guide, stitch the two rows together, stitching over each pin carefully as you go. Stitch all the rows together then remove the pins. Press all the horizontal seams towards the bottom of the patchwork.

Adding a border

1 Cut two strips the width of the patchwork and twice the depth of the border, plus 12mm (1/2in). With wrong sides together, press in half lengthways and press one long edge over by 6mm (1/4in). With right sides together, pin then stitch the unpressed edge to the top of the patchwork. Repeat on the bottom, then press seams outwards.

6mm (1/4in) turn-over

2 For the long sides, cut two strips the length of the patchwork, plus the top and bottom borders. Press and stitch as in Step 1. Begin stitching 6mm (1/4in) from the edge and finish 6mm (1/4in) from the bottom. Repeat on the other side, then press seams outwards.

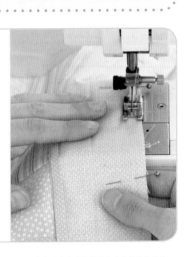

Adding wadding

Joining the layers

1 Cut the wadding and backing fabric to fit exactly between the pressed fold lines in the middle of the border strips. Lay wadding then backing fabric face up on the reverse side of the patchwork.

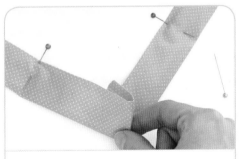

2 Fold the border along the fold lines at the top and bottom, and pin. Fold the sides to make neat corners. Slip stitch the border to the backing fabric.

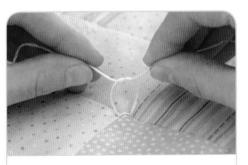

Using strands of embroidery cotton, backstitch through all layers at regular intervals at the intersections. To finish, tie a reef (square) knot at each stitch and trim neatly.

Patchwork bedspread PROJECT

Patchwork is a craft suitable for anyone who can use a sewing machine. This project is ideal if you are new to sewing by machine as all the seams are straight. If you can't find the exact fabrics used here, or wish to change the colour scheme, look for alternative fabrics with the same intensity of colour to achieve a similar overall look.

YOU WILL NEED

- 225cm (2½yd) olive green fabric (115cm/45in) wide
- 175cm (2yd) tiny blue spot fabric (115cm/45in) wide
- 75cm (30in) each of white polka dot fabric and wheel pattern fabric (115cm/45in) wide
- cutting mat
- patchwork ruler
- rotary cutter or dressmaking shears
- sewing machine
- cotton thread in matching colours
- iron
- glass-headed pins
- 145cm x 2m (57 x 79in) thin (2oz) polyester wadding
- 145cm x 2m (57 x 79in) backing fabric
- needle

1 Cut twelve 16cm (6¼in) squares of olive green fabric, 59 squares of tiny blue spot fabric, 22 squares of white polka dot fabric, and 24 squares of wheel pattern fabric.

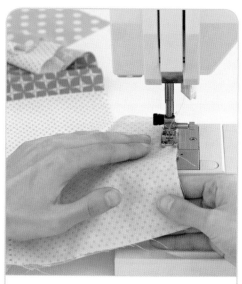

2 Arrange the squares as shown on the diagram on p.308. Following **sewing patchwork pieces** and **making a complete row** on p.54, stitch the squares together in rows.

3 Press the seam allowances on each row to one side. Following the diagram, press the seam allowances on alternate rows in the opposite direction.

4 Pin then stitch the first two rows together, following **joining rows** on p.55. Repeat for the other rows. Press all the horizontal seams towards the bottom of the patchwork.

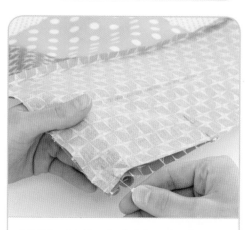

5 Following Step 1 of **adding a border** on p.55, stitch 15cm (6in) wide strips of olive green fabric to the top and bottom of the patchwork panel. Follow Step 2 to attach borders to the sides, then press.

6 Press the whole panel. With the patchwork face down, lay the wadding and backing fabric, face up, on top. Fold the border edges and corners over neatly and slip stitch. Following **joining the layers** on p.55, stitch ties through the layers at regular intervals.

Appliqué TECHNIQUES

Appliqué involves applying fabric shapes to a base fabric and stitching around the shapes. It's a great way of using small pieces of your favourite fabrics to embellish any fabric item. The simplest way to appliqué requires a product called bonding web, which is a thin web of dry glue with a paper backing. Bonding web allows you to create iron-on appliqué shapes very easily. If you are new to appliqué, keep the shapes simple at first before moving on to more complicated creations.

Creating the appliqué

1 Choose the image you want to use for your appliqué and select your fabrics. For this example, we are using a simple hand-drawn owl shape with separate wings. Cut out a piece of bonding web big enough for the owl's body and wings.

2 Place the bonding web over the body and the wings so that the glue side of the bonding web is facing down and the paper side is uppermost. Trace over the images using a pencil.

3 With the iron on a medium setting, iron the pieces of bonding web, glue-side down, onto the reverse of your chosen fabrics. If your fabric has a directional pattern, make sure that the pieces are positioned so that the pattern will be the right way up on the finished shape.

4 Cut out the fabric shapes, paying particular attention around the curves to make sure they are smooth.

Applying the appliqué

1 Peel the backing paper of the bonding web off the owl shape, making sure that the adhesive, now on the fabric, does not stick to itself.

2 Position the body of the owl onto the fabric you are attaching it to and iron it in position.

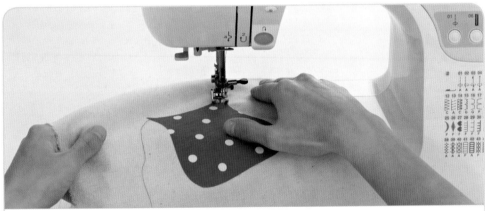

3 Sew around the shape by hand or with a sewing machine. You can use either a straight stitch or zigzag stitch to do this. If you are using a straight stitch, as shown here, keep your stitching 2 to 3 mm (1/10 to 1/8in) in from the edge of the shape.

4 Position and iron the wings in place and sew around them, as explained in Step 3.

Decorating the appliqué

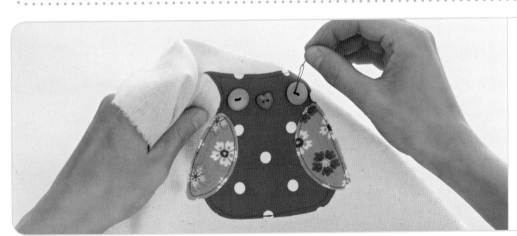

Embellishments such as buttons, sequins, and beads can be sewn on to add interest. Sew on two round buttons for the eyes using contrasting thread. Sew on an orange heart-shaped button for the beak using matching thread.

Appliqué throw PROJECT

A mixture of patterned and plain fabrics has been used to adorn this soft cream-coloured lambswool throw. Of course, you don't have to use the same fabrics that are used here, but when choosing your fabrics, spend time selecting ones that work well together. We have added an assortment of buttons to the flower centres to give the throw a charming homespun look.

YOU WILL NEED

- 4.5m x 50cm (5yd x 20in) bonding web
- pencil
- scissors
- 60 x 150cm (23 x 60in) each of plain light green linen fabric, grey/green floral cotton fabric, and pink floral cotton fabric
- 50 x 70cm (20 x 27½in) each of pale pink cotton fabric and green polka dot fabric
- iron
- 140 x 190cm (55 x 75in) plain cream woollen or fleece throw
- pins
- sewing machine
- cream, olive green, dark grey, and pink sewing threads
- 30 assorted medium-size buttons in grey, cream, red, and green
- sewing needle

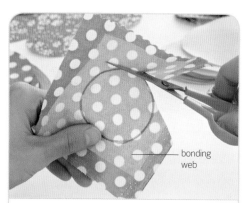

bonding web

1 Using the templates on pp.306-07, prepare 15 plain light green base circles, 15 smaller flowers in grey/green floral, 15 outer circles for them in pale pink, and 15 smaller inner circles for them in green polka dot. Then prepare 15 larger flowers in pink floral, 15 outer circles for them in green polka dot, and 15 smaller inner circles for them in pale pink.

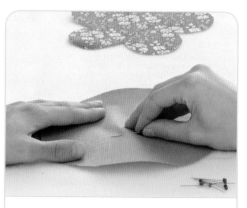

2 Peel away the backing paper of the bonding web and arrange a row of five alternating green circles and pink floral print flowers across the top of the throw, starting with a green circle. Pin them in position. Then arrange the second row, starting with a pink floral print flower. Iron them in position. Repeat these two rows twice more.

3 Sew around the edges of the green circles and pink floral print flowers in straight stitch. Peel away the backing paper on the grey/green flowers and iron them onto the green circles then stitch around these. When sewing the appliqués, keep cream thread in the bobbin and match the top threads to your fabrics.

4 Apply the two centre circles to each flower. Stitch around the pink circles in pink sewing thread and the green polka dot circles in olive green thread, remembering to keep cream thread in the bobbin throughout.

5 To finish, sew a button to each of the flower centres.

Bead embroidery TECHNIQUES

Beading is a great way to breathe new life into clothes and accessories. You can use almost any shape of small- or medium-size beads for beading. Small glass beads known as seed beads or rocailles, and bugle beads, which are small glass tubes, are the most popular and easy to work with. Also, as they are small, they will not weigh your fabric down too much. You can do beading on patterned fabrics to add detail to a pattern or you can create your own beaded motifs.

Preparing the design

1 Decide on the embroidery design and the item you want to embellish. Here we are using a simple hand-drawn flower on fine white linen fabric. Trace the design onto the fabric using a water-soluble pen.

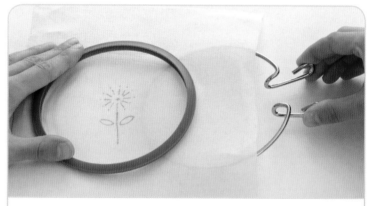

2 Place the fabric in an embroidery hoop and make sure the fabric is taut.

Applying the beads

1 The flower centre consists of a large bead with a small one on top. Using thread that matches the top bead, secure the thread at the flower centre. Take the thread through the large bead, then the small bead, and back down the large bead. Secure it.

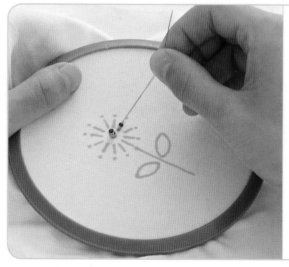

2 To apply beads to the petals, secure a length of pink thread at the inner edge of the first petal. Take the needle through a bugle bead and back into the fabric immediately at the end of the bead. Then take it out again a seed-bead width further on. Thread the seed bead on the needle and backstitch it in place.

3 Thread a second bugle bead on the needle and take the needle into the fabric at the end of the bead. Make a backstitch through all three beads, from the inner to the outer edge of the petal.

4 To apply the outer seed beads, use white thread so you can take the thread between the beads on the reverse of the fabric. Secure the first bead with two backstitches, then take the thread down and along the reverse of the fabric to the position of the next outer seed bead.

Stitching a line of beads

1 To make the stalk, secure green thread at the starting point. Thread four green seed beads onto the thread and take the thread down into the fabric just by the end of the last bead. (If you take it too near the starting point, the beads will not lie flat; if you take it too far away, the row of beads will be too slack.) Take the thread out to the front again, two beads back. Then take the thread forwards through those two beads.

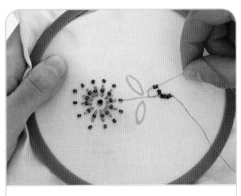

2 Pick up another four beads on the needle and repeat Step 1 until the line of the stalk is complete. Secure the thread.

Filling an area with beads

Finishing your work

1 Outline the leaves using the same techniques as for the stalk, but curving the line slightly as you go. Work two short rows of seed beads within the outline to fill.

2 Work a number of virtually invisible straight stitches over the beaded area to make sure the beads sit snug to the fabric and are secure.

Remove the hoop. Use a fine water spray to remove traces of water-soluble pen. Iron around the edges of the beaded motif or on the back. Wash gently by hand.

Beaded cardigan PROJECT

Seed beads in red and shades of green are transformed into two juicy-looking cherries that complement the gentle pink of this cardigan. While the beaded trim at the cuffs and hem is sewn directly onto the garment, the cherries and leaves are worked on a piece of pale pink organza, which is then fastened to the cardigan. This makes the embroidery easier to work and position. It also means you can easily stitch the motif to another garment later, should you wish.

YOU WILL NEED

- 18cm (7in) square of pale pink organza (or other finely woven, lightweight pale pink fabric)
- water-soluble pen
- embroidery hoop
- 10g (⅓oz) size 9 red seed beads
- 2g (⅛oz) size 9 emerald green seed beads
- 5g (¼oz) size 9 light green seed beads
- sewing needle
- red, green, and pink polyester sewing threads, to match the beads and cardigan
- fabric glue

- fine paintbrush
- scissors
- pale pink cardigan in a fine knit (lambswool, angora, and cashmere are all ideal)

1 Trace the cherry template on p.309 onto the organza using the water-soluble pen. Secure the fabric in the embroidery hoop. Outline the cherries with red beads, applying three beads at a time. Work two more rings of beads within the outline, then fill in the centre circles with a few short rows of beads. Secure the beads with safety stitches. Work a row of emerald green beads for the stalks. Work the outline of the leaves in light green beads and fill in with rows of beads.

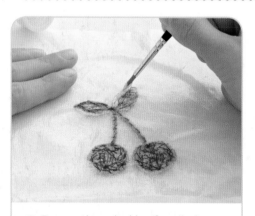

2 Remove the embroidery from the hoop. Working on the underside of the organza, paint a thin line of fabric glue around the entire outside edge of the embroidery and leave it to dry.

3 Cut away the fabric around the edges of the embroidery so no fabric is visible from the front. Place the motif in position and secure it to the cardigan using small oversewing stitches around the edge and pink sewing thread to match the cardigan.

4 Using pink thread and two backstitches for each bead, secure red seed beads at 1.5cm (⅝in) intervals around the cuffs, just at the top of the ribbing. Work the thread from one bead to the next, using tiny running stitches. Do not pull the thread too tightly.

5 Work two more rows above the rows just worked. Space the beads for the second row between the beads of the first row. The beads in the third row should be exactly above the beads in the first. Work the same beaded border around the ribbing on the lower edge of the cardigan.

Ribbon weaving TECHNIQUES

Ribbon weaving is a quick and easy way to create textured fabric panels that can be used for all sorts of fabric creations, from a cushion cover to a pretty bag. For your first attempt, choose satin ribbons in a plain weave. Once you've learned the basics you can experiment with sheer or silk ribbons and more interesting weave patterns, or you might think about embellishing the finished design with beads, sequins, or embroidery.

Weaving a ribbon panel

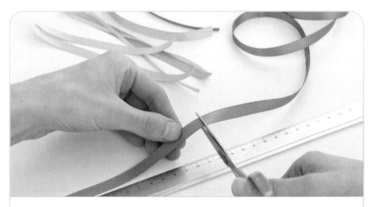

1 Cut strips of ribbon the length required, adding 5cm (2in) to each length to allow for seam allowances and slight loss of length caused by the weaving process. Cut enough ribbon strips to cover your panel when laid vertically side by side.

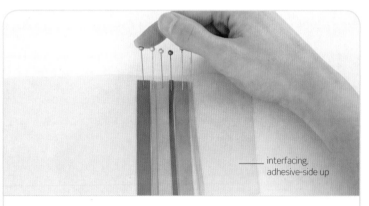

interfacing, adhesive-side up

2 Cut a piece of medium-weight iron-on interfacing slightly larger than the finished ribbon panel. Lay the interfacing on an ironing board or foam board, adhesive-side up, then lay the ribbons side by side vertically on top and pin them along the top edge. There should be no gaps between the ribbons.

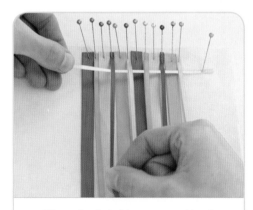

3 Weave the first ribbon across at least 1.5cm (⅝in) down from the top edges, lifting every other vertical ribbon to create a simple over-and-under weave. Pin the ribbon at both ends to hold it straight.

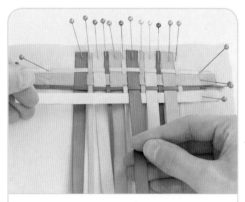

4 Weave a second ribbon across, lifting alternate vertical ribbons to those lifted for the first row. Pin the ends of the second ribbon. Continue weaving across the panel, ensuring the weave pattern is correct.

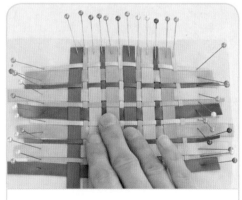

5 Occasionally pull gently on the vertical ribbons and push the centre of the horizontal ribbons up to keep them straight. Once the panel is complete, check the size and make sure the ribbons are square.

Attaching the fusible interfacing

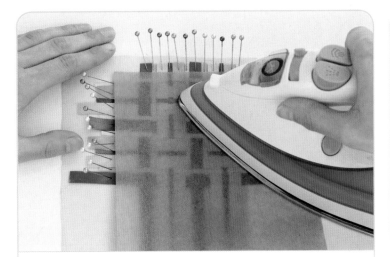

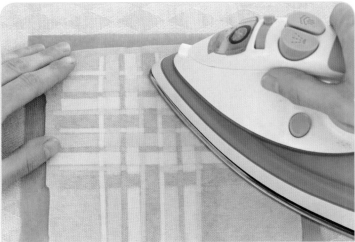

1 With most of the pins still in position, press the ribbons with a steam iron set to the appropriate temperature. For extra protection, cover the ribbons with baking parchment. Iron carefully, especially around the edges, so that the ribbons begin to stick to the interfacing.

2 Remove all the pins. Turn the panel over so that the ribbons are face-down. Press again over the back of the interfacing, making sure you hold the iron still for a second or two to allow the adhesive to melt a little. Finish by machine stitching around the edges of the ribbons to secure them in place.

Creating alternative weaves and finishes

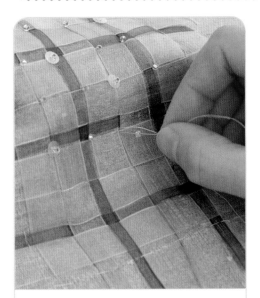

Sheer ribbons, which are not suitable for attaching with fusible interfacing, can be held in place by stitching at each intersection instead. Use embroidery thread. You can also add seed beads and even sequins to hold the ribbons together and embellish the panel.

You can create a variety of different weaves with ribbons. When using a mix of ribbon widths, a plain weave is best, but by weaving through two vertical ribbons at a time instead of one, for example, you'll create a basket weave. Weave one or two ribbons across each time.

To create a diagonal weave, start on the first row by lifting the first two vertical ribbons, then weave over and under two ribbons at a time. On the next and subsequent rows, begin the two over, two under weaving one vertical ribbon to the left each time you start a new row.

Evening clutch PROJECT

Transform an assortment of pretty satin ribbons into a chic clutch. Use a selection of different coloured ribbons in a variety of widths to create an interesting and balanced piece of woven ribbon fabric. Use a medium interfacing that will support the weight of the ribbons, ironing a second layer on top of the first if you want a firmer, more structured design.

YOU WILL NEED

- 7m (7½yd) each of blue, pink, and purple ribbons in different widths
- scissors
- 30 x 90cm (12 x 35in) black medium-weight iron-on interfacing
- glass-headed pins
- iron
- sewing machine
- dark blue cotton thread
- 50cm (20in) dark blue dupion silk (115cm/45in) wide
- needle
- snap fastener

1 Following **weaving a ribbon panel** on p.66, weave 30cm (12in) lengths of ribbon onto the adhesive side of the interfacing to make a woven panel measuring 25 x 23cm (10 x 9½in). Using a temperature to suit the ribbons, press with a steam iron first on the right side then on the back. Stitch around the edges to secure the ribbons. Make a second panel the same size.

2 With right sides together, pin a 30cm (12in) square of dark blue silk to each ribbon panel along the top edge. Stitch just above the first horizontal ribbon, then press the seams open. Trim the seams to 7mm (5/16in).

3 For the flap, with the dark blue silk uppermost, pin to mark 10cm (4in) down each short side. Stitch to the pins, then remove the pins. Snip the seams at the end of the stitching. Trim the seams and the two upper corners, then turn the panel through.

4 Stitch the silk and ribbon panels together down the sides to secure. Trim the flap panel to 24 cm (9¾in) deep and the other to 19cm (7½in). Tack along the bottom ribbon on each panel. Pin the panels right sides together. Stitch along the tacking thread and neaten the seam.

5 For each side panel, iron interfacing to the back of a 30cm (12in) square of dark blue fabric. Fold in half. Copy the side panel template on p.309 and cut it out. Pin the top of the template to the fold. Tack around the edge and trim to 6mm (¼in). Make a second side panel.

6 Pin the side panels to the side edges of the bag, beginning at the bottom of the flap. Tack in position, snipping into the side panels at the corner. Fold a ribbon over the raw edges, tack, and stitch neatly by hand or machine.

Wet felting TECHNIQUES

Felt can be made by applying heat, moisture, and friction to a mass of loose fleece fibres, which can then be manipulated to create flat or three-dimensional pieces. Unlike fabric, felt has no warp or weft, and can be cut without fraying. It is wonderfully soft and warm to the touch, and can be worked to the density of wood.

Carding

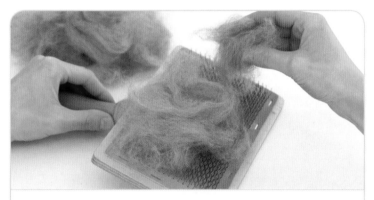

1 To make an even piece of felt, you first need to brush the fleece fibres so that they lie in the same direction. To do this, distribute a handful of fleece onto the left hand carder.

2 Holding the left carder in your hand, pull the right carder across the face of the left one. Use sufficient pressure to allow the teeth to slip between each other to comb out the fleece. Do this two or three times until most of the fleece has transferred over to the right carder.

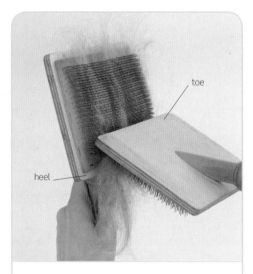

3 Transfer the fleece back to the left carder: to do this, put the toe of the right carder to the heel of the left carder, and push upwards.

4 Repeat the process three or four times, until the fleece is evenly spaced across the face of the left carder.

5 To remove fleece from the carder, place the heel of the right carder to the toe of the left carder and push downwards until the fleece comes away.

Colour-blending fibres

1 To blend coloured fleece fibres, spread fibres of different colours over the left carder.

2 Brush until you get the blend you want, adding extra fibres if desired. You can also blend different types of fleece together.

Preparing the work surface

Laying out the fibres

Lay a waterproof sheet over your work surface, place a bamboo blind on top, then a piece of net curtain.

1 Lay vertical tufts of carded fleece on the net, with a second layer at right angles to the first to help the fibres bond.

2 A third layer is not essential but will produce a thicker felt. Lay it at right angles to the second layer.

Fulling the felt

1 Pull the net over the laid-out fibres and sprinkle all over with warm soap solution to wet the fibres thoroughly.

2 Lightly brush olive oil soap over the net. Using your palms, gently rub the net up and down and side to side for 10 to 15 minutes, gradually applying more pressure.

3 Turn the net over, brush with soap again, and repeat the rubbing process on the other side for another 10 to 15 minutes. The fleece will turn into felt.

The pinch test

After working the felt on both sides, remove the net and do a pinch test – if the fibres move and pull away, you need to rub it some more. If the fibres hold together and are firm, you can remove the felt from the net.

Speeding up the felting process

1 Put the felt in a tub and pour boiling water over. This "shocks" the felt and speeds up the felting process. Wearing rubber gloves, press out the excess moisture with a wooden spoon.

2 Squeeze out the moisture and throw the piece of felt repeatedly onto the work surface to continue the felting process. Do this for about a minute.

Creating two-tone felt

horizontal fibres

vertical fibres

Lay even tufts of carded fleece onto the net. Lay the first colour vertically and the second colour at right angles to the first colour. To create patterns, pull out thin, wispy lengths of fleece and arrange them on top of the layered fleece fibres. Full the felt.

Using a template (for seamless felting)

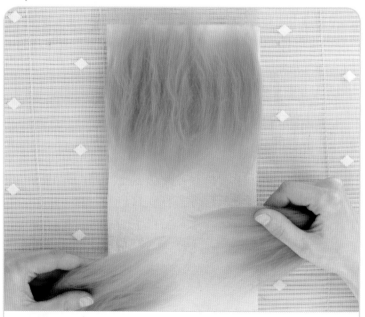

1 Place a template cut from heavy-duty plastic sheeting or foam carpet underlay on the net. Lay even tufts of carded fleece side by side over the template, working from top to bottom.

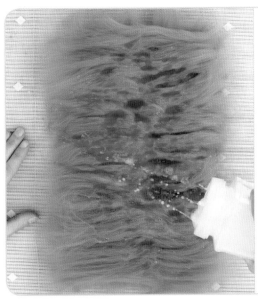

2 Lay a second perpendicular layer of fleece to cover the first, this time overlapping the edges of the template by about 3cm (1¼in). Sprinkle warm soap solution all over the fleece to wet the fibres thoroughly.

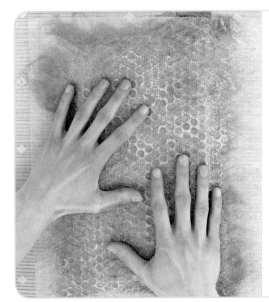

3 Place a sheet of bubble wrap on top of the wetted fibres. Use your hands to spread the moisture evenly across the fleece and remove the air.

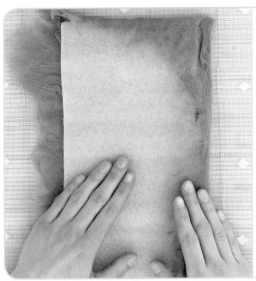

4 Remove the bubble wrap. Carefully turn the work over and fold the overlapping fibres onto the reverse side of the template.

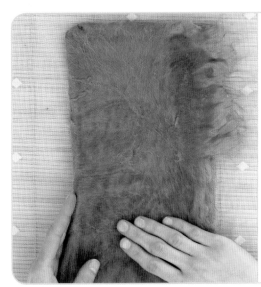

5 Lay two more layers of fleece over the reverse side of the template, creating a finer, wispy overlapped edge all round on the top layer. Carefully tuck the overlapped fibres under so that the whole template is encased in fleece.

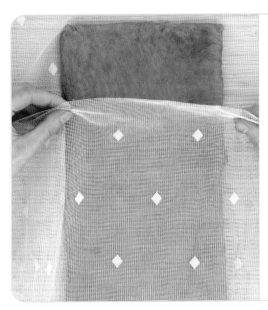

6 Wrap the template in the net, sprinkle with warm soap solution, and brush the surface of the net with olive oil soap. Rub both sides with the palms of your hands, paying particular attention to the edges.

7 Remove the net, do the pinch test (see opposite), then cut along one edge of the felted fleece using fine pointed scissors. Remove the template through the opening.

Felted book bag PROJECT

This felted book bag is worked around a template (see using a template on pp.72–73) so has no seams. Contrasting colours are used inside and out, and tiny felted flowers, made separately, are sewn to the outside of the bag with attractive stitched detail, using coloured wool yarn. The strap is hand rolled from a length of fleece roving and is sturdy enough to carry weighty books.

YOU WILL NEED

- 150g (5½oz) each of merino wool top in dark red and blue
- 50g (2oz) or 115cm (45in) blue fleece roving
- hand carders
- 38 x 46cm (15 x 18½in), plus two 6.5cm (2¾in) diameter circles of heavy-duty plastic sheeting or foam carpet underlay, for templates
- waterproof sheet

- bamboo blind
- net curtain
- warm soap solution in a dispenser
- olive oil soap
- fine pointed scissors
- blue and yellow wool yarn
- darning needle
- small amounts of pink, red, and green fleece

1 Following **using a template** on pp.72–73, lay out the carded dark red fleece on both sides of the template to form the inside of the bag. Repeat with the carded blue fibres for the outside of the bag, then follow **fulling the felt** on p.71.

2 Work the fibres until they hold together. Press and beat the felt to create a strong structure. Do the **pinch test** on p.72, then shock with boiling water to speed up the felting process.

3 Cut along one short side and release the template, then shape the sides and corners of the bag by pinching and manipulating the whole bag.

4 To make the strap, roll the blue fleece roving between wet, soapy palms, working along the whole length, to create a firmly rolled strap. Rinse thoroughly. When dry, use blue wool yarn to stitch the strap to the inside of the bag.

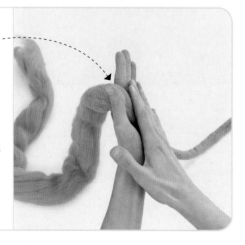

5 Using the circular templates and following **using a template** on pp.72-73, create four flowers using scraps of pink, red, and green fleece. To remove the templates, cut all the way round them, creating two flat circles per template.

6 Cut into the edge of each felted circle to create a scalloped edge and work with soapy fingers to set the edges. When dry, stitch the flowers onto the bag using yellow yarn to create flower centres.

Needle felting TECHNIQUES

Shaping and compressing fleece fibres using a long, barbed felting needle is a way to create three-dimensional shapes without the use of water, soap, and all that rubbing. Long, fine, barbed, and extremely sharp needles are poked into the fibres repeatedly to mesh them together, enabling detailed shapes to be made.

Forming a core

1 Use spare oddments of fleece for the core of a big project. Smooth out the fleece fibres with hand carders (see **carding** on p.70) as this will make the fleece easier to handle. Select your felting needles – you'll need a few as they tend to snap if bent.

2 Roll up the fibres into a loose ball and use a multi-needle tool to stab the fibres repeatedly over a block of dense foam sponge. Use a shallow, gentle stabbing motion at first, stabbing along the rolled edges to hold the fibres together. Stab all over to create the shape required, in this case, a ball.

3 As you continue stabbing the fibres, they will become more compact. Take care not to bend the needles, and always push them into the fleece in a straight line, to prevent them from snapping.

multi-needle felting tool

Creating shapes

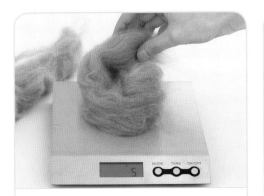

1 When creating shapes that need to be the same size, such as animal legs, use electronic scales to accurately weigh small amounts of fleece.

2 For specific shapes, arrange the fibres into the desired shape. For the legs of an animal, for instance, roll the fibres into a tube and stab them all round, turning as you go. Work up and down the sides, leaving unworked fibres at one end.

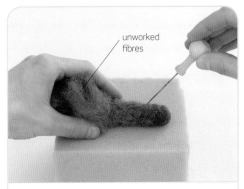

3 These unworked ends are used to attach the shape to another shape, in this case, the body of an animal.

Shaping features

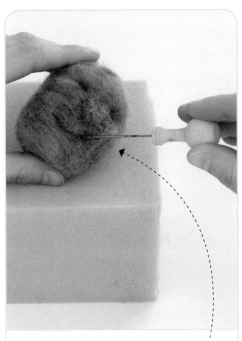

Use a single-needle tool for creating fine detailing, such as facial features. Stab the needle in repeatedly along the line of the detail you want. For curves and general shaping, stab the needle repeatedly across the area you wish to shape.

Creating patterns

1 You can work wispy pieces of fleece into needle-felted patterns. Carefully arrange the fibres on the surface of a felted piece of work.

2 Using a single-needle tool, make shallow stabs around the fibres to shape them into a pattern, then work across the whole pattern to push the fibres into the surface.

3 Continue in this way until the fibres have been worked into the item and the pattern is clearly visible.

Needle-felted sheep PROJECT

A sheep made from sheep's fleece is a wonderful thing. It's always useful to have a picture of the animal you want to make to use as a reference, so that you can achieve the right contours and dimensions. Needle felting is a very delicate craft, so time and patience are a must.

YOU WILL NEED

- visual references (optional)
- 35g (1¼oz) cream coloured fleece
- electronic scales
- hand carders
- foam block
- single-needle felting tool
- darning needle
- dark brown two-ply wool yarn

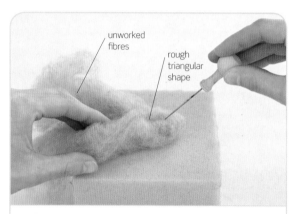

unworked fibres

rough triangular shape

1 Make two ear shapes from 5g (¼oz) carded fleece. Create a rough triangle and, with the fleece over a block of dense foam, work the felting needle along the centre to anchor the fibres, then roll the edges inwards and stab along each side. Leave unworked fibres at the base of both ears.

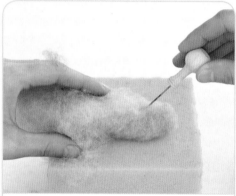

2 Make four legs from 12g (⅓oz) carded fleece. Roll each piece of fleece into a rough tube shape, then stab the fibres all round, turning the legs as you work. Leave unworked fibres at the top of each leg.

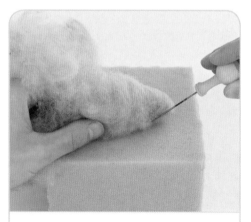

3 Now make a head with 5g (¼oz) carded fleece, leaving unworked fibres to attach the head to the body. Shape the nose and under the chin carefully.

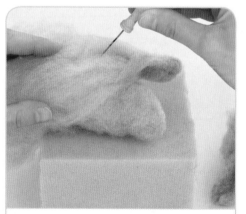

4 Attach the ears to the head by pinching them down the middle lengthways and laying the unworked fibres on either side of the head. Stab the felting needle through these fibres.

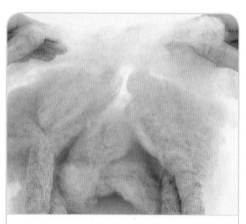

5 For the body, divide 12g (⅓oz) fleece into three and card each bundle. Lay out one bundle then place the unworked fibres of one front leg and one back leg on top of it, leaving the shaped ends protruding below the body. Place the next bundle on top, then the remaining front and back legs on top. Finally, place the last bundle over the top, to make five layers ready to be worked as a whole.

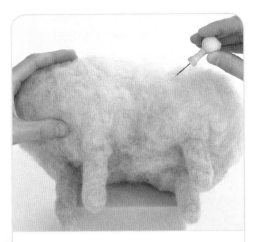

6 Lightly stab the fibres over the whole body and through all five layers, slowly compressing them to incorporate the legs and part-felt the body.

7 To attach the head, push the part-felted body into the splayed-out unworked fibres of the head, and stab the fibres so that they hold together. Continue to stab the fibres, gradually compressing them to create the body of the sheep.

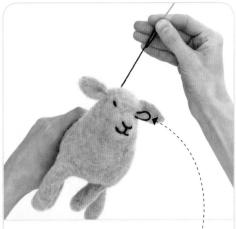

8 Stitch features onto the sheep's face using one long piece of dark brown wool yarn. Start by threading it up through the chin. To finish, take the yarn back into the body and snip off close to the body to hide the end.

Upholstery TECHNIQUES

Upholstering a drop-in seat pad is the simplest form of upholstery and is ideal for the complete beginner. With just a few basic upholstery materials you can breathe new life into old or tired-looking furniture. Once you've mastered the basic upholstery techniques, you can move on to more challenging projects.

PREPARING THE SEAT PAD

If you're using an old chair frame, you'll need to strip off any old materials using a mallet and ripping chisel. Make good any loose joints and fill any large tack holes with PVA wood glue and sawdust mixed to the consistency of porridge. Work the mixture into the tack holes and wipe off any residue on the surface of the frame.

Webbing the seat pad

1 Using good-quality black and white webbing, and working from the back to the front edge of the seat pad, position the webs so that they are no more than a web's width away from each other.

position tacks in a "W" formation

2 Turn the raw edge of the webbing over 2cm (³⁄₄in) and position it 1.5cm (⁵⁄₈in) in from the outside edge of the frame. Hammer in three 13mm (¹⁄₂in) improved tacks along the back edge of the web and two further tacks to form a strong "W" formation.

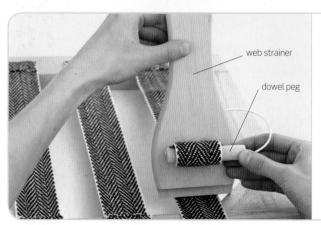

web strainer

dowel peg

3 Use a web strainer to tighten the webbing across the frame. With the handle facing away from you and the dowel peg hanging down, loop the webbing up through the slot in the web strainer. Insert the dowel peg in the webbing loop to apply tension.

4 Tension the webbing by pulling the web strainer over the front edge of the frame and position three 13mm (¹⁄₂in) improved tacks 1.5cm (⁵⁄₈in) in from the outside edge of the frame.

5 Cut the webbing off, leaving a 2cm (¾in) turn-back. Fold over the turn-back and hammer in two more 13mm (½in) improved tacks to form an invisible "W" formation. Fix all webs running in the same direction in this way.

6 Add a second set of webs at right angles to the first, weaving them over and under the first webs to provide good support. Tension and tack the webs into position as before.

Applying the hessian

Applying bridle ties

Lay medium-weight hessian over the webbing. Turn back the raw edges and attach the hessian to the frame with a row of 10mm (³⁄₈in) improved tacks inserted approximately 1.5cm (⁵⁄₈in) from the edges of the frame.

1 Using twine threaded through a curved spring needle, apply bridle ties to the hessian. These are large, loose backstitches about 10cm (4in) long, each of which you loop over the back of your fingers. These ties will hold the loose filling in place.

2 Position the bridle ties no more than 10cm (4in) apart. Make a row of ties along the outer edges of the hessian and apply more ties in the centre to provide good coverage.

Adding the filling

1 Apply a generous layer of loose hair filling to the hessian, tucking it under the bridle ties to hold it in place.

2 Tease the hair well to remove any lumps and create an even, soft but firm, consistency.

3 Create a good, even thickness about 4cm (1½in) deep. Fibre, foam, cotton, or wool felts are alternative fillings.

Adding the wadding layer

Cover the hair with two layers of skin wadding cut to the size of the seat pad. This will help to stop the hair working through the top covers.

2 Temporary tack the calico 1.5cm (⅝in) from the outside edge of the seat pad on all four sides, using 10mm (⅜in) tacks. Leave the corners until last.

Covering with calico or interliner/barrier cloth

1 Cover the wadding with calico or a fire-retardant interliner/barrier cloth, as appropriate. Cut the calico/barrier cloth 10cm (4in) larger all around than the seat pad. Turn the pad over, place it on top of the calico, and pull the calico taut. Temporary tack the calico/barrier cloth in place on the underside of the pad using 10mm (⅜in) tacks.

3 Using the tack lifter, lift and replace each temporary tack, tightening the calico/barrier cloth as you go, to form neat edges. There should be no filling on the outside edges of the seat pad or it may not fit back into the chair frame. Hammer all the tacks home.

Neatening the corners

1 Neaten the corners by pulling the calico/barrier cloth firmly over the centre point of each corner and hammering in a 10mm (³⁄₈in) fine tack at this point on the underside of the pad.

regulator

2 Using the end of the regulator, fold and crease the calico neatly to form a pleat on one side of the corner.

3 Open out the pleat and cut away any excess calico around the tack head.

4 Re-fold the pleat and tack in place using a 10mm (³⁄₈in) fine tack.

5 Trim off any excess calico back to the tacks.

6 Repeat this process for the other side of the corner and again on all three remaining corners.

UK FIRE SAFETY REGULATIONS

In the UK, chair frames made after 1st January 1950 must have fillings and fabrics that comply with the Furniture & Furnishings (Fire)(Safety) Regulations 1988. If your top fabric contains at least 75% natural fibres, you can use a Schedule 3 interliner/barrier cloth over the fillings. Alternatively, the fabric must be inherently fire retardant or back-coated fire retardant. Furniture made prior to 1950 falls outside the scope of the regulations.

Drop-in seat PROJECT

Traditional drop-in seat chair frames have a seat pad that can be easily popped out of the chair frame. When re-upholstering these pads, care must be taken not to allow any stuffing or unnecessary fabric to protrude along the sides of the seat pad or the pad may not fit back into the chair frame.

YOU WILL NEED

- drop-in seat chair
- black and white webbing
- scissors
- 10mm (³⁄₈in) and 13mm (¹⁄₂in) improved tacks and 10mm (³⁄₈in) fine tacks
- upholstery tack hammer
- web strainer
- medium-weight hessian
- twine
- curved spring needle
- loose hair filling (fibre, felts, or foam)
- skin wadding
- calico or fire-retardant interliner/ barrier cloth
- tack lifter
- regulator
- fabric of your choice
- bottoming cloth

1 Once you have prepared the seat pad (see pp.80–83), cover the calico with a general domestic-quality fabric of your choice, ensuring any pattern is positioned pleasingly.

2 Cut the fabric 10cm (4in) larger all around than the seat pad.

3 Fit the fabric in the same way as the calico, using 10mm (³⁄₈in) fine tacks, positioned 1.5cm (⁵⁄₈in) from the outside edge of the seat pad. Cut away any excess fabric back to the tacks.

4 Cut a piece of bottoming cloth to the size and shape of the underside of the seat pad. Lay the cloth over the fabric, covering all tacks and raw edges.

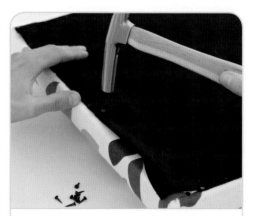

5 Turn the raw edges of the bottoming cloth under and tack to the underside of the seat pad, 1cm (³⁄₈in) from the outside edge.

6 Fold the bottoming cloth to form neat square corners and tack in place. Finally, fit the pad into the chair frame.

Papercrafts

Papercrafts

PAPERMAKING • PAPER MARBLING • PAPIER-MÂCHÉ • SCRAPBOOKING • LINO PRINTING

PAPER DECORATIONS • DÉCOUPAGE • PAPER PUNCHING • QUILLING

CARD-MAKING • BOX-MAKING • SCREEN PRINTING

Paper is such a familiar and humble material, it's easy to overlook how versatile it can be when it comes to crafting. In this chapter, you'll learn ways to transform paper into stationery, gifts, and decorative items. Because much of the paper used in these projects is recycled, the cost is minimal but the results are sensational.

Paper is an intrinsic part of our everyday lives. There are newspapers, magazines, catalogues, brochures, letters that are delivered to our door, brown paper parcels, cardboard cartons, and shoe boxes with their accompanying layers of tissue paper.

Paper accounts for about a third of municipal waste; at best it is recycled by pulping but at worst it is consigned to landfill. Once you've leafed through these pages and can see for yourself what can be done with a few pieces of paper and card, you'll view this modest and most basic of materials in a different light.

This chapter explains a wealth of paper-crafting techniques, as well as offering a number of inspiring and achievable projects, including a stationery set, postcards, homewares, and decorations.

With writing paper conjured up from paper pulp and petals or adorned with printed motifs, you can be at the forefront of a letter-writing revival. Instead of hoarding old photographs and letters in a drawer, use scrapbooking techniques to create an heirloom album. With a shoe box and a few scraps of giftwrap, you can make a keepsake box. And if there's something to celebrate, make your own greetings cards and gift boxes, or decorate a party venue with bold and colourful paper pompom decorations.

Paper might not be the first thing that comes to mind when you think of home accessories, so a punched lampshade or a quilled paper picture is likely to be something of a talking point. It's time to rescue all that paper from the recycling bin. Scissors at the ready? Get snipping and ripping!

Papercrafts TOOLS AND MATERIALS

Scissors, sticky tape, paper, and glue are the kind of items you'll find in most households, so when tackling papercraft projects you won't need to make a large investment in specialist equipment. Try out the projects with the tools and materials you already have to hand before going out and buying any extra items.

Papermaking

Shredded waste paper Use waste paper without too much dark printing, such as bank statements. Keep to one main colour if possible. Paper that has already been recycled, such as most newspaper, does not work so well as the fibres are too short.

Food colouring You can use powdered or liquid food colourings or even icing paste to correct the colour of homemade paper if the pulp looks a little drab.

Decorative additions Use dried flower petals and leaves; short scraps of colourful yarn, lace, or fabric; snippets of Angelina fibre; glitter; confetti; and sequins – almost anything small and flat – to add interest to homemade paper.

Mould and deckle A mould is a frame with netting stretched over it that holds the paper pulp. A deckle is the same size as the mould and sits on top of it. The deckle helps trap the pulp and shape the paper sheets. Both are available from craft shops, or you can make your own (see p.96).

Blender or food processor This makes mashing paper pulp effortless. You could use a potato masher instead, but it's hard work and takes a long time.

Absorbent cloths Use J cloths or old flannelette sheets cut a little larger than the mould to drain and dry homemade paper sheets. If the cloths are textured, your paper will be too.

Paper marbling

Good-quality paper
Use cartridge paper or watercolour paper for marbling. The paper need not be expensive but it does need to be sturdy enough to be handled when wet.

Acrylic or marbling paints
Acrylics work well but will probably need thinning with a little water; special marbling paints are better.

Cocktail sticks or twigs
Use these to drag the paint into swirls and patterns. The slimmer the stick, the more elegant the lines and swirls will be.

Fungicide-free wallpaper paste or marbling size
Mixed with water, this will form a jelly-like surface on which the marbling paints float.

Paintbrushes or pipettes Use these to distribute the paint. Pipettes work better when creating lines and large dots, but paintbrushes produce tiny dots and interesting splatters.

Wide-tooth comb Use an Afro comb or make an equivalent by taping halved cocktail sticks onto a 15cm (6in) ruler. This forms a comb-like tool that can be used to produce fan and feather patterns.

Papier-mâché

Recycled items Save packaging such as plastic containers, cardboard tubes, and plastic carrier bags, which can be combined to form basic shapes.

PVA glue Polyvinyl acetate adhesive, also known as white glue or woodworking adhesive, can be used straight from the container for glueing items together or it can be diluted to use as a paste for final layers.

Masking tape Use decorator's masking tape or sticky tape to join components when making a base for papier-mâché objects.

Newspapers Combine strips of old newspapers or pages from telephone directories and similar types of absorbent paper with wallpaper paste. This forms a paper pulp which, when dry, hardens to a tough shell.

Tissue paper Instead of painting designs on the surface of a papier-mâché object, you can use coloured tissue paper to form a final layer or to apply cutout shapes.

Wallpaper paste This is used to create the paper pulp and should be made by mixing with water, according to the instructions on the packet.

91

Scrapbooking

Ribbons and borders Ribbons can be used to attach labels, to tie into bows, or to create borders. Self-adhesive ribbons are also available.

Albums Modern scrapbooks are available in a variety of formats, with 30 x 30cm (12 x 12in) being the most popular. Some have pages bound in, while many are loose-leaf.

Printed and decorative papers Choose from a wide variety of patterned and plain papers, and papers with deckle edges to add interest to plain scrapbooking pages.

Deckle-edged scissors Use scissors with shaped blades to cut decorative edges on paper. Various shapes are available, from the familiar pinking (zigzag) blades, to scallops, wave shapes, and many others.

Card and paper Plain coloured card and paper are useful for creating backgrounds.

Charms and accents These little items – jewels, sequins, tiny frames, and other specially manufactured decorations – add the final flourish to scrapbooking pages.

Adhesives Various glues are used for different applications. A glue stick will stick papers and photographs, while glue dots are useful for applying small decorative elements.

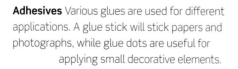

Small envelopes These can be used for hidden journalling (see p.111) and they are also useful for storing small components ready for use in scrapbooking projects.

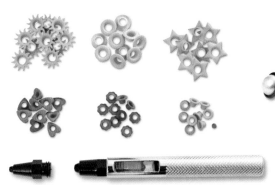

Eyelets and eyelet setter Eyelets are used to create neat holes in a page, which are useful for threading with ribbons and cords. An eyelet setting tool usually combines a hole punch and a tool for attaching the eyelet.

Brads Otherwise known as paper fasteners, these consist of a stud with two prongs on the back, which are inserted into a hole punched in paper. The prongs are then opened out and flattened, keeping the brad in place. Use them to hold components on a page or simply as decoration.

Page protectors For loose-leaf albums, you'll need plastic sleeves – also known as page protectors.

Rubber stamps Choose picture stamps for adding decorative touches, and alphabet and word stamps for captions and titles. Use an ink pad or brush pens to apply multiple colours to stamps.

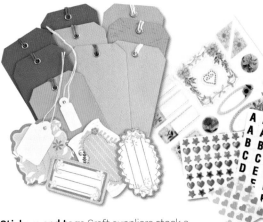

Stickers and tags Craft suppliers stock a wealth of stickers – flat, dimensional, matt, shiny, holographic, metallic, plush, and so on – to decorate scrapbooking pages, as well as labels and tags, all of which can be used in imaginative ways.

Lino printing

Lino cutting tools Buy a selection of three or four tools – including narrow, medium, and wide gouges – and a couple of safety handles.

Inks Specialist lino printing inks are available in a range of intermixable colours. Choose water-based inks as they do not contain solvents and are easy to clean off.

Carbon paper Use this with a hard pencil (such as an H or 2H) for transferring designs to the surface of the lino.

Lino This is available in pre-cut squares and rectangles, or buy a large piece and cut it yourself.

Roller Buy a roller in a width to suit the size of lino you are using.

Paper decorations

Paper All kinds of paper can be used – you can recycle magazine pages for bunting and cardboard boxes for card cutouts – but tissue paper and crepe paper are particularly useful and come in a range of vivid, eye-catching colours.

Découpage

Small scissors Choose small, sharp scissors with pointed blades for getting into corners and cutting out the tiniest areas of a design.

Paper Use printed papers that have a pattern of separate, distinct motifs that can easily be cut out. Many craft suppliers sell papers that have been specially designed for découpage.

Varnish The paper surface of the découpage needs to be sealed to protect it, so varnish is important. Choose a water-based varnish as it is solvent-free and you can wash the brush used to apply it with water.

Découpage medium This is the best choice of adhesive to stick down paper cutouts. It is easy to apply with a paintbrush and has a milky appearance so that you can visibly ensure an even coating. It allows the paper to be repositioned as needed and doesn't make the paper buckle.

Paper punching

Lever punches These come in a range of sizes to punch a variety of shapes. Regular punches punch the shape close to the edge of the paper; long-arm punches reach further in.

Anywhere punches These come in two parts which align with the paper in between, using strong magnets. Shapes can be punched anywhere and at any angle on the paper.

Spring-loaded punches These punches are used to cut small holes for decoration or to insert brads or eyelets.

Eyelet/hole punch This hand-held punch is designed to be used with a small heavy hammer. Hold the tool upright with the paper on a punching mat and hit sharply with the hammer to cut a hole.

Paper There is a wide variety of paper in different weights and thicknesses. Choose a paper suitable for the project. Some papers are soft and difficult to punch through; others are crisp and punch cleanly.

Punching mat Small cutting mats are specially made to use with eyelet/hole punches. Ordinary cutting mats would be irreparably damaged if used to punch holes.

Quilling

Paper You can buy ready-cut paper strips, which saves time and effort.

Quilling tools A quilling tool is a plastic stick with a slit in the top for inserting the end of a paper strip. Tools are often sold in sets, with slits of various sizes to accommodate papers of different widths.

Box-making

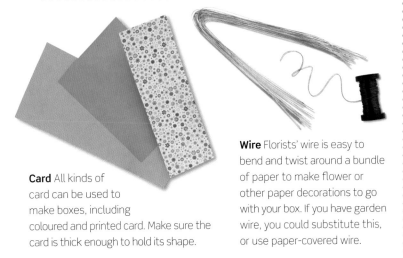

Card All kinds of card can be used to make boxes, including coloured and printed card. Make sure the card is thick enough to hold its shape.

Wire Florists' wire is easy to bend and twist around a bundle of paper to make flower or other paper decorations to go with your box. If you have garden wire, you could substitute this, or use paper-covered wire.

Screen printing

Silk screens These wood or metal frames have a monofilament mesh and are used with a squeegee. A 90T mesh is standard for screen printing onto paper. The higher the number, the finer the mesh.

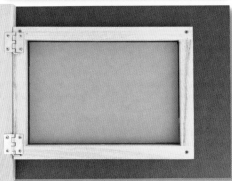

Base sheet and hinges The base sheet is attached to the screen with hinges so you can lift the screen up and down easily. The base sheet holds the card and stencil in place.

Thin acetate Use thin acetate or plastic for a durable stencil. Alternatively, you can use 70–90gsm printer paper. This will make several prints before starting to absorb the ink and becoming unuseable.

YOU WILL ALSO NEED...

Ruler Use a metal ruler for cutting; a plastic ruler is also useful for measuring and drawing straight lines.

Scissors These are an essential tool for cutting paper. Use a large, sturdy pair for cutting large sheets of paper and card; use smaller scissors for more detailed work.

Sticky tape This is useful for securing paper, for example, when wrapping a gift. Double-sided sticky tape can often be used instead of glue, for sticking down pieces of paper invisibly and securely.

Adhesives A glue stick is useful for paper, while an all-purpose glue forms a strong bond for attaching sequins, gems, and other small items to paper.

Cutting mat A self-healing cutting mat is essential when cutting card and paper using a metal ruler and craft knife. These mats are usually printed with a grid of straight lines so they are also useful for accurately measuring lines and angles.

Craft knife Cuts straight lines more accurately than scissors. Make sure you change the blade regularly.

Paintbrushes Save your best artist's brushes for watercolours and use cheaper brushes for varnishes, acrylic, household paints, and PVA glue.

Tweezers Use these to position small components such as jewels, sequins, and small stickers.

Iron An iron on a medium setting is used to flatten and smooth homemade paper sheets once dry.

Squeegee This is used for pushing the ink through the screen onto the card. It can be made from rubber or plastic and should fit inside the frame of the silk screen. A square-edged blade is best for working on paper.

Scrubbing brush This is used for cleaning the screen once you have finished printing. Always do this as soon as you have finished printing, before the ink dries. Nylon bristles are best.

Screen printing inks There are both water- and spirit-based varieties of ink. Water-based inks are good for beginners and are easy to wash out of the screen. They come in a range of colours, which can be mixed together.

Papermaking TECHNIQUES

Paper has come a long way since the ancient Chinese first made paper in the second century BC. The Egyptians used papyrus, our ancestors used animal skins, but we gradually developed a process of making an even surface to write or draw on from pulped fibres. To make your own paper, use paper such as printer paper that's already been pulped once.

Making a mould and deckle

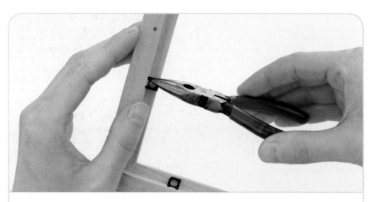

1 You will need two sturdy picture frames of roughly the same size to make a mould and deckle. If one is slightly larger, it should be the mould. Remove any hooks, clips, or wires from the frames.

2 To make the mould, stretch netting or fine mesh (plastic mosquito mesh works well) tightly across the flat side of the frame and staple all around the edge. This side is the top of the mould.

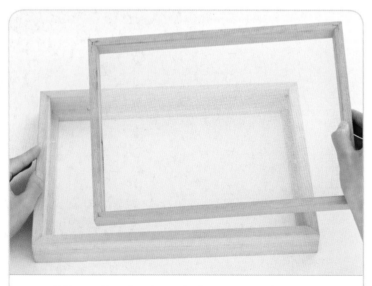

3 Hold the mould so that the netting is uppermost. Place the deckle flat side down on top of the mould. The deckle "frames" the paper pulp, forming a neat edge all round.

Selecting paper to use

Some papers work better than others for papermaking. Suitable papers include bank statements, printer paper, old letters, and other non-glossy papers without too much dark printing. Papers that aren't suitable are glossy papers, such as magazines and colour supplements, or recycled paper, such as newspapers and kitchen paper, whose fibres are too short. Try to stick to one dominant colour.

Shredding and soaking paper

Building a couching mound

Shred the paper into short 1cm (³/₈in) wide strips. Soak in a tub of water for at least a couple of hours – overnight is better – to allow the water to penetrate the fibres.

1 Lay some open newspapers on your work surface. Build a pile of newspapers, one folded over the next, concertina-style, about 5 to 8cm (2 to 3in) high and a little wider and longer than the mould. There should be no dip in the centre or water will pool there.

2 Drape several old towels over the mound of newspapers and roll them up around the edges. This is the "couching mound", on which you'll lay your sheets of paper to drain.

Making paper pulp

Angelina fibres

1 Half-fill a large shallow tray with cold water. Scoop some of the soaked paper into a food processor, cover with water, and blitz until it resembles a paste. Empty the paste into the tray. Repeat until the water in the tray is like a thickish soup.

2 If you're planning to add other fibres, glitter, or Angelina, stir them in now. Yarn and/or flower petals can also be added to the mix, or you can add them later if you want to control what their final position will be. Stir the mixture thoroughly.

Making paper from pulp

1 Hold the mould and deckle together, with the deckle flat side down, on top. Slide them into the tray of pulp at a 45° angle. Scoop up some of the pulp. Carefully withdraw the mould and deckle, shaking gently as you do so. This will help distribute the pulp evenly, which avoids holes in the paper.

2 Let the water drain through the netting, then tilt the mould and deckle gently towards one corner to allow the excess water to run off.

3 Lift off the deckle, then carefully lay an absorbent cloth over the pulp.

4 Align the edge of the mould with the edge of the couching mound. Quickly flip the mould containing the pulp on top of the mound.

5 Run your fingers over the netting: the pulp will start to come away from the mould and stick to the cloth beneath.

6 Carefully peel away the mould. Start by lifting one corner or side: the pulp should remain on the cloth. Run your hand over any obstinate areas to help release the pulp from the net. Leave the pulp to drain.

Draining and drying the paper

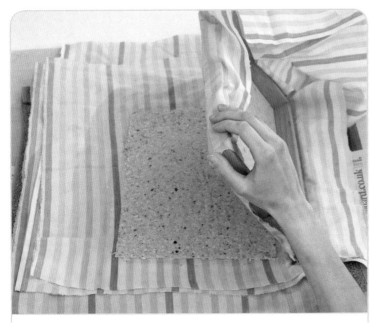

1 Cover the sheet of paper with cloth and start work on the next sheet. Build up a pile of cloths and sheets, one on top of the other, on the couching mound. When the "pulp soup" gets thin, blitz some more soaked paper and add it to the pulp mix.

heavy weight

2 Once you've used up as much of the pulp as you can and before the sheets of paper get too thin, lay one final cloth and a newspaper or towel over the top of the mound. Then lay a chopping board on top, pile some weights onto it, and leave for 10 minutes to squeeze any remaining water out of the sheets.

3 Remove the weights and chopping board and carefully peel off the top cloth.

4 The sheet of paper usually adheres to the cloth beneath it. Peg it onto a line or drying rack to dry. Lift and peg each successive cloth with paper attached. Leave to dry overnight or for a few days if the weather is damp.

5 When the paper is dry, remove it from the cloth. If it doesn't come away easily, iron it with the cloth face upwards, then peel the cloth off. If the paper has curled at the edges, press it flat with a medium-hot iron.

Petal writing paper PROJECT

Make some unique and decorative paper to write a special letter to a friend or to mount a precious picture on. Handmade paper is easy to make but hard to beat when it comes to making an impression. Use paper that you would otherwise recycle and add dried petals and scraps of coloured or metallic thread to create a really special effect.

YOU WILL NEED

- paper to shred (see p.96)
- shredder
- tub
- food processor
- large shallow tray
- red or pink food colouring (optional)
- newspaper
- old towels
- mould and deckle
- dried flower petals
- short scraps of coloured thread (optional)
- absorbent cloths a little larger than the mould
- chopping board
- heavy weight
- iron

1 Shred and soak the paper. Make the pulp following **making paper pulp** on p.97. If the pulp looks greyish, stir in a little red or pink food colouring. Follow **building a couching mound** on p.97.

2 Slide the mould and deckle into the tray and scoop up some pulp. Shake to distribute the pulp evenly, then tilt the mould and deckle to allow excess water to run off.

3 Scatter dried petals around the edge of the paper so they won't obscure any writing. You may wish to scatter a little more pulp over the petals, or lay some scraps of thread over them to "fix" them to the paper.

4 Lift the deckle then carefully place an absorbent cloth over the paper, taking care not to disturb the petals.

5 Flip the cloth and mould over onto the couching mound to drain. Run your fingers over the netting to dislodge the sheet of paper, then gently lift the mould off. Place absorbent cloth over the sheet of paper.

6 Continue making sheets until the pulp gets too thin, then drain the paper using a heavy weight on a chopping board to help squeeze out the water. Hang up to dry. When dry, iron the reverse side of the sheets, so as not to scorch or disturb the petals.

Paper marbling TECHNIQUES

Marbling is a great way to experiment with paper, colour, and pattern. Every piece of hand-marbled paper is unique, although with practice you'll be able to make similar patterns reliably. The patterns can be as simple or as complicated as you choose. If you enjoy this craft, you'll probably also like fabric marbling (see pp.26–29).

Preparing the size

"Size" thickens the water the paint will float on. To make it, mix wallpaper paste or marbling size with water, as directed on the packet, and pour into a large shallow tray to fill it to 2 to 3cm (approx 1in). Leave to set for about 30 minutes.

Adding the paint

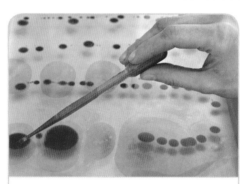

1 Load a pipette or paintbrush with acrylic or marbling paint and gently flick, drip, or trail it onto the set size. It will spread quite fast, so work quickly. If the paint sinks, thin it with a little water, shake until you reach the right consistency, and try again.

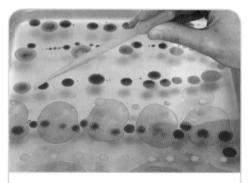

2 If you're using more than one colour, rinse the pipette or paintbrush, dry it with kitchen paper, then reload it with another colour. Flick onto the surface of the size, in between the blobs or trails of the first colour.

Creating patterns and effects

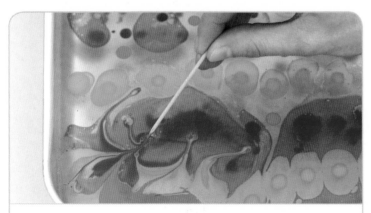

1 For a veined-marble effect, drag a cocktail stick randomly once or twice through the paint.

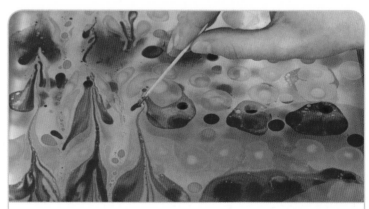

2 For a flame-like pattern, drag a cocktail stick over the surface of the paint, from one edge of the tray to the other, then move the cocktail stick towards the centre and drag it back in the opposite direction. Repeat to make more lines/rows of pattern.

3 To make more complex patterns, after Step 1, drag the cocktail stick to and fro over the surface at right angles to your first patterns to break them into smaller "flames".

4 To add a further dimension, drag a wide-tooth comb over the flames to produce a series of repeating loops. Each pattern is unique and it's great fun to experiment, but be careful not to overwork the pattern as the paints will mix together and end up looking muddy.

Marbling the paper

1 Hold the paper (120gsm is ideal) at either edge so that it dips a little in the middle. Lower it onto the paint so that the centre of the paper touches the paint first, followed by the edges. This prevents bubbles of air getting trapped underneath the paper.

2 Leave the paper for at least 10 seconds so it absorbs as much paint as possible. Then lift it out and rinse off the size under gently running cold water for a few seconds; stop if the paint starts to wash off.

3 Place the marbled paper face up on a towel to dry. Drag a sheet of kitchen paper or newspaper over the surface of the size to blot up any leftover paint, then add more paint and repeat the process to produce another sheet.

4 When the paper is dry, iron it on a medium heat to flatten it out.

Marbled book cover PROJECT

Turn an inexpensive notebook into something unique and special with a few sheets of hand-marbled paper, a little glue, and bookbinding tape. You could transform a plain hardback diary, notebook, or address book into the perfect gift.

YOU WILL NEED

- A5 hardback notebook
- 2 x A4 sheets of handmade marbled paper in matching colours (see techniques on pp.102–03)
- 1 x A4 sheet of handmade marbled paper in a contrasting colour (see techniques on pp.102–03)
- ruler
- PVA glue stick
- scissors
- craft knife
- 5cm (2in) wide bookbinding tape

spine

1 Slide the notebook under a sheet of marbled paper and centre the pattern on the front of the book. Leave at least 2.5cm (1in) from the edges of the sheet to the outside edges of the book.

2 Run your fingers around the outside edges and corners of the book to crease the paper. Run your thumbnail up the crease near the spine.

3 Cut the paper 2.5cm (1in) beyond the creases, and cut straight up the line made with your thumbnail. Apply PVA glue to the front cover and position the paper with the "thumbnail" crease by the spine and the other creases at the edges of the book. Press the paper to the cover and smooth it.

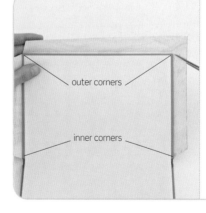

outer corners

inner corners

4 With the book open, snip the paper at an angle at the inner corners and cut away a 120° wedge at the outer corners. This ensures the paper overlaps neatly when folded to the inside.

5 Apply PVA glue around the edges of the inside cover. Fold the top and bottom edges of the marbled paper firmly onto the glue, then fold the outside edge over and smooth into position. Make sure all edges are well stuck down.

6 To neaten the inside cover, cut the contrasting sheet of marbled paper 5mm (¼in) smaller all round than the book cover. Apply PVA glue to the inside cover and stick the contrasting sheet down so that it covers the folded-over edges of the first sheet.

7 Repeat Steps 2, 3, 4, and 5, using the matching paper to make the back cover. Cut some bookbinding tape 2cm (¾in) longer than the spine. Lay it flat on your work surface, sticky-side up, centre the spine, then press the spine on the tape. Turn the book to one side and smooth the tape around the corner onto the flat surface; it should overlap onto the marbled paper. Repeat for the other side. Crease the tape either side of the spine.

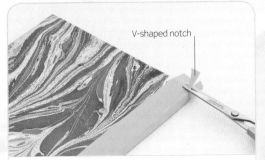

V-shaped notch

8 Cut V-shaped notches in the tape at the top and bottom of the spine indents and fold it over the front and back cover. You may be able to fold the tape in at the spine in the same way; if there isn't space, trim the tape and fold it over on itself to avoid a raw edge.

9 To make the corners, cut four 5cm (2in) lengths of bookbinding tape. Place one sticky-side up on the work surface. With the book open, position one corner diagonally over the tape so that a triangle of tape shows on either side, with a sliver of about 1mm (¹⁄₁₆in) still visible at the tip to allow for the thickness of the cover. Press the cover onto the tape, then fold the triangles to the inside cover. They should just about meet in the middle. Repeat for all corners.

Papier-mâché TECHNIQUES

The term papier-mâché is French for "chewed paper", and describes a variety of techniques where paper is saturated with paste and moulded into a shape which, when dry, forms a hard, durable shell. It is remarkable what a magical transformation can be achieved with old newspapers and paste, which makes papier-mâché a great recycling craft, ideal for creating decorative objects for the home such as vases, bowls, boxes, pencil pots, plaques, and trays.

Making a base

1 Select suitable plastic or cardboard containers that can be joined together to create interesting, one-off shapes.

2 Use an all-purpose glue to join the components together.

3 Use plastic bags, rolled into sausages or crumpled up, to pad out the basic form. Stick these in place with sticky tape.

Preparing the papier-mâché

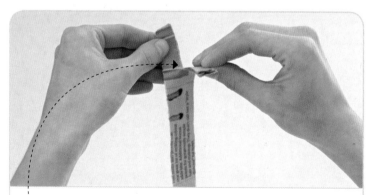

1 The paper should be absorbent: use old newspapers or pages torn from telephone directories. Tear the paper into manageable strips – don't cut it; the torn edges, when overlapped, will form a smooth surface without too many ridges.

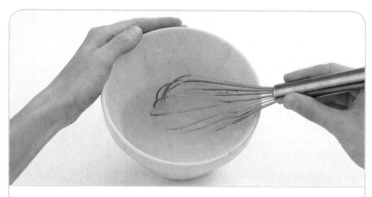

2 Mix wallpaper paste in a bowl, following the instructions on the packet. Most pastes contain fungicides, so if you have sensitive skin, you may wish to wear rubber gloves. Protect your work surface with newspaper or plastic sheeting.

Building layers

1 It's important to ensure that each paper strip is saturated with wallpaper paste. Dip it into the paste and use your fingers to remove surplus paste.

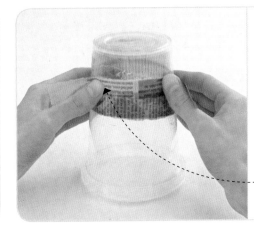

2 Apply the paper strip to the object and smooth it out with your fingertips, expelling air bubbles. Make sure you cover not only the surfaces but also all the edges and joins.

3 Build up lots of layers – at least eight or nine – to ensure a successful result.

tissue paper

4 Newsprint creates a neutral grey surface but if you wish to cover this up, apply a few layers of tissue paper; this will help to disguise the print and also creates a smoother surface.

Decorating the object

1 Allow the papier-mâché to dry completely before decorating. If there are any ridges or bumps, lightly sand the surface using fine sandpaper.

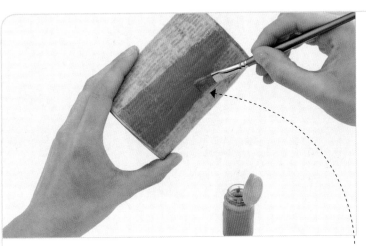

2 If you wish to decorate the surface of the papier-mâché object, you can paint it with water-based paints such as poster paints, watercolours, gouache, acrylics, or even household emulsion. Apply an (optional) undercoat of white paint if you want to use very light colours.

3 Once you have decorated the item, finish by sealing it with several coats of water-based varnish.

Papier-mâché bowl PROJECT

This decorative bowl is made from a disposable plastic receptacle – the kind sold in supermarkets containing salads – and the cardboard plinth from the centre of a ball of knitting yarn, plus a couple of plastic bags to pad out the rim. You can create a stylish bowl from these humble components, and decorate the surface using coloured tissue paper and a smattering of metal leaf.

YOU WILL NEED

- plastic bowl
- cardboard cylinder
- all-purpose glue
- 1–2 plastic bags
- sticky tape
- card
- scissors
- wallpaper paste
- newspaper, torn into strips
- PVA glue
- medium and large soft paintbrushes
- coloured tissue papers
- metal leaf size
- metal leaf
- water-based varnish

1 Glue the cardboard cylinder to the base of the bowl. Roll up one or two plastic bags and tape them under the rim of the bowl. Cut a circle of card to fit the base of the cylinder and glue or tape it in place.

2 Mix up wallpaper paste. Dip strips of newspaper in the paste, squeeze off excess paste with your fingers, and apply the saturated strips to the inside and outside of the bowl and all over the plinth, smoothing out each strip as you go.

3 Continue in this way until the whole piece is covered, then repeat until you have built up at least eight or nine layers. Leave to dry completely (this can take several days or even weeks, depending on temperature and humidity).

4 Once dry, brush the surface of the entire piece with PVA diluted with water to the consistency of single cream, then apply pieces of coloured tissue paper, brushing each one with diluted PVA. Apply two or three layers of tissue, then leave to dry.

5 Cut out circles from tissue paper in a contrasting colour, and glue these in place, using more of the diluted PVA. Leave to dry for several hours or overnight.

6 Once the tissue layers are dry, paint the rim with metal leaf size. Leave for 10 minutes, then apply metal leaf over the size, rubbing down gently with clean fingers. Use a large, soft brush to brush away any excess. Protect with two or three coats of varnish.

Scrapbooking TECHNIQUES

For decades, even centuries, people have enjoyed preserving paper scraps, tickets, greetings cards, postcards, and other memorabilia in albums. The new generation of scrapbooks are, essentially, highly decorated personalized photograph albums. The vast array of scrapbooking materials for sale in most craft shops and online is an indication that the craft is enjoying a huge revival. Here are some tips on how to make a basic scrapbook page to which you can add your own personal touches.

Choosing materials

1 A photograph or other image forms the focal point of an album page. Use a colour or theme from the photograph when selecting papers to form the background of the page. Materials with a high acid content will deteriorate over time, so make sure you use acid-free papers and card, as well as a suitable acid-free adhesive.

2 If you can't find paper of a suitable colour, make your own. Use water-based paints – watercolours, gouache, or acrylics – to paint a wash on white acid-free paper.

Cropping images

1 Photographs are the focal points and need to be shown to their best advantage. Use two L-shaped pieces of card to help decide how to crop pictures to eliminate distracting clutter.

2 Once you have decided on the format for your photograph, use a steel ruler and a craft knife to trim off unwanted areas. Protect your work surface by using a cutting mat.

3 Enhance pictures by sticking them onto pieces of card that are bigger than the image, forming a border all round. Experiment with edging tools to create decorative borders.

Making a border

1 Look out for decorative papers with printed borders that can be cut out for special pictures. As when selecting a background, choose harmonious colours.

2 Use small sharp scissors to cut out intricate shapes. Once you have cut out your border pieces, place them on the photograph to see if adjustments are needed.

3 Use a suitable acid-free adhesive to stick your photograph onto the background, then stick the border in place, trimming off any excess paper where pieces overlap.

Making embellishments

decorative punch

Craft supply shops are well stocked with ready-made embellishments but you can make your own, cutting out paper shapes freehand with scissors or using a decorative punch. This is a great way to utilize paper scraps left over from other projects.

Applying brads and eyelets

Punch a hole through all layers of paper where you wish to apply a brad or eyelet. Brads can be added by hand – just insert into the hole and spread out the metal prongs on the reverse. To add an eyelet, use a special setting tool and a hammer.

Making a hinge

A strip of paper with one end glued to the background makes a good hinge. You could fold the paper to create a concertina, which is useful for a series of pictures or a long caption that wouldn't otherwise fit across the width of the page.

Hidden journalling

"Journalling" refers to words, usually in the form of captions, stories, or poems. If these are personal or too long to fit on the page, write or print them on a separate piece of paper and fold it, then place it in an envelope glued to the background. This is a useful device for any items that you wouldn't wish to glue directly to the page.

Scrapbook page PROJECT

Old family photographs are the starting point for this scrapbooking project, which uses printed papers and a range of simple but effective techniques to create a nostalgic atmosphere that will stand the test of time. Use these step-by-step instructions only as a rough guide, adding your own creative touches to make your scrapbook really personal.

YOU WILL NEED

- ring binder scrapbook with plain pages
- old family photographs or postcards
- plain and printed papers
- metal ruler
- craft knife
- cutting mat
- glue stick
- self-adhesive paper lace
- photo corners (optional)
- dimensional decorative stickers
- ribbon
- small envelope
- rubber stamp and ink pad

1 Gather all your materials together before you begin. Once you have selected the photographs you wish to use, choose papers and other materials such as stickers, ribbons, labels, and rubber stamps that suit the theme and colour scheme.

2 Cut printed papers to fit the dimensions of the page and stick these in place. For best effect, also arrange some slightly smaller contrasting papers on top to make a multi-dimensional backdrop. Glue in place.

3 To make a frame, cut self-adhesive paper lace longer than the frame you wish to create. Peel off the backing and stick in place, with the ends overlapping at corners. Make diagonal cuts across the corners, then peel away the excess to form a neat mitre.

4 Once the frames are in place, stick down the photographs. If they are originals, you may wish to use photo corners to avoid damaging the paper; or make photocopies and stick these down. Add a sticker to each corner of the frame.

5 Add more stickers and tie a handmade label to the top of the ring binder with ribbon. Apply glue to the front of an envelope and stick it onto the page, then slip in a sheet of paper with your "secret journalling" (see p.111). A rubber-stamped heart on the flap adds a final flourish.

Lino printing TECHNIQUES

Lino printing can produce a similar effect to a traditional woodcut but lino is easier to carve than wood. The parts you cut away remain the colour of the surface you are printing on and uncut areas create the printing surface. Remember when you transfer your design to the lino that it will be reversed once it is printed. Cut away enough lino to create clear areas of print surface: lines that are too thin will become clogged with ink and may not print clearly.

Transferring your design

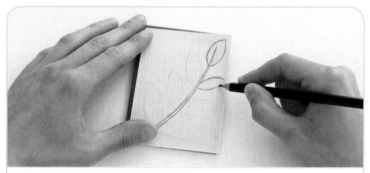

1 A simple design can be drawn straight onto the surface of the lino using a soft pencil. Make sure that the lino is clean and free from grease and dust. Alternatively, you may prefer to draw your design on paper first; this is useful if tracing a design from a printed source. Choose a thin, smooth paper such as tracing paper or layout paper.

2 Place a piece of carbon paper face down on the lino and place your drawing face down on top of the carbon. You should be able to see the lines of your drawing. Trace over these lines using a hard pencil to transfer the drawing onto the surface of the lino.

Cutting lino

1 Lino can be bought ready-cut, but if you want a particular size, place the lino on a cutting mat and use a metal ruler and craft knife to make several shallow cuts into the lino until you have cut right through it.

2 The lino has a hessian backing. If you fold the cut lino, you can cut through the hessian. You can use a craft knife for this step or you may prefer to use scissors.

3 When it comes to cutting the design, use a narrow V-shaped gouge for thin lines. Be sure to cut these lines deeply enough, so that they do not become clogged with ink when you come to print your design.

4 A U-shaped gouge is perfect for clearing large areas. Once you have finished cutting the design, brush away all the scraps of lino and make sure the printing surface is clean and dust-free.

Printing

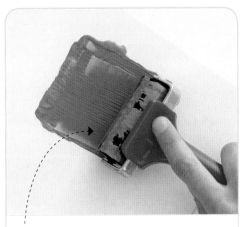

1 Roll out lino printing inks on a wipe-clean surface, such as a sheet of glass or a ceramic tile. Water-based inks are the best choice for most purposes and colours can be mixed to create the desired shade.

2 Once the roller is covered with an even layer of ink, roll it across the surface of the lino cut until it is evenly coated.

3 Place the paper on top of the inked lino and rub gently with the curved bowl of a spoon, or similar object, to press the ink onto the paper.

4 Carefully peel away the paper from the lino to reveal the print. This is the time to assess your print and decide whether or not you wish to cut away more of the lino.

Adding another colour

1 Once you have made the desired number of prints in your first colour, you can add a second colour. Wipe the ink from the surface and cut away more of the design.

2 Mix a second colour, darker than the first, then roll the inky roller over the lino.

3 Press the printed paper onto the lino, making sure the design lines up. Peel away the paper to reveal the two-colour print.

Stationery lino print PROJECT

If you want to reproduce the same image several times over to use on invitations, place cards, or, as here, on a set of decorated stationery, then lino printing offers the perfect solution. You can print the design onto as many sheets of paper and envelopes as you wish: just apply ink to the lino before making each print. Presented in a box, this paper and matching envelopes make a lovely gift.

YOU WILL NEED

- tracing paper or layout paper
- pencil
- carbon paper
- 7.5cm (3in) square of lino
- V-shaped and U-shaped lino cutting tools
- blue water-based lino printing ink
- small sheet of glass or ceramic tile
- roller
- A5 writing paper
- spoon
- C6 envelopes

1 Transfer the bird design (see template on p.309) to the surface of the lino, following **transferring your design** on p.114.

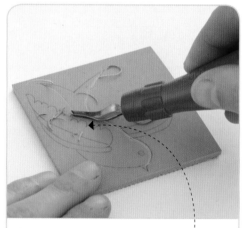

2 Cut along the lines using a narrow V-shaped gouge, then use a slightly wider V-shaped gouge and go over the lines again to ensure that they are sufficiently deep and wide (so that they do not become clogged with ink when printing).

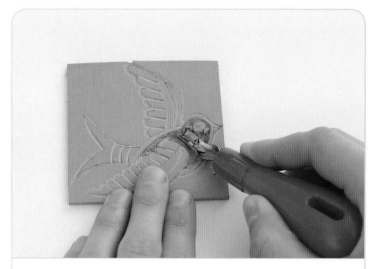

3 Using a wider U-shaped gouge, cut away excess lino from the areas that will not be printed (see white areas on the template).

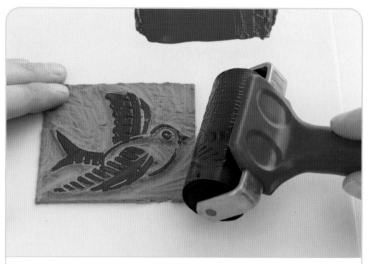

4 Squeeze a little ink onto the glass or tile and roll out, using the roller. Once the roller is charged with a thin, even layer of ink, roll it across the surface of the lino.

5 Place a sheet of A5 paper on the lino; make sure the lino is under the correct area of the paper (in this case, the top right-hand corner) and smooth over the paper using the back of a spoon. Repeat Steps 4 and 5 until you have the desired amount of printed paper. Use the lino to print on the envelopes, too.

Paper decorations TECHNIQUES

For parties and festivals the world over, people love to use decorations to create an atmosphere of celebration – and paper and card are the ideal choice. It's amazing how you can transform your home with tissue paper, string, scraps of card, and some deft snips of your scissors. Use the techniques on this page, along with your own imagination and creativity, to make stunning decorations, whatever the occasion.

Concertina folding

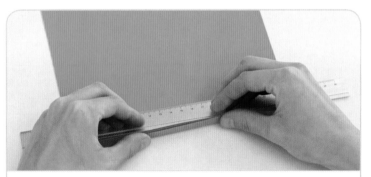

1 This basic paper-folding method is useful for all kinds of projects, such as the tissue paper pompoms on pp.120–21. Position a ruler across a sheet of paper to determine the width of the fold, then fold the paper against the edge of the ruler. Run over the fold with a blunt object to make sure it is really crisp.

2 Flip the paper over and repeat the folding process. Continue until the whole sheet has been folded into a concertina. You can create a number of decorative effects by tying a length of ribbon around the folded paper, then fanning out the folds above and below.

Making paper bunting

1 Bunting is a great way to use paper scraps left over from other projects – you can even use pages cut from magazines and brochures. Fold over one edge of the paper then cut out triangle shapes on a cutting mat, using a metal ruler and craft knife.

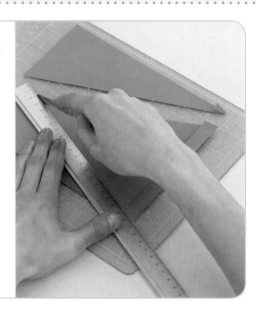

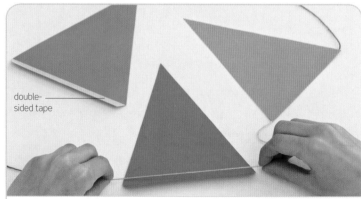

double-sided tape

2 Open out the fold and lay a strip of double-sided sticky tape across it. Lay a length of string or cord just below the tape, then peel off the tape backing, and fold the paper over, pressing to stick down the flap.

Making cardboard cutouts

1 Even the most humble, everyday materials can be transformed into decorations. Draw shapes on cardboard and cut them out with a craft knife.

2 Punch a hole in each cardboard cutout. Thread a length of string or cord through the hole and tie in a knot, ready for hanging up.

3 Use dimensional paints and gems to decorate each cutout.

Making temporary decorations

1 Make a template of a simple shape - such as a flower - then draw around the template on the paper backing of decorative self-adhesive paper or foil, then cut out the shape.

2 Peel off the paper backing and stick the shapes onto mirrors, vases, windowpanes, and other objects, as temporary decorations that can be peeled off.

Making paper "straw"

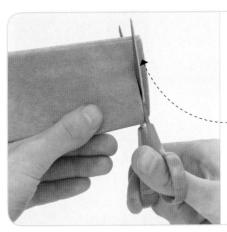

1 Fold a sheet of tissue paper several times, until it is a manageable size but not too thick, then cut across it into very thin strips.

2 Fluff out the strips, pick them up, and gently crumple them in your hands, then tease them out again. Use the resulting "straw" to line gift boxes (see pp.140–41) or as a nest for small gifts, baubles, or other decorations.

Tissue paper pompoms PROJECT

Tissue paper seems so fragile but it is more robust than it appears and is the ideal choice for bold decorations for parties and festivals. These paper balls – reminiscent of giant dandelion seed heads – can be suspended from the ceiling or from tree branches on invisible threads, or used as a table centrepiece. They will withstand a gentle breeze indoors or outdoors, though not strong winds or rain. Choose colours to match your theme.

YOU WILL NEED

- sheets of coloured tissue paper, 76 x 50cm (30 x 20in)
- scissors or craft knife
- ruler
- spoon, or similar smooth object
- 50cm (20in) lengths of florists' wire
- invisible thread

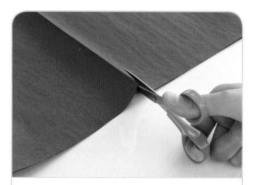

1 To make a small pompom, fold a sheet of tissue paper in half, in half again, and in half once more. You will have eight layers. Cut along the folds using scissors or a craft knife to make eight sheets measuring 25 x 19cm (10 x 7½in). Place the sheets in a neat stack.

2 Starting at one short end, make concertina folds at intervals of about 1.2cm (½in). Crease each fold as you make it by running the bowl of a spoon or the handle of your scissors along its length.

3 Bind the centre of the strip by bending a length of wire in half and twisting it firmly around the paper. Form a loop with the wire and tuck in the ends so they don't protrude.

4 Cut the ends of the strip in a pointed or curved shape, depending on the effect you wish to create.

5 Use your fingertips to tease out the folds of tissue, one at a time, working towards the centre, to form a ball shape. Tie a length of invisible thread to the wire loop, for hanging.

6 To make a larger version, use eight whole sheets of tissue paper, placed on top of each other in a neat stack. Follow the instructions for the smaller version but make the folds slightly wider – about 2.5cm (1in).

Découpage TECHNIQUES

Découpage is the craft of decorating an object with paper cutouts glued in place. If you take the time to apply many coats of varnish over the paper cutouts, they will appear to sink into the surface and will look as though they are part of the object and not merely stuck on. Choose from the wide range of printed papers available: gift wrap, magazine pages, catalogues, and brochures – and even papers with repeat motifs printed specifically for découpage.

Choosing your materials

Look for papers that have printed motifs that are separate and do not overlap with other parts of the design. This will provide you with individual elements to cut out. Make sure you have enough of your chosen motifs: buy two or more sheets of paper, if necessary.

Cutting out the motifs

1 Rough-cut the paper: this means cutting out each motif roughly, leaving a border of paper all round.

2 Using small scissors with pointed blades to ensure accuracy, cut out each motif very carefully. For best results, keep the scissors quite static and move the paper, rather than the other way round.

3 Make sure you cut away any areas of background within the motif. This is particularly important if, say, the background is white and the object you are sticking the motif onto is coloured.

Arranging and glueing the cutouts

1 Try out your design before sticking anything down. Move the cutouts around until you are happy with the arrangement.

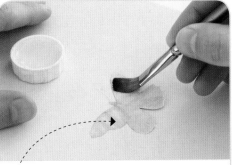

2 Brush découpage medium or PVA glue diluted with water to the consistency of thin cream onto the back of each cutout. Make sure each piece is thoroughly covered and there are no dry areas.

3 Place the glued cutouts in place and smooth out the paper, expelling any air bubbles. Use the same brush you used to apply the medium to the back of the cutouts.

Varnishing the piece

When the cutout is stuck down, leave it to dry, then apply a coat of clear varnish. You can choose a matt or gloss varnish, depending on the effect you want to achieve. Apply several coats of varnish, allowing each one to dry before applying the next.

Adding embellishments

1 To highlight small areas of the design, stick on flat-backed gems, which will add texture and sparkle.

2 Glitter also adds a touch of sparkle to a finished design. Simply apply dabs of glue using a cocktail stick to the areas you wish to highlight.

glitter

3 Then sprinkle on glitter, tip off any excess, and leave to dry thoroughly.

Keepsake box PROJECT

You can use découpage to decorate a number of different objects. A plain cardboard box is an ideal candidate for this technique. Choose one that is sturdy and well-proportioned, and look for printed papers with attractive flower heads and leaves – such as these pansies – to combine into an elegant floral arrangement to decorate the lid and sides of the box.

YOU WILL NEED

- printed papers
- small scissors with pointed blades
- cardboard box with lid
- soft paintbrush
- découpage medium or PVA glue diluted with water to the consistency of thin cream
- water-based gloss varnish

1 Cut out motifs roughly from printed paper then, using small scissors, cut out each one neatly, including areas between the leaves, stems, and petals.

2 Arrange the cutouts on the box until you are satisfied with the design. Take time to assess whether you have enough cutouts or whether you need to make more.

back of cutout

3 Using a soft paintbrush, apply découpage medium or diluted PVA glue all over the back of the cutout that will form the basis of your arrangement.

4 Place the pasted cutout in position on the box lid and smooth out, using the brush still loaded with medium. Repeat to complete the arrangement with the remaining cutouts.

5 Apply cutouts to the sides of the box in a similar way, avoiding the upper part which will be covered by the sides of the lid.

6 To protect the paper cutouts and to create an attractive finish, brush the box with several coats of varnish – ideally about six or more coats – leaving each coat to dry thoroughly before applying the next.

Paper punching TECHNIQUES

Punching is a decorative technique that is used to add patterns to paper and thin card. Not all papers punch successfully: mulberry papers, tissue paper, and some natural fibre papers are too soft. Punches won't punch through paper or card that is too thick either, so try out your punch on sample papers first to ensure a good result.

Making a template for a conical lampshade

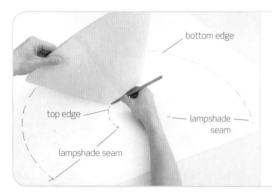

1 Place the lampshade on a large piece of paper with the seam aligned near the long edge of the paper. Mark the position of the seam, then roll the lampshade, marking the trajectory of the bottom edge with a pencil, until you get to the seam again. Mark the position of the seam at the other end. Roll the shade again as before, this time marking the top edge and seam.

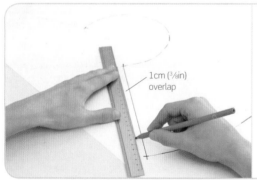

2 Draw a smooth curve along the top and bottom trajectory lines. Join the seam marks with a ruler, adding a 1cm (³⁄₈in) overlap at one end. Cut along the lines.

3 Check the size and shape of the sleeve by placing it over the lampshade. Make any necessary adjustments, then use as a template to cut the coloured paper sleeve.

Punching

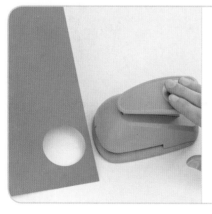

1 Most punches have a slot for the paper and a lever to punch the shape. Standard punches punch close to the edge of the paper; long-arm punches punch further in from the edge. Working on a flat surface, slot the paper into the punch, and press the lever firmly.

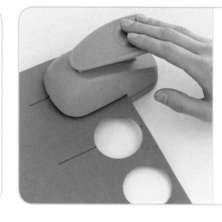

2 To space punched shapes accurately, use the side of the punch as a guide (align the edge of the punch with the edge of the previous shape, for example) or mark with a pencil before starting. You may need to mark the punch too to position it accurately.

3 To punch a shape out of patterned paper or to position text in the centre of a shape, turn the punch upside down. Slot the paper into the punch so that you can see the pattern positioned correctly, then press the lever.

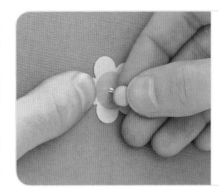

4 Punching creates an aperture as well as a cut-out shape. Use the shape as an embellishment: stick it onto a background, or punch a small hole through the shape and the background, and insert a brad or eyelet to secure.

Using an "anywhere" punch

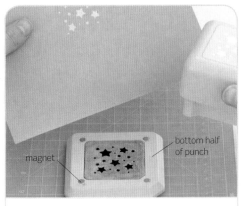

magnet

bottom half of punch

1 Larger "anywhere" punches use magnets to align the top and bottom halves of the punch on the paper. Place the bottom half on a cutting mat, then place the paper on top. lower the top half until the magnets attract and the punch is positioned exactly.

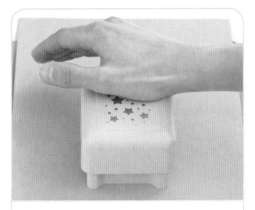

2 Press the top half of the punch with the heel of your hand, or preferably with both hands. If the punch is not lined up correctly it won't punch. Lift off the top half of the punch to see the punched shape.

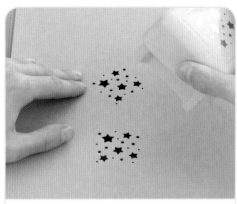

3 "Anywhere" punches can punch at any angle: either rotate the base of the punch to the required position or turn the paper. When punching shapes close together, make sure you don't punch into a previous shape.

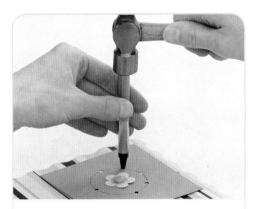

4 To punch a hole anywhere on a surface, use a hammer punch and mat. The tips are interchangeable for different sizes of holes. Use a special punching mat as this type of punch will damage a regular cutting mat.

5 Spring-loaded eyelet punches can punch holes anywhere. Position the punch on the paper with a punching mat underneath, pull up to tension the spring, and release. The spring creates a hammer action that punches a hole in the paper.

Looking after your punches

Punches need some maintenance. If the punch sticks, punch through several layers of wax paper to lubricate it. If the punch is blunt, punch repeatedly through several layers of aluminium foil to sharpen it.

Punched lampshade PROJECT

A plain white lampshade can be transformed by covering it with a coloured paper sleeve. Add interest by punching holes in the paper so that the colour of the lampshade shows through. Here, a pretty star punch was used to create a night sky effect on fabulous lavender blue paper, but there are lots of different punch designs that could be used on other colours of paper.

YOU WILL NEED

- plain lampshade
- white paper for the template
- pencil
- ruler
- lavender blue paper
- scissors
- 4cm (1½in) starry night "around the page" punch
- eraser
- double-sided sticky tape

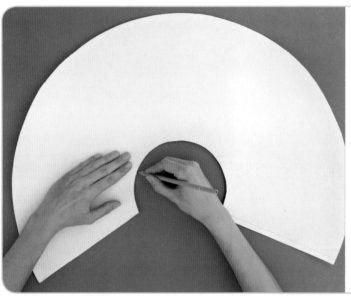

1 Follow **making a template for a conical lampshade** on p.126. Use the resulting template on the right side of the lavender blue paper to make the lampshade sleeve. Mark the 1cm (³⁄₈in) overlap at one end on the coloured paper then cut out.

2 Following **using an "anywhere" punch** on p.127, punch around the entire bottom edge of the sleeve, marking each start point 4cm (1½in) – or the size of your punch – from the last with a light pencil mark.

one-third mark

3 Fold the white template into thirds and use it to pencil mark the right side of the coloured sleeve into thirds. Cut a number of of 4cm (1½in) squares and arrange them in a regular and/or random pattern on the first third of the sleeve. Draw light pencil lines around each square.

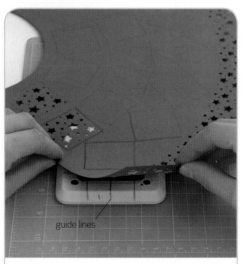

guide lines

4 Line the punch up with one of the marked squares. You can mark the edges of the punch for accurate positioning. Hold the paper while you align the punch with the horizontal and vertical lines of the marked square. Punch the shape. Repeat to punch each square.

seam

5 Work around the sleeve, marking more squares on each third of the sleeve. Once all the squares have been punched, rub out the pencil lines. Using double-sided sticky tape, stick the overlap under the edge of the seam. Place the sleeve over the lampshade.

Quilling TECHNIQUES

Quilling, sometimes called paper filigree, is the centuries-old art of creating decorative shapes from narrow strips of paper. Various shapes can be formed, usually by first rolling the strips into tight coils, then allowing them to unroll slightly and pinching them. These can then be combined to make patterns, using the various shapes and colours to good effect. No special tools are needed – you can roll the strips around a cocktail stick – though quilling tools and pre-cut paper strips are readily available from craft suppliers.

Cutting paper strips

Basic quilling

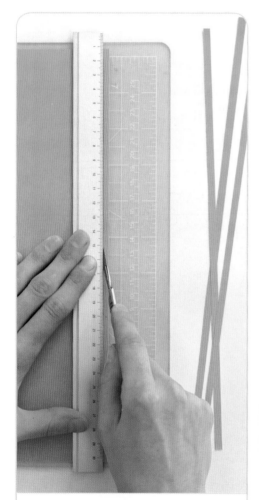

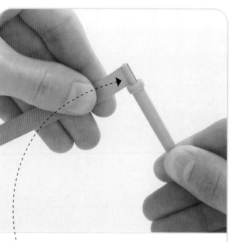

1 Insert one end of a paper strip into the slit in the quilling tool (or wrap the end around a cocktail stick).

2 Twirl the tool with one hand while guiding the paper strip with the other, to wind the paper into a tight coil.

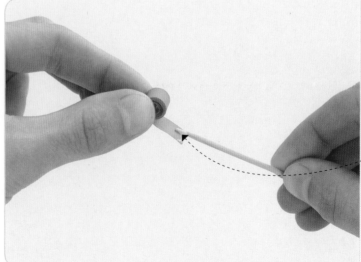

3 Slip the paper coil off the tool. If you want to use the quilled strip as a tight coil, use a cocktail stick to dab a spot of PVA glue to the end of the strip and stick in place.

Use a metal ruler and craft knife over a cutting mat to cut narrow strips from a sheet of coloured paper. Strips can be any width, though 3mm (1/8in) is the most popular size.

Creating shapes

1 Allow the coiled paper to relax slightly to make a round coil that is more open in appearance, then glue the end in place.

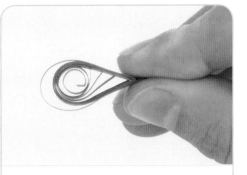

2 To create a teardrop shape – useful for flower petals and leaves – allow the coiled paper to unwind slightly before glueing the end in place, then pinch the coil in one place between finger and thumb.

3 To create a shape reminiscent of an eye – known as a marquise – allow the coiled paper to relax slightly, glue the end, then pinch the coil in two places, as shown.

4 For a triangular shape, pinch a coil that has relaxed slightly in three places. This shape is useful for flower motifs and leaves.

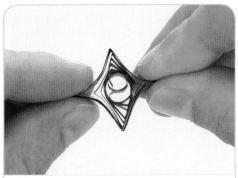

5 A relaxed coil pinched in four places is known as a star.

6 Create this heart shape by rolling a paper strip from both ends, then crease the centre of the strip so that the coils face each other.

Glueing and arranging

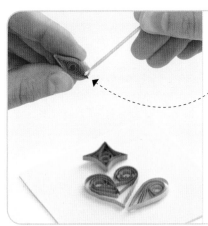

1 Use small dabs of PVA glue – which becomes transparent once dry – to glue shapes to a background.

2 Combine various shapes to make motifs that can be used to decorate greetings cards, labels, pictures, and book covers.

Quilled paper picture PROJECT

You will need only the most basic materials – strips of coloured paper, a quilling tool or cocktail stick, a piece of backing card, and glue – to create a decorative quilled picture. To display your work of art, choose a fairly deep frame, or mount the picture using a deep mount that accommodates the thickness of the paper strips and prevents them from touching the glass.

YOU WILL NEED

- 3mm (⅛in) wide paper strips in blue, yellow, red, green, and pale green
- quilling tool
- PVA glue
- cocktail sticks
- 25 x 20cm (10 x 8in) backing card

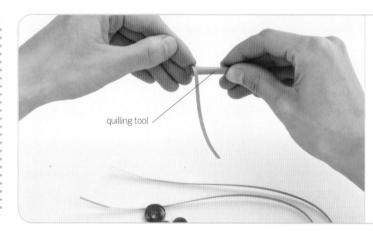

quilling tool

1 Make 15 coils in blue: make three tight coils, eight a little more relaxed, and four more relaxed still. Glue the ends in place.

2 Make three tight coils in yellow, then make seven teardrop shapes in red for the petals, glueing the ends in place.

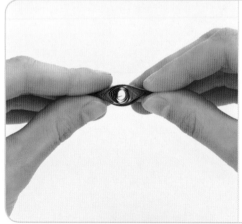

3 Make six leaves using green paper strips and glue the ends.

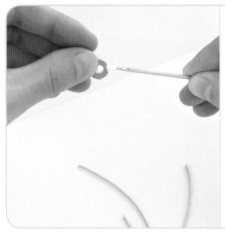

4 Fold pale green strips in half lengthways to create stems. Apply glue sparingly along the edges of the paper and place on the backing card, using the final image as a guide. Glue one yellow coil to form a flower centre.

5 Arrange the other quilled shapes in position. When you are happy with the arrangement, glue each shape in place.

Card-making TECHNIQUES

Homemade greetings cards are fun to make and show the recipient that you really care. Traditionally sent on special occasions such as birthdays and Christmas, they can also be sent to convey all kinds of messages – such as "thank you" and "good luck", or to convey various sentiments. Best of all, making your own cards requires only the most basic materials and this craft really allows you to express your creativity in a unique and individual way.

Making basic cards

1 There is a wide range of card available to buy, both plain and patterned. For card-making, choose card stock that is sturdy but not too thick.

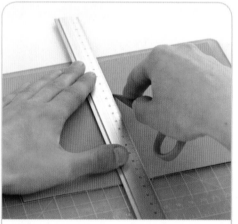

2 A rectangle of card folded in half makes a basic, single-fold card. To make folding easier and neater, score the centre line using the back blade of a pair of scissors and a metal ruler.

3 Cut a piece of paper to the same dimensions as the card or slightly smaller, and fold it in half, for an inner leaf on which to write your message. Punch two holes through both layers, on the centrefold.

4 Thread the ends of a length of ribbon through the holes of both layers and tie with a bow.

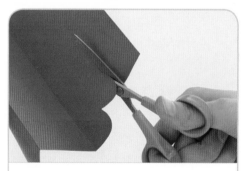

5 Additional folds create further design possibilities: a two-fold card gives six surfaces for decoration (three on the front and three on the back). Cut the corners in an interesting shape to add another dimension.

6 This scalloped edge creates an attractive effect. It can be left plain or decorated with stickers.

Making pop-ups

1 Pop-ups add an extra dimension to a single-fold card. Cut two slits at right angles to the folded edge, then score between the ends of these slits, parallel to the edge of the card, to create a rectangular "flap".

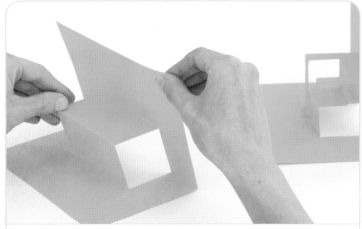

2 Fold across the scored lines to create the pop-up. By cutting and scoring a second set of lines, you can create another level of pop-up. Experiment on scrap paper first to make sure both sets of scored lines work together correctly.

Adding extra decorative elements

1 Combine shapes cut from plain and patterned card scraps to make components to decorate your card.

deckle-edged scissors

2 Use fancy scissors to cut decorative edges. Deckle-edged scissors are available from most craft suppliers, with a wide selection of different blades.

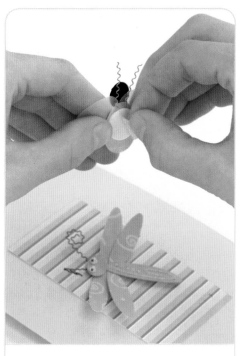

3 To add texture and interest, use small pieces cut from thick card, or use dimensional sticky pads to raise components off the surface of the card, creating a 3D effect.

Pop-up cake card PROJECT

Suitable for a number of different occasions, such as a greetings card or an invitation for a birthday, anniversary, or wedding perhaps – this pop-up card is impressive but uses the simplest techniques to maximum effect. All you need are some colourful card scraps, a steady hand, and a sharp craft knife. Vary the colour scheme to suit your own tastes and the occasion.

YOU WILL NEED

- 2 plain coloured pieces of card measuring 24 x 17cm (9¾ x 6¾in)
- metal ruler
- scissors
- pencil
- cutting mat
- craft knife
- printed and white card scraps
- deckle-edged scissors
- double-sided sticky tape
- hole punch
- narrow ribbon
- stickers
- glue stick

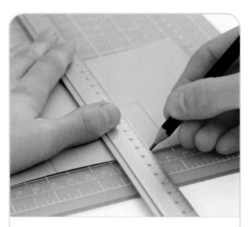

1 Score across the centre of one of the cards and fold in half. Measure 5cm (2in) in from each side and make two 5.5cm (2¼in) cuts at right angles to the folded edge at each of the marked points. Measure 1.5cm (⅝in) in from the cut lines and make two more 3.5cm (1⅜in) cuts.

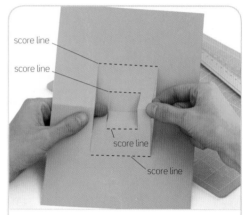

score line
score line
score line
score line

2 Score between the ends of the two pairs of parallel cuts. Open out the card, folding the larger pop-out inwards and the smaller, inner one outwards, as shown.

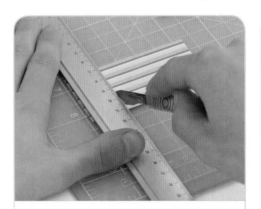

3 Using striped card, cut a rectangle 10 x 5.75cm (4 x 2½in) for the bottom tier. For the top tier, cut a piece 7 x 4.5cm (2¾ x 1¾in) then cut away strips to form candles. For the middle tier, cut a piece 8 x 4.5cm (3¼ x 1¾in) and cut away corners to create a tab to slot into the middle of the inner pop-up.

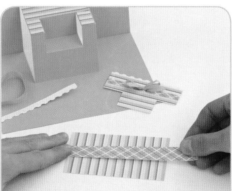

4 From the striped card, cut a piece to cover the top of the pop-up. From contrasting card, cut strips to fit across the tiers. Using deckle-edged scissors, cut strips of white card for borders. Punch pairs of holes in the centres of the card strips, insert short lengths of ribbon, and tie in bows.

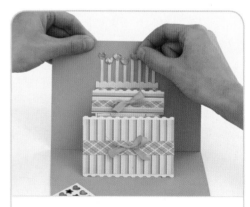

5 Stick the strips onto the tiers using double-sided sticky tape, then stick the tiers to the pop-ups, checking to make sure that the card can still be folded. Decorate the candles and surrounding card with stickers.

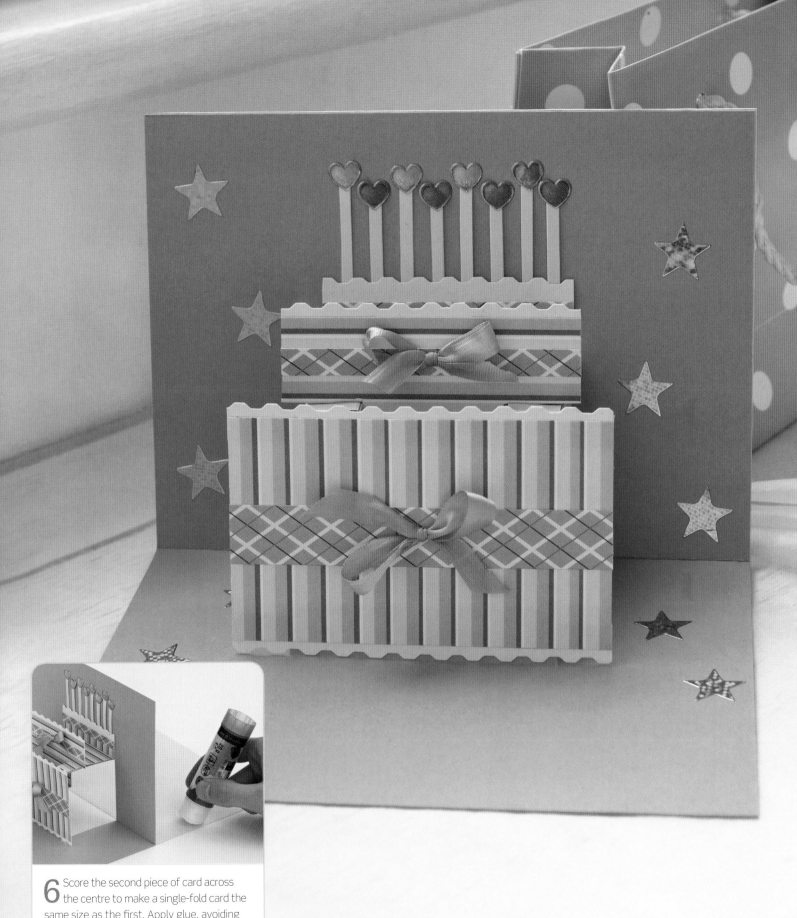

6 Score the second piece of card across the centre to make a single-fold card the same size as the first. Apply glue, avoiding the pop-ups, then stick the two cards together to form a neat outer layer.

Box-making TECHNIQUES

Box-making is also known by the French term "cartonnage" and covers a variety of techniques. In its simplest form, this craft consists of cutting a form from flat card using a template, cutting out the shape, scoring and folding, then assembling it into a box. Gift boxes are readily available from stationers and craft shops but it's much more fun – and cheaper – to make your own.

Choosing materials

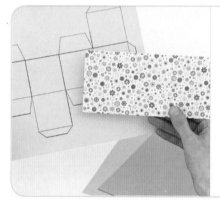

Choose your materials carefully. For a small box, thin card will do, but for a bigger box, the card needs to be slightly thicker. Photocopy the template on p.310 onto the wrong side of the card, enlarging it to the desired size, or copy then trace it onto the card.

Cutting

1 Place the card on a cutting mat and cut out the outline of the box using a craft knife and metal ruler. Take care not to cut along the internal fold lines.

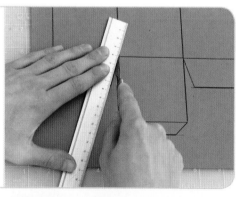

2 If you prefer, you can use scissors to cut out the outline.

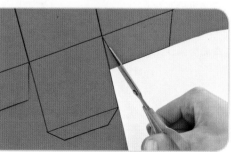

Scoring

1 For a neater finish, score along the fold lines before folding them. Make sure the drawn lines are on the inside of the box and, using a metal ruler as a guide, run the blunt edge of a craft knife blade over the fold lines.

2 Once you have scored all the fold lines, fold inwards along each one.

3 For really crisp fold lines, run along the folds with a smooth instrument, such as the back of a spoon. The proper tool for this job is a bone folder, so use this if you have one.

Making labels

Use card offcuts to make labels. Cut small rectangles of card then trim off two corners. Apply a round sticker and punch a hole in the centre of the sticker. Add a loop of cord. Leave plain or decorate with a paper cutout.

Making decorative bows

1 To make a bow, cut two strips of crepe paper with the grain running widthways. Use one strip for the loops and one for the tails, cutting the ends in a V-shape. Place the loop in the centre of the tails.

2 Cut a third strip and fold in each long edge to the centre. Wrap this piece twice around the centre of the bow, then cut off excess and glue or tape the cut end to the underside of the bow.

Making paper flower decorations

1 Make a paper flower centre by wrapping two or three layers of tissue paper around a ball of wadding. Using fine wire, bind the ball to one end of a length of thick paper-covered wire.

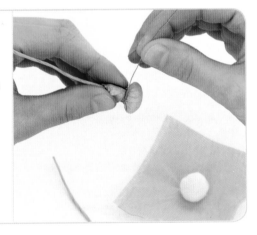

2 Cut petals from crepe paper with the grain running lengthways down each. Flute the edges then gently stretch the centre of each petal to create an attractive curl.

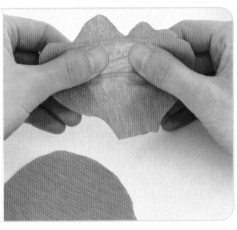

3 Wrap the base of each petal around the flower centre, one at a time, fastening with fine wire. Use a total of about 10 or 12 petals.

4 Conceal the base of the petals by wrapping with a strip of tissue paper backed with double-sided tape. Continue wrapping the strip around the length of the stem to cover it.

Small gift box PROJECT

This little box is the ideal way to present small, awkwardly shaped gifts. Use the template on p.310 to create as many boxes as you like, in different sizes and using different coloured card. A3 card is widely available in a range of colours and printed patterns. Choose coordinating tissue paper to make paper straw (see p.119) to stuff inside the box.

YOU WILL NEED

- A3 plain or patterned card
- cutting mat
- craft knife
- metal ruler
- scissors
- double-sided sticky tape
- tissue paper, for the paper straw (optional)

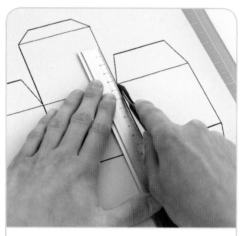

1 Transfer the box template on p.310 to the back of a sheet of A3 card, then score along all internal fold lines using the back of a craft knife blade and a metal ruler.

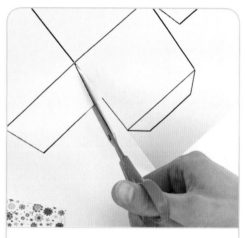

2 Cut out the box using the craft knife or, if you prefer, scissors. Take care not to snip into the internal fold lines.

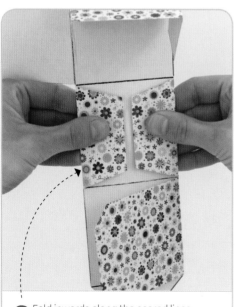

3 Fold inwards along the scored lines, making sure each crease is sharp.

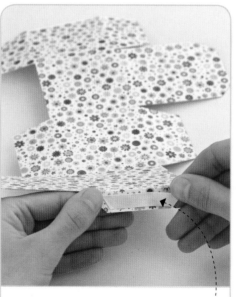

4 Apply a piece of double-sided sticky tape to the right side of the end flap.

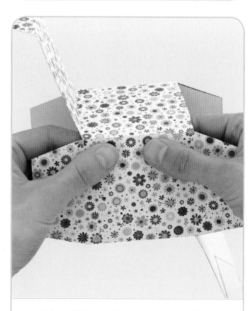

5 Peel off the backing paper from the tape and press the end flap into position to form the four sides of the box.

6 Fold the two pairs of larger flaps inwards. Decide which will be the top and bottom, then stick a strip of double-sided tape to each of the larger flaps on the base and press the square base onto these flaps. Tuck in the smaller side flap, leaving the top open, ready for filling.

Screen printing TECHNIQUES

Screen printing is a fun way to create multiple copies of a simple image. Cut out the stencil from a sheet of thin acetate and place it between the frame and the card on which you're printing, then pull the ink across the screen with the squeegee to print the image.

Preparing the screen

1 Wash the screen by scrubbing it on both sides with a nylon brush and a solution of detergent and warm water. Do not soak. Rinse thoroughly, pat dry with kitchen paper, and leave to dry flat.

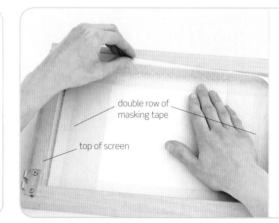

double row of masking tape

top of screen

2 Protect the edges of the screen by taping lengths of masking tape on the front and the underside of the screen. Apply a double row of tape across the top and bottom to create a wider area onto which the inks can be prepared. The unmasked area of the screen is the "canvas".

Preparing the stencils

second stencil

first stencil

1 Here we're making a two-colour print, with two red leaves and three yellow leaves, for which we'll need two separate stencils. Using a marker pen, trace the first part of the design (two leaves) on the centre of a sheet of thin acetate. Place another sheet of acetate directly on top of the first sheet and trace the second part of the design (three leaves).

2 Cut out the stencils over a cutting mat using a craft knife. Make sure that the stencils stay flat and do not crease. Always keep your fingers away from the blade.

Registering the print

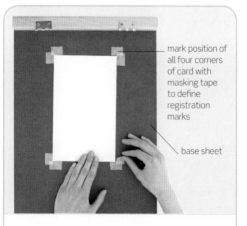

mark position of all four corners of card with masking tape to define registration marks

base sheet

1 Registering ensures that the card and stencil are always in the same relative positions, allowing you to make multiple prints. Place the first blank piece of card on the base sheet and mark the position of all four corners with masking tape. (The card should be smaller than the stencil so that unwanted ink doesn't bleed onto it.)

mark position of all four corners of stencil with masking tape to define registration marks

card registration marks

2 Place the first stencil on top of the card so that the design is centred, and mark the position of all four corners of the stencil with masking tape.

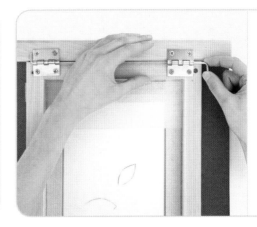

3 Insert the hinge pins to join the screen to the base sheet. Lower the screen onto the card and the stencil, making sure they remain lined up with their registration marks.

Making the first print

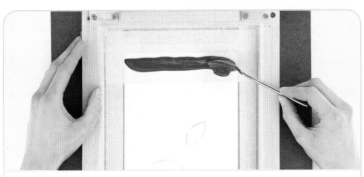

1 Using well-mixed screen printing ink, spoon a line of ink along the width of the masking tape at the top of the screen. Use the squeegee to pull the ink across the screen, angling the top of the squeegee towards you to push the ink through the screen. You may need to do this twice to ensure the ink is pushed through the screen.

2 Use the squeegee to move the leftover ink back to the top of the screen. Lift the screen and remove the printed card. Insert a new blank piece of card and repeat until you have as many copies of the first stencil as you need.

Cleaning up

Before adding the second colour, you must clean the equipment first. Use the squeegee to remove excess paint from the screen, then remove the masking tape. Working quickly so that the paint doesn't dry, use a nylon brush and running water and detergent to wash the screen, squeegee, and stencil. Pat dry with kitchen paper, then allow to dry naturally.

Adding a second colour

Place a previously printed and dried card on the base sheet so that it is lined up with the existing registration marks. Place the second stencil on top of the card so that it too is aligned to its registration marks and the design is centred. Protect the edges of the screen with masking tape, and repeat the printing process, this time using a second colour ink. Repeat until you have a complete set of cards. Clean up your equipment as soon as you have finished.

Screen printed postcards PROJECT

The technique of screen printing is ideal for making multiple printed copies of a design. Here, it is used to make two-colour postcards. You can display the finished postcards in a frame or print the design on a larger piece of card and fold it to make a birthday card for a cat lover.

YOU WILL NEED

- silk screen 90T mesh, 36 x 25cm (14 x 10in) outside measurement
- nylon scrubbing brush
- detergent
- 2.5cm (1in) wide masking tape
- scissors
- 2 sheets of thin acetate
- marker pen
- cutting mat
- craft knife
- 15 x 10cm (6 x 4in) white postcards
- base sheet and hinges
- water-based screen printing inks
- spoon
- 18cm (7in) rubber or plastic squeegee
- kitchen paper

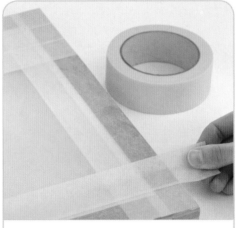

1 Following **preparing the screen** on p.142, wash the screen and leave it to dry flat. Then tape lengths of masking tape first on the front and then on the underside of the screen. Apply a double row of tape across the top and bottom of the screen where the ink will be prepared.

2 Refer to the template on p.311 and prepare two stencils, one for each element of the postcard, following **preparing the stencils** on p.142. Ensure that the two stencils form the whole picture when you hold the sheets together with the edges lined up so that you can use the same registration marks for both stencils.

3 Place a postcard on the base sheet and mark the position of all four corners with masking tape. Lay both stencils over the postcard so that the design is centred and mark the corner positions too. Remove the butterfly stencil.

4 Stir the ink, then spoon a line of ink along the width of the masking tape at the top of the screen. Use the squeegee to pull the ink across the stencil, following **making the first print** on p.143.

5 When you have made enough prints using the first stencil, remove the masking tape then wash the screen, squeegee, and stencil in warm soapy water. Pat dry and leave to dry flat.

6 Once the prints have dried, prepare the screen with masking tape again and repeat this process using the second stencil to add the second colour.

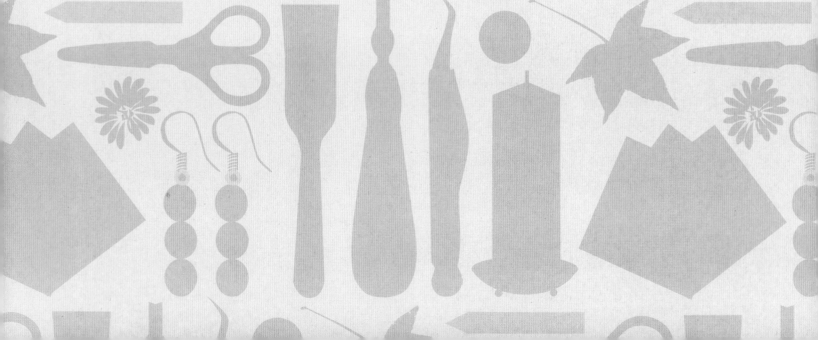

Jewellery

Jewellery

BEADING • SILVER WIREWORK • COLD ENAMELLING • LOOM WEAVING

POLYMER CLAY • AIR-DRY CLAY • METAL CLAY

It's surprising how easy it is to create fabulous jewellery with just a few tools and components. From stringing beads to make a necklace, to actually making the beads yourself, the following pages contain all you need to know to get you started.

Part of the fun of making your own jewellery is seeking out the materials for your chosen project: bead shops are a treasure trove of enticing beads and findings that are fun and easy to put together, and usually inexpensive too. Of course, the Internet gives access to an even wider selection.

In addition to beads and findings, there's a whole host of specialist materials, such as air-dry clay, polymer clay, and metal clay. These versatile materials are widely available and make the craft of making jewellery particularly exciting.

If you're looking to make a special piece of jewellery, semi-precious beads are not as costly as you may think. Also, consider taking apart old jewellery to reuse the beads: it's a wonderful way to achieve a vintage style and give new life to a treasured but broken piece of jewellery.

Now is your chance to experiment with techniques that are new to you. If you're a keen needle worker, the loom-woven cuff on pp.172–73 is sure to appeal, as the beads are woven with a needle and thread on a bead loom using an age-old weaving technique. If you already enjoy modelling with clay, there are projects for making your own beads, a pendant, and a brooch using a variety of clays that are a far cry from the lumpy modelling materials you may remember from a few years ago.

All the projects in this chapter are very adaptable – for instance, if you're making a necklace, you could also make a shorter version for a matching bracelet. Your own homemade beads can be strung as necklaces or bracelets, or hung from ear wires to make beautiful earrings. Be inspired to take the techniques further and create your very own designs. Handcrafted jewellery pieces are always welcome gifts and can be given an extra-personal touch by making the piece in the recipient's favourite colours and style.

Jewellery TOOLS AND MATERIALS

You may find that you already have some of the tools and materials needed to make jewellery. For comfort and safety, always work on a well-lit, clean, flat surface, and keep sharp tools and materials beyond the reach of young children and pets.

Beading

Flexible beading wire This strong nylon-coated wire is available in different thicknesses. Cut the wire with wire cutters and store it in coils as any kinks cannot be removed.

Wire Wire for making jewellery comes in different thicknesses and finishes such as silver- and gold-plated, sterling silver, and coated copper. 0.6mm (24 gauge) wire is suitable for many applications.

Bead reamer A diamond-tipped bead reamer will enlarge a hole in beads of various materials or file a jagged edge of a hole which could snag thread. For best results, moisten the reamer and bead with water before use.

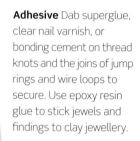

Adhesive Dab superglue, clear nail varnish, or bonding cement on thread knots and the joins of jump rings and wire loops to secure. Use epoxy resin glue to stick jewels and findings to clay jewellery.

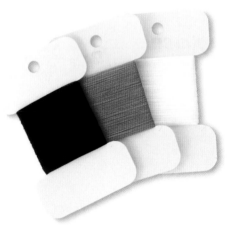

Embroidery scissors Use small, sharp scissors such as embroidery scissors just for snipping thread or fabric. Paper will blunt them quickly and never use them to snip wire.

Bead stringing thread This flexible, synthetic thread is very strong. It comes on a reel in a limited range of colours and thicknesses.

Beading needles These are very thin with a long eye. They are prone to bend and break easily, so have a selection to hand. Long and short beading needles are available.

Cord, thong, and narrow ribbons Thread beads with large holes onto suede, leather, or cotton thong and narrow ribbon. Shiny, round cord called rattail comes in 1 to 3mm (1/16 to 1/8in) thicknesses and lots of colours.

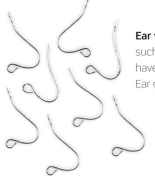

Ear wires These come in various styles such as fish hooks and ear studs, which have a loop below to suspend beads. Ear clips are available for unpierced ears.

Tag ends These three-sectioned metal pieces fold into thirds to secure the ends of ribbon, cord, and thong. The loop at the top can be fixed to a jump ring.

Fastenings Necklace and bracelet fastenings come in all sorts of styles and finishes, from simple bolt rings or a ring and bar to elaborate clasps festooned with jewels.

Jump rings Use these tiny findings to join fastenings to necklaces and to link components. Open and close jump rings sideways; do not pull the rings open outwards as they may weaken and snap.

End bars Finish a multi-strand necklace by fixing each flexible beading wire with a crimp to a hole of the end bar. End bars can also be used to suspend beads from ear wires.

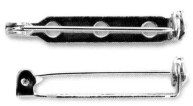

Headpins Headpins resemble long dressmaking pins. They are 2.5 to 5.5cm (1 to 2¼in) in length. Beads are threaded onto a headpin, then a loop is made at the top for hanging the bead.

Calottes Finish necklaces strung on thread with calottes, which consist of two hinged cups with a loop attached. The knotted thread ends are enclosed securely in the cups.

Bails Squeeze the claws of a bail through the holes of a drop bead. Some bails are very decorative and can coordinate with the style of the beads.

Ballpins These serve the same purpose as headpins but have a ball or decorative shape at the end which can be an added feature of your jewellery.

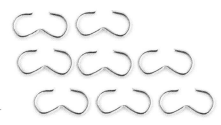

Brooch backs Stick a brooch back to the underside of a handmade clay design with strong epoxy resin glue. Allow the glue to dry completely before handling.

Crimps These tiny metal cylinders finish the ends of flexible beading wire on necklaces. Fix crimps with crimping pliers or snipe-nose pliers.

Figure-of-eight connectors Use these small components to join bezels that have a loop at each side to make a bracelet. They can also be used in place of jump rings.

Charms These small, decorative figures, usually made of metal, have a loop at the top ready for fixing to jewellery.

Chain This can be bought by the metre in various thicknesses and styles. Make a charm bracelet by fixing charms suspended on bails and jump rings to the chain, then fasten the ends with a clasp.

Jewellery stones and chatons To add sparkle, press jewellery stones and chatons into clay jewellery. Chatons have a gold foil backing. Flat-backed stones can also be glued to bezels and blanks.

Spacer beads Often made of metal, spacer beads can be placed between large beads. They are often an inexpensive way of adding more beads to a necklace.

Pearls Pearls have been popular for making jewellery for hundreds of years. Cheap realistic imitations are available in gentle colours and different shapes.

Tiny beads Use seed, rocaille, or Delica beads of the same size for weaving on a bead loom. Place a tiny bead between large beads of a necklace to help the necklace drape neatly.

Glass and plastic beads These come in an endless range of shapes, sizes, and colours. Plastic beads are lightweight, which is a consideration when making elaborate earrings.

Crystals Swarovski crystals are the best quality crystals and so sparkly that just a few will set off a piece of jewellery beautifully. Facetted shapes such as bicones are particularly effective.

Drop beads and pendants These beads have a hole across the top and can be hung on bails to make pendant beads. Use handcrafted glass drop beads as a focal point on a necklace.

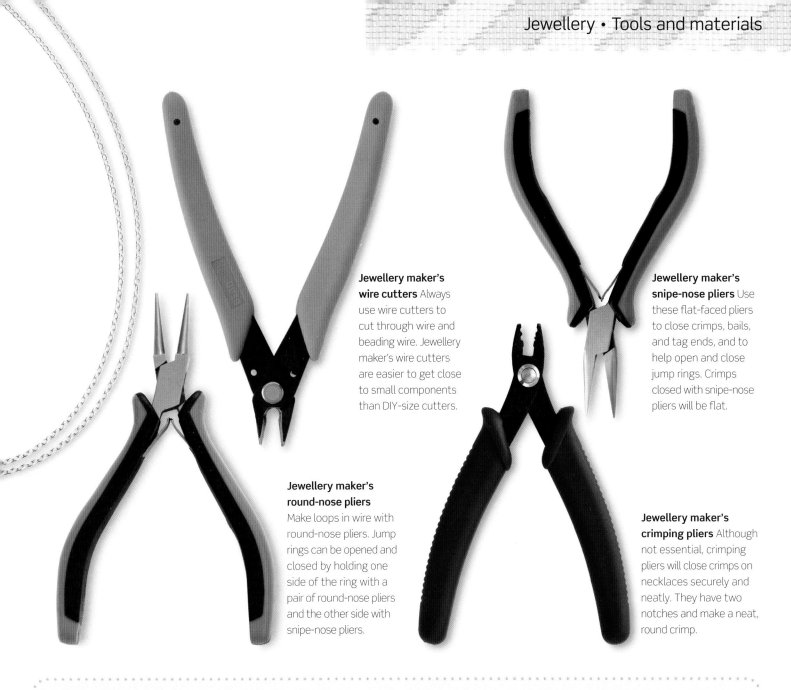

Jewellery maker's wire cutters Always use wire cutters to cut through wire and beading wire. Jewellery maker's wire cutters are easier to get close to small components than DIY-size cutters.

Jewellery maker's round-nose pliers Make loops in wire with round-nose pliers. Jump rings can be opened and closed by holding one side of the ring with a pair of round-nose pliers and the other side with snipe-nose pliers.

Jewellery maker's snipe-nose pliers Use these flat-faced pliers to close crimps, bails, and tag ends, and to help open and close jump rings. Crimps closed with snipe-nose pliers will be flat.

Jewellery maker's crimping pliers Although not essential, crimping pliers will close crimps on necklaces securely and neatly. They have two notches and make a neat, round crimp.

Cold enamelling

Cold enamel colours These can be mixed to create your own shades. The enamels harden in the air so there is no need for a kiln.

Cold enamel hardener Cold enamel colour must be mixed with hardener before use. For best results, always follow the manufacturer's instructions and leave to dry for 24 hours.

Jewellery blanks or bezels For a professional finish, apply cold enamel to ready-made metal bezels and blanks. A bezel has a rim to apply your decoration within; a blank is completely flat.

153

Loom weaving

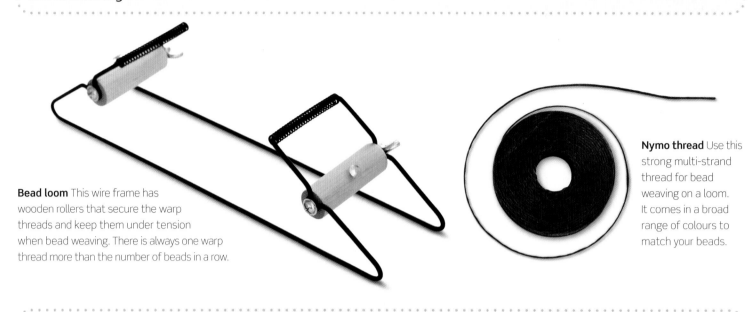

Bead loom This wire frame has wooden rollers that secure the warp threads and keep them under tension when bead weaving. There is always one warp thread more than the number of beads in a row.

Nymo thread Use this strong multi-strand thread for bead weaving on a loom. It comes in a broad range of colours to match your beads.

Polymer clay/air-dry clay/metal clay

Sanding tools Gently sand hardened clay to smooth any jagged edges with fine sandpaper and sanding pads. A needle file is useful for getting into intricate corners.

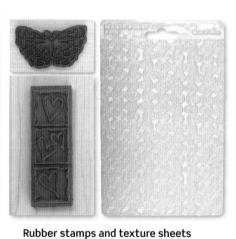

Rubber stamps and texture sheets There is a huge choice of ready-made rubber stamps and texture sheets available to press onto the surface of metal clay to create a design or texture.

Non-stick sheet A plastic stationery file divider is an ideal surface to work polymer clay, air-dry clay, and metal clay on. A Teflon sheet, or even playing cards, can also be used for metal clay.

Polymer clay This synthetic clay is hardened by baking in a domestic oven. There is a huge choice of colours, including glitter, translucent, and metallic versions.

Air-dry clay As the name suggests, the appeal of air-dry clay is that it hardens in the air. Some air-dry clays shrink a little as they dry out. Keep the clay wrapped in clingfilm and in an airtight container when not in use.

Tissue blade This long, thin blade is great for cutting all kinds of clay. A tissue blade is ideal for cutting straight lines or can be bent to cut a gentle curve. Keep the blade in a sealed container when not in use.

Cutters Small metal cutters allow you to stamp shapes from clay quickly and neatly. Cutters are available from craft and cookware shops.

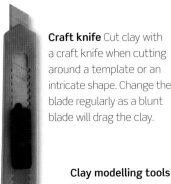

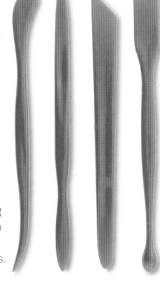

Craft knife Cut clay with a craft knife when cutting around a template or an intricate shape. Change the blade regularly as a blunt blade will drag the clay.

Clay modelling tools An inexpensive set of clay modelling tools or synthetic clay shapers are very handy for shaping and smoothing clay. Even dressmaking pins can be used to create fine details.

Firing brick and mesh To protect your work surface, place metal clay pieces on a sheet of stainless steel mesh over a heatproof fibre brick while heating them with a torch. A small stainless steel cage, usually supplied with the steel sheet, can be placed over the clay.

Tweezers Position small components such as jewellery stones on fresh clay with a pair of tweezers. Use the tips of the tweezers to embed the stones in the clay.

Wooden skewers Slip polymer clay beads onto wooden skewers for support while baking in the oven. Rest the sticks on the edges of a baking tray.

YOU WILL ALSO NEED...

Tape measure Use a flexible tape measure to judge necklace lengths and to measure lengths of beading. Popular necklace lengths are 40cm (16in), 45cm (18in) and 52 to 63cm (20½ to 25in).

Masking tape A piece of tape wrapped temporarily around the end of beading wire or thread will stop beads slipping off when threading.

Graph paper Work out a design on graph paper if you want a patterned length of bead weaving, with each square on the graph paper representing a bead.

Measuring cups Plastic drinking cups can be used to mix cold enamelling materials but for accuracy, use mixing cups with measure markings to measure quantities.

Mixing sticks and cocktail sticks Use purpose-made mixing sticks or cocktail sticks to mix cold enamel colours. Cocktail sticks are also used to pierce holes in clay and to apply superglue or clear nail varnish to secure jewellery findings.

Polishers and burnishers Polish metal clay with a stainless steel or brass brush, polishing pad, polishing paper, or polishing cloth to give it a shine. Burnish the metal with a metal crochet hook or the back of a teaspoon.

Clingfilm To stop clay from drying out, wrap spare clay in clingfilm while modelling the clay. For extra protection, store clay wrapped in clingfilm in an airtight container.

Non-stick roller Roll clay out flat with a non-stick roller. Small lightweight versions are available from craft shops. Keep the roller clean and only use it for craftwork.

Badger balm and olive oil Lightly smear badger balm or olive oil on your hands and tools when working with metal clay; they will stop the clay from sticking.

Talcum powder A light dusting of talcum powder on air-dry and polymer clay, or on your hands and roller stops the clay from sticking.

Beading TECHNIQUES

A few basic techniques are all you need to assemble handcrafted jewellery. Keep pairs of jewellery wire cutters, snipe-nose pliers, and round-nose pliers to hand – they will help you achieve a neat finish to your jewellery. Although initially fiddly to handle, professional-looking wire loops can be made and jewellery findings attached quickly and efficiently with a little bit of practice.

Making a single loop

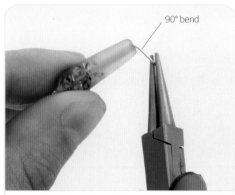

90° bend

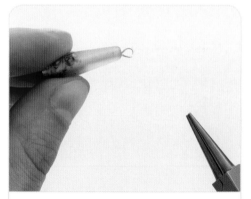

1 Slip a bead onto a headpin or ballpin, slipping a seed bead on first if the hole in your bead is too big. Snip off the excess wire 8mm (5/16in) above the bead with wire cutters.

2 Hold the end of the wire with a pair of round-nose pliers. Bend the wire away from you at a right angle on top of the bead.

3 Turn your wrist to curl the wire towards you, making a loop. Release the wire, then grab it again to continue rolling it into a loop resembling a closed circle. A dab of superglue on the join will give added security.

Making a wrapped loop

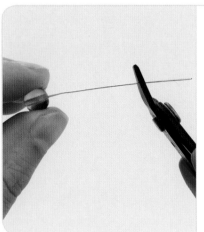

1 Slip a bead onto a headpin or ballpin. Snip off the excess wire with wire cutters, leaving 4cm (1½in) above the bead.

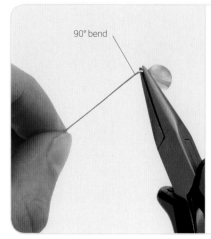

90° bend

2 Hold the wire with a pair of snipe-nose pliers, resting the jaws on the bead. Use your fingers to bend the wire over the jaws at a right angle.

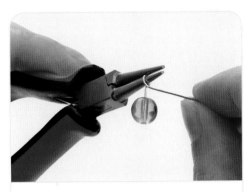

3 Using round-nose pliers, loop the wire around the jaw of the pliers so that the wire is at right angles to the wire emerging from the bead.

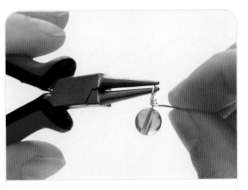

4 With the round-nose pliers through the loop to hold the piece steady, use your fingers to wrap the extending wire neatly around the wire emerging from the bead.

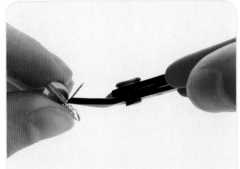

5 Snip off the excess wire close to the bead with wire cutters. Squeeze the snipped end close to the wrapped wire with snipe-nose pliers.

Attaching a bail

1 A bail has a claw on each side to hook onto a pendant or drop bead. Gently pull the claws of a bail open until the gap between them is large enough to slip a drop bead or pendant onto one claw. Slip the bead or pendant onto one claw.

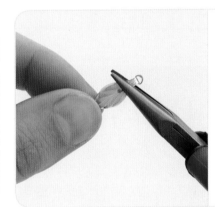

2 Squeeze the bail closed with snipe-nose pliers. Depending on the style of the bail, you may need to attach a jump ring to it (see below) to keep the component facing forwards.

Attaching a jump ring

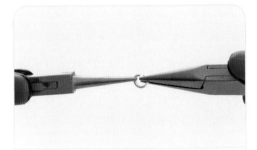

1 Jump rings join fastenings to necklaces and link components. Holding the jump ring between two pairs of pliers, gently pull one pair towards you until the ring opens wide enough to enable you to slip your jewellery component on.

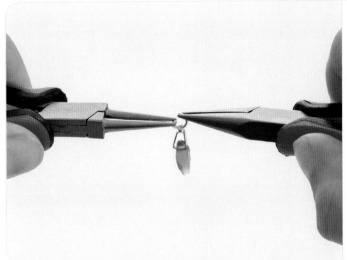

2 To close, hold the open ring between two pairs of pliers and push one pair towards the other, aligning the join. For extra security, dab the join with superglue or clear nail varnish, using a cocktail stick to deliver a tiny amount.

Threading beads

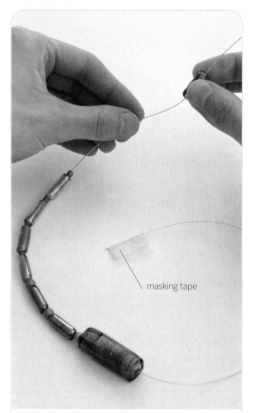

masking tape

Wrap masking tape around one end of the beading wire or thread to stop beads slipping off. Thread on the beads, working outwards from the centre of your work. This allows you to add or remove beads either side of the centre to achieve the desired length.

Attaching a crimp

1 A crimp is a tiny metal cylinder used to fix the ends of flexible beading wire. Slip one crimp then one jump ring onto the wire. Pull the end of the wire back through the crimp until the crimp sits 4mm (³⁄₁₆in) from the last bead and the jump ring 4mm (³⁄₁₆in) from the crimp.

2 Place the crimp in the inner notch of a pair of crimping pliers. Squeeze the pliers closed; the squashed crimp will be crescent-shaped. If you do not have crimping pliers, squeeze the crimp flat with snipe-nose pliers.

3 Position the crimp in the outer notch of the crimping pliers. Squeeze the pliers closed to round the shape of the crimp. Turn the crimp and repeat to improve its shape.

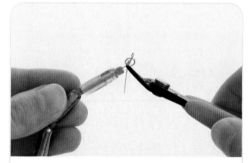

4 Snip off the excess wire as close as possible to the crimp with wire cutters. If making a necklace, repeat at the other end.

Fixing calottes

1 A calotte has two hinged cups with a loop attached. The knotted ends of strung beads are enclosed in the cups for a neat finish. Insert the thread at each end of a necklace through the hole in a calotte. Tie the thread in a large knot and cut off the excess thread. Glue the knot in one cup of the calotte with superglue.

2 Squeeze the calotte cups closed with a pair of snipe-nose pliers. Slip the loop of the calotte onto a jump ring. Close the loop and repeat at the other end of the necklace, if this is what you're making.

Attaching a necklace fastening

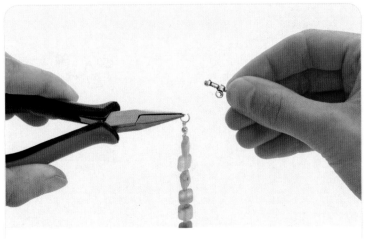

1 Use two pairs of pliers to open the jump ring at one end of the necklace. Slip the loop of one half of a necklace fastening onto the jump ring.

2 Close the jump ring using the two pairs of pliers. Apply a tiny dab of superglue or clear nail varnish to the jump ring join for extra security. Repeat at the other end of the necklace.

Attaching a tag end

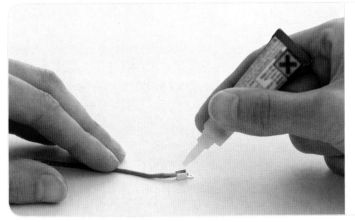

1 A tag end is a three-fold metal strip that secures the end of a thick threading material. Place the end of a cord, thong, or fine ribbon in the centre of a tag end. Glue in position with superglue. Allow the glue to dry.

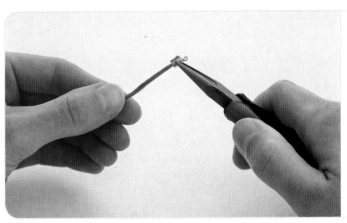

2 Fold one side of the tag end over with snipe-nose pliers, then the other side. Squeeze the tag end tightly closed with snipe-nose pliers. Fix a jump ring to the loop of the tag end.

Attaching an ear wire

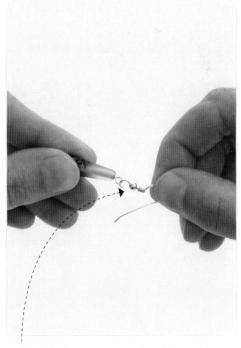

Open the loop on an ear wire with round-nose pliers. Hook the loop of the earring component onto the loop of the ear wire. Close the loop with the pliers.

Beaded pearl necklace PROJECT

A pair of delicate heart-shaped beads anchors two strands of pearls at the front of this beautiful necklace featuring classic pearls in gentle colours. Pearl beads often have very tiny holes, so use the slimmest beading needles for this project. Remember to thread on the same number of pearls either side of the hearts.

YOU WILL NEED

- 160cm (64in) white bead-stringing thread
- embroidery scissors
- masking tape
- 2 short beading needles
- 2 x 1.2cm (½in) heart-shaped pearl beads
- 128 x 3mm (⅛in) natural round freshwater pearls
- 104 x 4mm (³⁄₁₆in) peach rice freshwater pearls
- 6 x 7mm (⁵⁄₁₆in) natural round pearls
- 2 gold calottes
- snipe-nose pliers
- 2 x 4mm (³⁄₁₆in) gold jump rings
- round-nose pliers
- gold toggle and ring necklace clasp

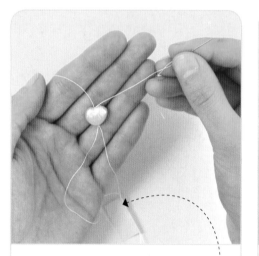

1 Cut two 80cm (32in) lengths of stringing thread. Join the threads with masking tape at their centre to stop the beads slipping off. As you'll be threading beads outwards from the centre, you'll be able to make changes to the beading sequence if you wish. Thread each thread onto a short beading needle. Thread both threads through the tip of a 1.2cm (½in) heart-shaped pearl bead.

2 Separate the threads and thread sixteen 3mm (⅛in) natural round pearls onto one thread and thirteen 4mm (³⁄₁₆in) peach rice pearls onto the other. Insert both threads through a 7mm (⁵⁄₁₆in) natural round pearl. Repeat this sequence twice. Separate the threads and thread sixteen 3mm (⅛in) natural round pearls onto one thread and thirteen 4mm (³⁄₁₆in) peach rice pearls onto the other.

3 Check the necklace length and how the pearls sit in a mirror. If necessary, add or remove pearls. Tape the beaded thread ends and remove the masking tape at the centre of the necklace. Thread on the second heart and pearls to match the first half of the necklace.

4 Insert both threads at each end of the necklace through a calotte, then slip the loop of each calotte onto a jump ring. Slip the loop of the toggle clasp through the jump ring and close. Repeat on the other side with the second half of the clasp.

Silver wirework TECHNIQUES

Fixing beads on twisted wires or binding an item with wire threaded with beads is a great technique for decorating plain jewellery and accessories such as a hair comb, headband, or bangle, or to make pretty pendants to hang on a necklace or ear wires. Use 0.4mm (28 gauge) or 0.6mm (24 gauge) wire and always start and finish the wire on top of your work, so it won't scratch skin or clothing.

Making a bunch of twisted stem beads

1 Thread one bead onto wire, leaving a tail 5.5cm (2¼in) longer than the intended length of the longest twisted stem. Hold the bead and twist the wires together to 5cm (2in) from the tail end.

2 Bend the long end upwards and thread on another bead. With the bead just below the level of the first bead, twist the wires together under the bead until you reach the bottom of the first twisted stem.

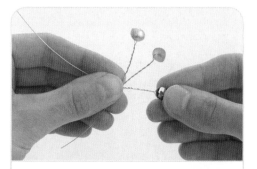

3 Again, bend the long end upwards. Thread on another bead and hold the bead just below the level of the second bead. Twist the wires together under the bead until you reach the bottom of the other twisted stems.

Binding with a bunch of twisted stem beads

1 Bend the short tail of wire of the bunch around the item to be bound, finishing on the outward-facing surface. Snip off excess wire. Squeeze the end flat with snipe-nose pliers.

2 Bind the long tail of wire of the bunch under and over the item a few times, pulling the wire taut as you work.

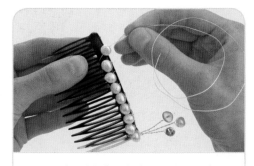

3 Continue binding the long tail around the item, adding beads if you wish. (See Steps 2 and 3 of **binding with wire and beads**, opposite.)

Binding with wire and beads

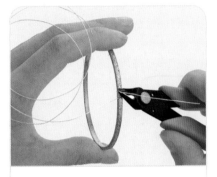

1 Leaving a 5cm (2in) tail, bind wire around the item four times to secure it. Snip off the tail on the outer surface with wire cutters. Squeeze the end flat with snipe-nose pliers.

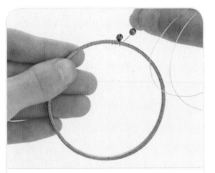

2 Thread on a bead and hold it against the outer surface. Again, bind the wire around the item, pulling the wire taut as you work. Continue adding beads and binding.

3 If you run out of wire, bind the wire four times around the item, finishing on the outer surface. Snip off excess wire. Squeeze the wire end flat against the surface with snipe-nose pliers, then bind a new length of wire over the end of the last wire. Continue adding beads and binding.

Finishing a continuous binding

When you reach the end, bind the wire four times around the wire at the start. Finish with the end on the outer surface. Snip off the excess. Squeeze the end flat against the surface with snipe-nose pliers.

Finishing a straight edge binding

When you reach the end, bind the wire four times around the item, finishing with the end on the outer surface. Snip off the excess wire. Squeeze the end flat against the surface with snipe-nose pliers.

Making a pendant

1 On a bunch of twisted stem beads, snip the short tail of wire level with the end of the twisted wires. Bend the other tail to a right angle.

2 Hold the tail with round-nose pliers close to the right angle. Roll the wire around the jaw of the pliers to make a loop. End with the tail at a right angle to the twisted wires.

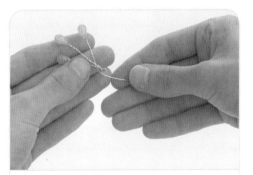

3 Wrap the tail neatly around the twisted wires. Snip off the excess. Squeeze the end flat against the wrapped wire with snipe-nose pliers.

Sparkly tiara PROJECT

Make this pretty tiara to set off an outfit for a special occasion. Bunches of twisted stem beads stand proud of the headband and the sides of the band are bound with wire and beads. Bead shops sell plain tiaras ready to decorate, or use a narrow headband instead. A mixture of crystal, glass, semi-precious chips, and pearl beads have been used here, adding a touch of glamour.

YOU WILL NEED

- 8m (9yd) 0.4mm (28 gauge) silver-plated wire
- wire cutters
- selection of 3–6mm (1/8–1/4in) crystal, glass, semi-precious chips, and pearl beads in assorted colours
- silver-plated tiara or 5mm (1/4in) wide silver headband
- snipe-nose pliers

1 Snip a 1m (40in) length of wire. Follow **making a bunch of twisted stem beads** on p.162. Hold the bunch of twisted stems at the front edge of the centre of the tiara. Bind the short tail over and under the tiara. Finish on top of the tiara and snip off excess wire if necessary. Squeeze the end against the tiara with snipe-nose pliers.

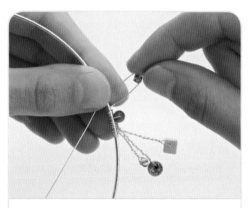

2 Bind the long tail of the wire under and over the tiara four times. Thread on a bead to sit on top of the tiara. Bind the tiara four more times. Hold the tail upwards and thread on one bead 2cm (3/4in) above the tiara. Bend the tail downwards. Twist the wires together until you reach the tiara. Repeat Steps 2 and 3 of **making a bunch of twisted stem beads** on p.162 using the same length of wire.

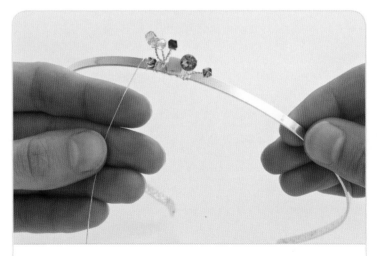

3 Bind the tiara four more times. Continue the sequence of adding beads, binding the tiara, and making twisted stem beads as you work outwards from the centre of the tiara.

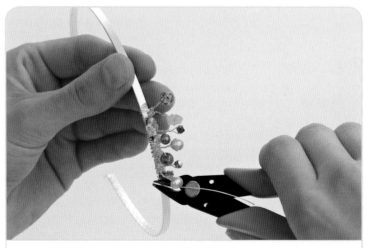

4 If you need to finish a length of wire and add a new length, follow Step 3 of **binding with wire and beads** on p.163. Continue making twisted stem beads and binding with beads for 8.5cm (3³/₈in).

5 Snip a 150cm (60in) length of wire. Follow **binding with wire and beads** on p.163 to bind and bead the tiara, finishing 2cm (¾in) from the end of the tiara. To finish, follow **finishing a straight edge binding** on p.163. Decorate the second half of the tiara to match, starting by binding the short tail of the wire around the centre of the tiara.

Cold enamelling TECHNIQUES

No special equipment is needed for cold enamelling, yet with just the addition of a hardener, the enamels set rock hard with an attractive glossy sheen. There is a large range of enamel colours, which can be mixed to create new shades. Apply the enamels to metal jewellery bezels or blanks. Interesting effects can be achieved by swirling contrast-coloured enamels on a background colour or by applying glitter for extra sparkle.

Mixing colours

If you wish to mix your own colours, do so before adding hardener. Pour the enamel colours or drop them with a mixing stick or cocktail stick into a mixing cup. Mix the colours evenly with the stick.

Adding hardener

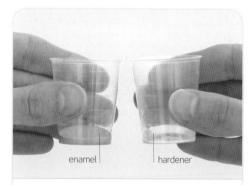

enamel | hardener

1 The enamel must be mixed accurately – two-parts of enamel colour to one-part of hardener. Pour two-parts of colour into a mixing cup. Pour one-part of hardener into another mixing cup.

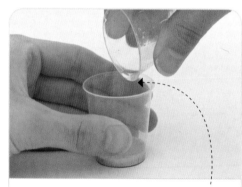

2 Pour the hardener into the colour and mix. Leave to stand for 10 minutes to ensure there are no air bubbles. The mixture will remain workable for one hour. Prepare a second colour at the same time if wanted.

Cleaning metal

While the colour is standing, clean the bezel or blank with white spirit on a soft cloth. This degreases the surface.

Applying cold enamel

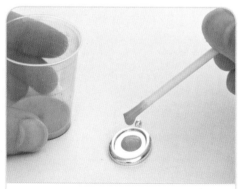

1 With the bezel or blank on a flat surface, apply the enamel to the recess with a mixing stick or cocktail stick.

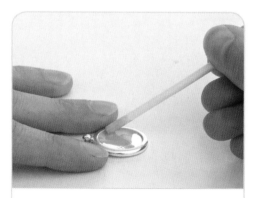

2 Distribute the enamel up to the outer edges, butting it against the frame of the bezel. Set aside for 24 hours.

Keeping a bezel level

plastic clay support

Often a bezel cannot be kept flat when applying the enamel and while it cures, such as on a ring for example. To keep the bezel level, support it on plastic clay.

Applying a second colour enamel

1 If a second prepared colour is applied immediately after its standing time on top of the first, it will spread on the surface. Apply the colour with a cocktail stick and swirl to distribute it.

2 Alternatively, leave the second colour to stand for a further 10 minutes, then apply it. You will not be able to spread it so much.

Applying enamel in relief

Apply a background colour and leave to dry for 24 hours. Use a cocktail stick to apply other colours in dots or swirls to the background colour. The other colours will stand proud of the surface. Set aside for 24 hours.

Applying glitter

1 Apply a background colour to a bezel and leave to dry for two hours. With the bezel on scrap paper, sprinkle fine glitter onto the background colour. Do not shake off the excess glitter. Set aside for 24 hours without touching.

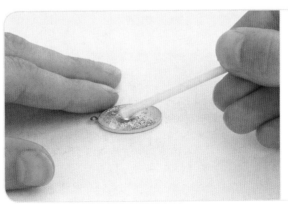

2 Mix clear cold enamel with hardener (see **adding hardener**, opposite). Apply the clear enamel on top, completely covering the background colour and the glitter. Set aside for 24 hours.

Linked bracelet PROJECT

This charming bracelet is simple to make and is a great introductory project to cold enamelling. The enamelling is applied to bezels that have a loop at each side. These are linked together with figure-of-eight connectors. This bracelet has five bezels and is approximately 18cm (7in) in length. To shorten the bracelet, use fewer bezels; to lengthen it, add more bezels or link extra jump rings at one end.

YOU WILL NEED

- light blue and mint green cold enamel colours
- 3 mixing cups
- cold enamel hardener
- mixing sticks (optional)
- cocktail sticks
- 5 silver 3cm (1¼in) oval bezels with a link at each side
- white spirit
- soft cloth
- 6 silver figure-of-eight connectors
- snipe-nose pliers
- round-nose pliers
- 2 silver jump rings
- silver ring and bar fastening

1 Prepare light blue and mint green cold enamel colours with hardener following **adding hardener** on p.166. While the colours stand, clean the bezels with white spirit on a soft cloth. Apply the light blue colour to the recesses of the bezels with a mixing stick or cocktail stick.

2 Set the bezels and mint green enamel aside for 10 minutes. Using a cocktail stick, swirl a circle of the mint green colour on the light blue background colour. Set aside to cure for 24 hours.

3 With the bezel face down, slip one loop of a figure-of-eight connector through one loop of the bezel. Squeeze the loop of the connector closed with snipe-nose pliers. Attach the other loop of the connector to another bezel. Repeat to link all the bezels.

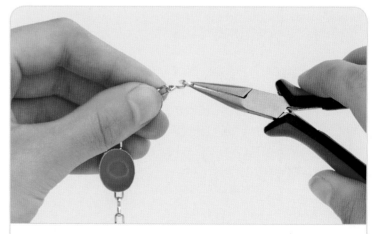

4 Fix a figure-of-eight connector through the end loops of the first and last bezels and close with snipe-nose pliers. Slip a jump ring through the end loop of the first connector.

5 Slip the loop of the bar of the fastening onto the jump ring. Close the jump ring using two pairs of pliers. Repeat to fix a jump ring to the end loop of the last connector and the ring of the fastening to that jump ring.

Loom weaving TECHNIQUES

Loom-woven beads produce a flat band of beads. You'll need one warp thread more than the number of beads in a row. Create designs by following beading charts drawn on graph paper, with each square representing a bead. Sew the weaving to a band of soft leather or imitation leather to make into a cuff or choker, and fasten with ribbon, or see pp.172–73 for how to make a toggle fastening.

Preparing the loom

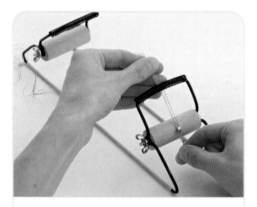

1 Cut warp threads at least 30cm (12in) longer than the intended length of the weaving. Knot the threads together at one end. Divide the bundle in half and slip the knot under the nail on one of the rollers.

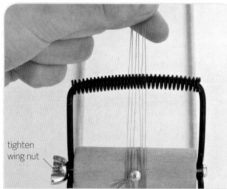

tighten wing nut

2 With the threads taut, turn the roller until they extend 15cm (6in) beyond the second roller. Tighten the wing nut to hold the roller in place. Place one thread in each groove of the spring.

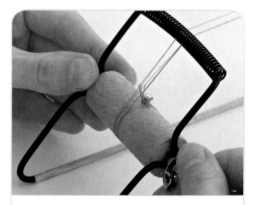

3 Knot the other ends of the warp threads and slip the knot under the nail on the second roller. Loosen the wing nut of this roller and wind the roller to take up the slack. Tighten the wing nut.

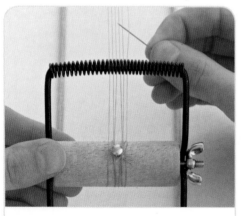

4 Sit the threads in the grooves of the second roller, separating the threads with a needle. Tighten the tension again if necessary by loosening the wing nut, turning the second roller, and tightening the wing nut again. The threads should be taut.

Loom weaving

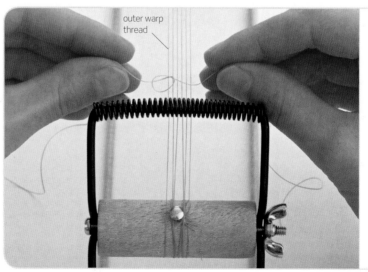

outer warp thread

1 Thread a long length of thread onto a long beading needle: this will be the weft thread. Tie the weft thread to one outer warp thread close to the second roller, leaving a trailing end 15cm (6in) long.

2 Using the beading needle, thread on beads for the first row. Refer to a chart if beading a specific design. There are six warp threads here, so thread on five beads.

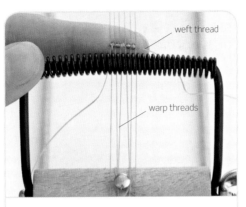

weft thread

warp threads

3 Slip the beads along the weft thread, position the thread at right angles under the warp threads, then press the beads up between the warp threads with a finger.

4 To secure the first row, take the needle back through the beads, making sure that it passes above the warp threads. Pick up the next row of beads and repeat.

Adding a new weft thread

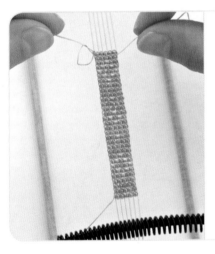

When the weft thread starts to run out, weave it back through a few rows of beads. Tie a new long weft thread to an outer warp thread, leaving a 15cm (6in) trailing end. Continue adding beads and weaving as before.

Reaching the first roller

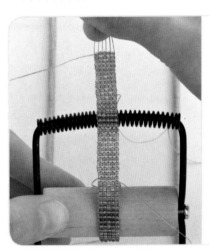

When you reach the first roller, loosen the tension on both rollers. Roll the weaving onto the first roller, tighten the tension, and continue weaving until the weaving is the required length.

Finishing the sides and ends

1 Loosen the tension on the rollers and remove the work. Weave the trailing ends of the weft threads back into the work by inserting the thread on a needle in and out of a few rows of beads. Cut off the excess threads close to the weaving.

2 With a short beading needle, weave each warp thread back through the work, weaving them over and under the weft threads. Cut off the excess threads close to the weaving.

171

Loom-woven cuff PROJECT

Make this pretty cuff of loom-woven beads in colours to match a favourite outfit. The cuff closes with a pair of toggle and loop fastenings. Bead the subtle pattern of diagonal stripes by following the easy-to-use beading chart on p.309. The cuff measures 18cm (7in) in length. To lengthen or shorten it, add or decrease rows of beads at each end of the chart.

YOU WILL NEED

- loom
- lilac Nymo thread
- scissors
- 10g (1/3oz) lilac seed beads or size 15 Delica beads
- 4g (1/5oz) green seed beads or size 15 Delica beads
- 10g (1/3oz) purple seed beads or size 15 Delica beads
- long beading needle
- short beading needle
- 2 x 8mm (5/16in) lilac beads

1 Follow **preparing the loom** on p.170, using 17 x 45cm (18in) lengths of warp threads. Use a 1m (40in) length of weft thread to start weaving the design on p.309, following **loom weaving, adding a new weft thread**, and **reaching the first roller** on pp.170–71. Follow **finishing the ends** on p.171, leaving the third, fourth, thirteenth, and fourteenth warp threads free at each end of the weaving.

2 For the toggle, thread the third and fourth warp threads onto a short beading needle. Thread on two lilac seed beads, one 8mm (5/16in) bead, and one lilac seed bead. Take the needle back through the 8mm (5/16in) bead and the two seed beads. Adjust the toggle to sit against the end of the weaving.

3 Separate the two threads. With one of the threads on a short beading needle, insert the needle through the fourth bead from the edge in the last row of weaving, then sew through the toggle again to secure.

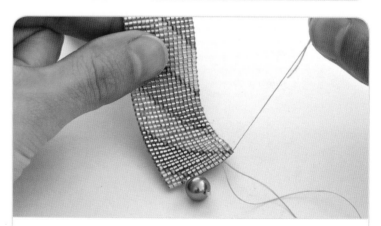

4 Take the threaded needle back into the last row of beads in the cuff, weaving it over and under the weft threads. Trim away the excess. Thread the other thread on the needle and insert it through the same bead as in Step 3, but starting from the opposite direction. Weave the thread as before and trim the excess.

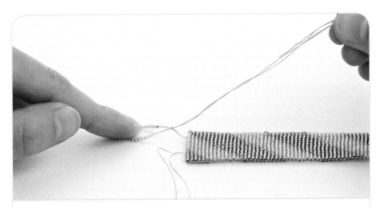

5 Repeat to make a toggle with the thirteenth and fourteenth warp threads. To make a loop at the other end of the cuff, thread the third and fourth threads onto a short beading needle. Thread on 22 lilac seed beads. Insert the needle back through the first seed bead.

6 Adjust the loop to sit against the end of the weaving. Check to see that the loop will slip snugly over the toggle and adjust if needed. Separate the two threads and thread one on a short beading needle. Insert the needle through the fourth bead in the last row of the weaving, then sew through the loop again to secure. Follow Step 4 to secure the threads. Repeat to make a second loop with the thirteenth and fourteenth warp threads.

Polymer clay TECHNIQUES

Polymer clay is a great modelling medium for making beads. Canework or millefiori beads – plain beads covered with thin decorative slices from canes of coloured clay – evoke the look of Venetian glass. To begin, knead the clay a little to produce a soft, pliable clay. Wash your hands regularly while you work to avoid mixing one colour into another.

Blending colours

Twist together logs of clay in different colours. Stretch and twist the clay, double it over, and repeat to create a marbled effect. You can use the clay at this stage or continue blending it to achieve an even colour.

Rolling a clay sheet

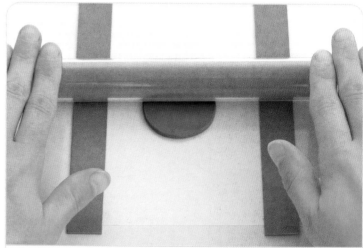

To roll clay to a specific thickness, place it on a non-stick sheet with a strip of card either side. Roll out using a non-stick roller. Vary the thickness of the card or layer the strips for thinner or thicker sheets of clay.

Making a jelly-roll cane

1 Roll two 1mm (¹⁄₁₆in) thick sheets of different coloured clays. Stack the sheets and cut to a 5cm (2in) square using a tissue blade. Flatten two opposite edges with a non-stick roller.

2 Starting at one flattened edge, roll the layers tightly and evenly. Roll the cane on a flat surface to smooth the join. Cut the ends of the roll level.

Making a flower cane

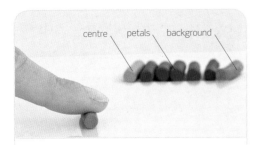

centre   petals   background

1 Roll eight 6mm (¼in) thick logs – one for the centre, five for the petals, and two for the background. Trim the logs to 3cm (1¼in).

2 Roll a 1mm (¹⁄₁₆in) sheet of a fourth colour for the outer petals. Cut it into five 3 x 2cm (1¼ x ¾in) rectangles and wrap one around each of the petal logs. Roll to smooth the joins, then trim to 3cm (1¼in) long.

3 Arrange the petal logs around the centre log with the outer petals facing outwards. Cut the background logs lengthwise into quarters. Place a quarter between each petal log. Roll the cane a few times to smooth the circumference.

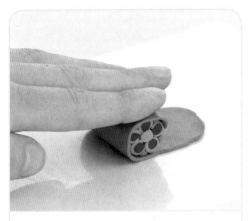

4 Roll a 2mm (¹⁄₁₀in) thick sheet of the background colour and wrap it around the flower. Roll the cane to smooth the join. See below to make pendants or continue to roll the cane to lengthen it. Cut the ends level.

Making plain and canework beads

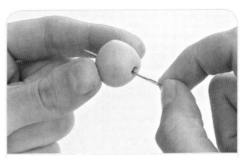

1 Roll a ball of clay and pierce a hole through the centre with a thick needle. Enlarge the hole with the needle and reshape. You can use scrap clay if the bead is to be covered in canework.

2 For canework beads, cut thin slices of jelly-roll cane and press them to the beads, butting the slices together. Fill gaps with tiny bits of matching clay. Roll the beads to smooth them, then re-pierce the hole.

Making pendants

Cut discs of canework 4mm (³⁄₁₆in) thick from a flower cane. Pierce a hole at the top with a thick needle. Bake the pendants flat on a baking sheet following the manufacturer's instructions. After baking, fix a bail through the hole (see p.157).

Baking beads

Thread beads onto a wooden skewer or thick wire for support while baking. Rest the skewer across an ovenproof bowl, then bake in a domestic oven following the manufacturer's instructions.

Polymer clay beads PROJECT

Make this pretty necklace to show off a set of canework beads. The beads are graduated in size and include spotted beads, which are quick and simple to make. Placing small, plain clay "spacer" beads between the larger beads emphasizes each decorative bead and helps them lay in a gentle curve. Of course, you could use glass or metal spacer beads for a change of texture.

YOU WILL NEED

- non-stick sheet
- light grey, dark blue, turquoise, and mid-blue clay, plus scraps of any colour
- 2 strips of 2mm (¹⁄₁₀in) thick card
- non-stick roller
- tissue blade
- thick needle
- wooden skewer or thick wire for baking
- 80cm (32in) flexible beading wire
- masking tape
- 2 silver crimps
- 2 silver jump rings
- crimping or snipe-nose pliers
- necklace fastening

1 Working on a non-stick sheet, blend a 3.5cm (1³⁄₈in) ball of light grey and a 1.5cm (⁵⁄₈in) ball of dark blue clay to achieve a mid-grey clay. Blend a 2cm (³⁄₄in) ball each of light grey and turquoise clay to make a light turquoise clay.

2 Follow **making a flower cane** on p.175 to make a flower cane with a dark blue centre, light turquoise petals, light grey outer petals, and mid-blue background. Roll to 8mm (⁵⁄₁₆in) thick. Make a plain 2cm (³⁄₄in) bead using scrap clay and pierce a hole through the centre with a thick needle. Press flower cane slices in a row around the middle of the bead.

3 Follow **making a jelly-roll cane** on p.174 to make a jelly-roll cane with light grey clay inside and mid-blue clay outside. Cut a 4cm (1¹⁄₂in) length of the cane and roll to 6mm (¹⁄₄in) thick. Roll the remaining cane to 8mm (⁵⁄₁₆in) thick. Cut slices from the smaller cane and press to the bead above and below the flowers. Roll the bead to smooth it, then re-pierce the hole.

4 From scrap clay, roll four 2cm (³⁄₄in) beads, four 1.5cm (⁵⁄₈in) beads, and four 1.2cm (¹⁄₂in) beads. Apply flower cane slices to two beads of each size and 8mm (⁵⁄₁₆in) jelly-roll cane slices to the remaining beads.

5 To make the spotted beads, roll four 1.5cm (⁵⁄₈in), four 1.2cm (¹⁄₂in), and four 1cm (³⁄₈in) balls of mid-blue clay. Pierce holes through the beads with the needle. Roll a 1mm (¹⁄₁₆in) thick log of light grey clay, cut it into slices, and press to the mid-blue beads. Roll the beads to embed the spots then re-pierce the holes. Now make twenty-six 6mm (¹⁄₄in) light grey spacer beads.

6 Follow **baking beads** on p.175, then thread the beads onto flexible beading wire. Graduate outwards in size from the centre, with the largest bead at the centre and a spacer bead between each decorated bead. Follow **attaching a crimp** on p.158 and **attaching a necklace fastening** on p.159 to complete the necklace.

Air-dry clay TECHNIQUES

Some air-dry clays are in two parts – the clay and a hardener – which helps the clay dry rock hard. If you want to blend the colours to produce the exact shade you want, do so after mixing in the hardener. Then break off the amount of clay needed and store the rest in an airtight container. Be aware that some air-dry clays shrink as they dry.

Using two-part clay

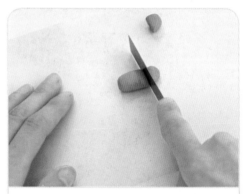

If your clay is in two parts, cut off equal amounts of each and knead together until blended, following the manufacturer's instructions. One part might be shinier than the other; once mixed, there should be no shiny streaks running through the clay.

Blending colours

Blend colours after mixing a two-part clay. Twist together different coloured logs of clay, stretching, twisting, and doubling them over to achieve an evenly mixed shade. Keep any mixed leftover clay wrapped in clingfilm in an airtight container until needed.

Rolling a clay sheet

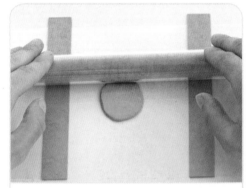

Place the clay on a non-stick sheet between two strips of card. To stop the clay sticking, sprinkle talcum powder on a non-stick roller. Roll the clay. If you need to vary its thickness, use thicker or thinner strips of cards.

Using a template

1 Cut out the template from baking paper and place it on the rolled-out clay. Cut around the template using a craft knife, then remove the template.

2 Peel away the excess clay and store it wrapped in clingfilm in an airtight container so that it doesn't dry out.

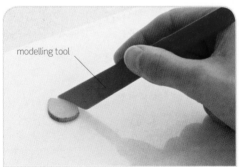

modelling tool

3 Pat the cut edges of the shape with a straight-sided clay modelling tool to neaten the edges. With the blade flat against the surface, slip a tissue blade or the blade of a craft knife under the clay to lift it.

Using a metal cutter

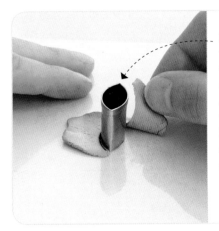

Press the cutter firmly onto the rolled-out clay. Peel away the excess clay and store it wrapped in clingfilm in an airtight container. Remove the cutter and slip a tissue blade or the blade of a craft knife under the shape to lift it.

Making a small hole

With the clay lying flat, insert a thick needle through the clay to make a hole. To do the same on a three-dimensional piece, hold the piece carefully and pierce a hole through the clay with a thick needle.

Using a bezel

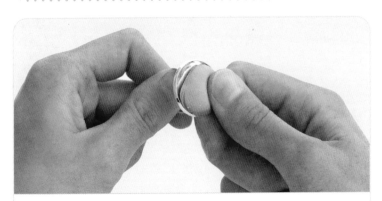

Choose a clay that will not shrink and use a bezel with a rim that overhangs the recess. Press the clay onto the centre of the bezel, then smooth it outwards with your thumb to fit under the rim of the bezel.

Using jewellery stones and chatons

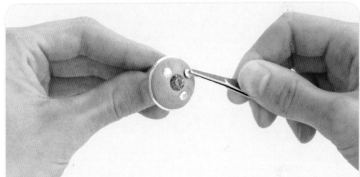

Place a jewellery stone or chaton on the clay using tweezers or a moistened fingertip. If necessary, gently nudge the stone into position with tweezers. Press the stone into the clay with the tips of the tweezers.

Forming three-dimensional shapes

For a three-dimensional shape, place the clay over a suitably shaped item, such as a drinking straw or a teaspoon for a curved shape. Alternatively, rest the clay on a scrunched-up piece of clingfilm.

Drying air-dry clay

To dry the clay to a hard, durable finish, follow the manufacturer's instructions and set it aside, usually for about 24 hours. If necessary, the hardened clay can be gently smoothed by sanding with fine sandpaper or a needle file.

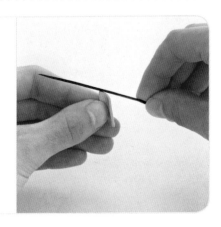

Air-dry clay pendant PROJECT

Make a cascade of delicate blooms from air-dry clay to hang as pendants from a long necklace. Each flower has a cluster of sparkling crystal chatons at the centre and hangs on headpins between silver and crystal beads. For best results, make the flowers in batches of three at a time so that your clay is easy to work with and does not dry out.

YOU WILL NEED

- baking paper
- pencil
- scissors
- 20g (³⁄₄oz) each of white and amethyst air-dry clay
- craft knife
- clingfilm
- non-stick sheet
- strips of 1mm (¹⁄₁₆in) thick card
- talcum powder
- non-stick roller
- straight-sided clay modelling tool
- round-ended clay modelling tool
- 18 x 1mm (¹⁄₁₆in) light amethyst chatons
- tweezers
- thick needle
- 5cm (2in) silver headpin
- 2 x 2.5cm (1in) silver headpins
- wire cutters
- round-nose pliers
- glue
- 90cm (35in) flexible beading wire
- 32 x 4mm (³⁄₁₆in) light amethyst bicone crystal beads
- 260 silver rocaille beads
- 2 silver crimps
- 2 jump rings
- crimping or snipe-nose pliers
- necklace fastening

1 Trace the flower template on p.309 onto baking paper and cut it out. If using a two-part clay, mix the two halves following **using two-part clay** on p.178. Blend a 1.5cm (⁵⁄₈in) ball of white clay and a 1cm (³⁄₈in) ball of amethyst clay to make a pale amethyst shade. Divide the clay into three equal pieces. Wrap two pieces in clingfilm.

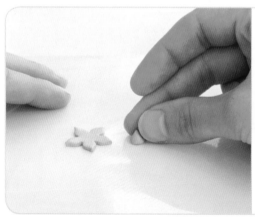

2 Roll the third piece of clay out to 1mm (¹⁄₁₆in) thick, following **rolling a clay sheet** on p.178. Use the template to cut one clay flower. Pull away the excess clay. Remove the paper template, pat the edges to smooth the clay with the straight-sided clay modelling tool. Roll a 5mm (¹⁄₄in) ball of clay using some of the excess clay from the flower, then squeeze the ball into a cone shape. Wrap any leftover clay in clingfilm.

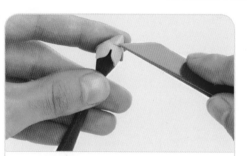

3 Lift the flower by slipping the blade of a craft knife underneath it. Smooth the flower over the rounded end of the round-ended clay modelling tool. Press the cone on top. Smooth the cone onto the flower with the straight-sided clay modelling tool to hide the join.

4 Lift the flower off the tool and splay the petals open. Holding the flower between your fingers, place three chatons on the flower centre and gently press them into the clay with the tips of a pair of tweezers.

5 Pierce a hole through the cone with a thick needle. Use the two pieces of clay set aside in Step 1 to make two more flower pendants, then repeat the steps with a fresh piece of clay to make three more. Set the pieces aside to harden. Follow **making a single loop** on p.156 to fix four flowers on a 5cm (2in) headpin and each of the two remaining flowers on 2.5cm (1in) headpins.

6 Thread the long headpin, three crystal beads, one short headpin, then a sequence of one crystal bead and 10 silver rocaille beads 13 times onto flexible beading wire. Repeat on the other half of the necklace. Follow **attaching a crimp** and **attaching a necklace fastening** on p.159 to finish.

Metal clay TECHNIQUES

Metal clay is a fabulous material that looks uninspiring to begin with but once fired, becomes a beautiful precious metal. The clay is made from fine particles of pure metal mixed with organic binders and water. The clay can be fired on a gas hob or with a gas torch, making it suitable for home use, or it can be fired in a kiln.

Preparing metal clay

Only break off enough clay for your needs and keep the rest wrapped in clingfilm and sealed in an airtight container. Wrap the clay you are using in clingfilm and knead for a few seconds to soften it.

Rolling metal clay

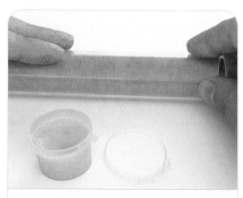

1 Smooth badger balm or olive oil sparingly onto a non-stick roller to stop it sticking.

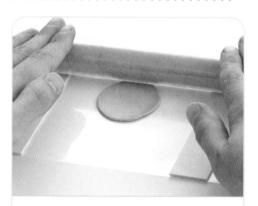

2 Place the clay on a non-stick surface with a strip of card at least 2mm ($^1/_{10}$in) thick on either side. Roll the clay, resting the ends of the roller on the card strips.

Adding texture

Rub a little badger balm or olive oil on a rubber stamp or texture mat, then press it firmly and evenly onto the clay to make an imprint. Lift off the stamp or mat.

Using a cutter

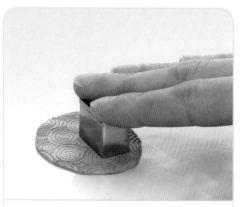

1 Smooth badger balm or olive oil sparingly onto a metal cutter. Press the cutter firmly onto the clay. Pull away the excess clay, then lift the cutter.

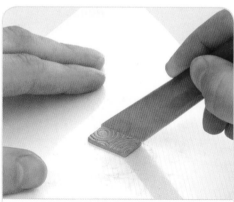

2 Wrap excess clay immediately in clingfilm and store it in an airtight container. Pat the edges of the cut shape with a flat-sided clay modelling tool to neaten them.

Making a hole

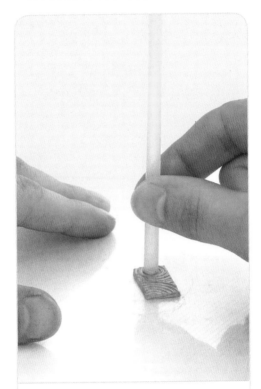

The clay will shrink by 8 to 10% after firing, so make the hole large enough to accommodate whatever will be inserted through it. Pierce the clay with a drinking straw or with a thick needle.

Sanding the clay

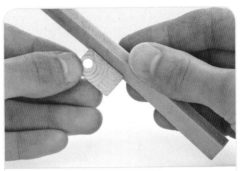

1 Leave the piece to dry for a few days. Handle the clay gently as it is brittle, and sand any rough edges with a sanding pad.

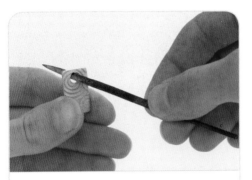

2 Use a needle file to even out or enlarge holes. The piece can be sanded once fired but it is easier to do so now.

Firing on a gas hob

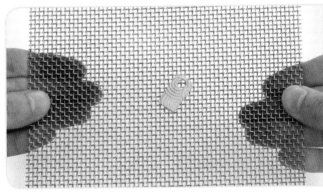

Place the clay on a sheet of stainless-steel mesh. Place the mesh on a gas burner and turn the heat on fully – the clay will smoke for a few seconds. Heat for 10 minutes, then turn off the gas and leave the clay to cool.

Polishing the metal

1 After firing, brush with a soft brass brush for a satin finish. For a mirror finish, polish with dampened coarse polishing paper, then with dampened fine polishing paper.

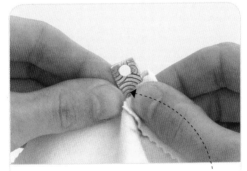

2 Give a final polish with a polishing cloth; this will highlight any raised areas. Burnishing with a metal crochet hook or the back of a teaspoon will also produce a shine.

FIRING SAFETY NOTE

Always refer to the clay manufacturer's firing instructions. Pieces no larger than 3cm (1¼in) in diameter can be fired on a gas hob. The clay must be bone dry before firing or it could "pop" and burst. For safety, place a stainless-steel mesh cage over the clay when firing.

The clay can also be fired with a butane gas torch or in a kiln. To fire with a gas torch, place the completely dry clay on a ceramic fibre brick, which in turn is placed on a fireproof surface. Direct the flame at a 45° angle, 5cm (2in) away from the clay. Move the flame around the piece and fire, following the clay manufacturer's instructions.

Metal clay brooch PROJECT

This charming bird brooch is 99.9% silver and would make a delightful gift, although you may decide to keep it for yourself! The bird has a satin finish, while its wing is highly polished to a mirror shine. The simple decoration is created with humble dressmaking pins. As a finishing touch, beaded ballpins are suspended below the bird like a pair of whimsical "legs".

YOU WILL NEED

- baking paper
- pencil
- scissors
- 12g (½oz) silver metal clay
- non-stick sheet
- 2 strips of 2mm (¹⁄₁₀in) thick card
- badger balm or olive oil
- non-stick roller
- craft knife
- clingfilm
- medium artist's paintbrush
- jar of water
- thick needle
- flat-sided clay modelling tool
- plain dressmaking pin

- glass-headed pin
- fine sandpaper
- needle file
- sheet of stainless-steel mesh
- soft brass brush
- polishing papers
- polishing cloth
- 2 x 3.5cm (1³⁄₈in) sterling-silver ballpins
- 2 x 5mm (¼in) blue beads
- 2 x 4mm (³⁄₁₆in) sterling-silver rice beads
- round-nose pliers
- brooch pin
- epoxy resin glue

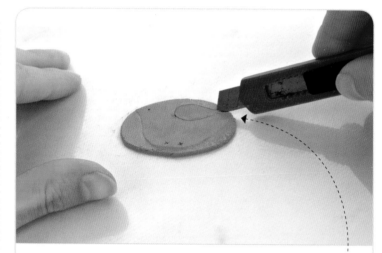

1 Trace the wing and bird templates on p.309 onto baking paper and cut out. Follow **preparing metal clay** and **rolling metal clay** on p.182, rolling the clay 2mm (¹⁄₁₀in) thick. Place the templates on the clay and cut around them with a craft knife. Peel off the templates. Lift off the excess clay and store it wrapped in clingfilm in an airtight container.

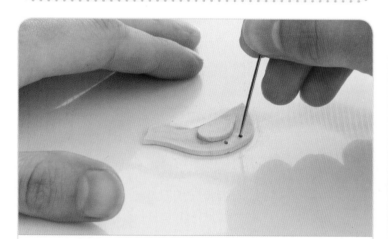

2 Lift the wing by slipping the craft knife underneath it. Moisten the underside with water. Position the wing on the bird. Referring to the template, pierce two holes at the crosses with a thick needle. Wiggle the needle to enlarge the holes, remembering that the clay will shrink when fired.

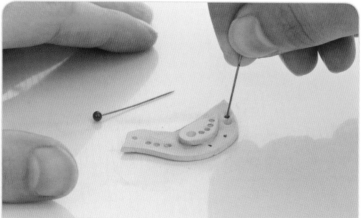

3 Pat the edges of the bird with the flat-sided clay modelling tool. Use the head of a dressmaking pin to make the bird's eye. To add other decorations, press the head of a glass-headed pin into the body and wing, then the head of a dressmaking pin.

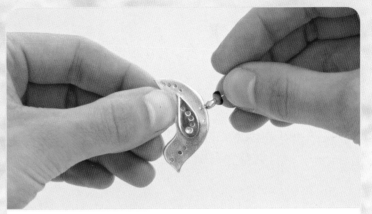

4 Follow **sanding the clay** and **firing on a gas hob** on p.183. Polish both sides of the bird with a soft brass brush. Polish the wing with dampened polishing paper, starting with a coarse paper and finishing with a fine paper. Carefully give the wing a final polish with a polishing cloth.

5 Follow **making a single loop** on p.156 to fix a blue bead and a silver rice bead onto both silver ballpins. Open the loop of one ballpin and slip it through one hole on the bird. Close the loop with round-nose pliers. Repeat to fix the second ballpin. Follow the glue manufacturer's instructions to stick a brooch pin to the back of the bird.

Ceramics and glass

Ceramics and glass

ETCHING GLASS • PAINTING GLASS• PAINTING CHINA • PAINTING TILES • MOSAICS

Decorating your home is about personalizing your space in a way that says something about you – and here are some great ways to do just that. The following pages provide a rich mix of techniques for decorating glass and ceramics. The techniques are easy but using them will make you feel very accomplished.

These techniques definitely fall under the category of "designer DIY". Whichever you choose – glass etching, painting, stencilling, or mosaics – you can produce some decorative and functional items for your home.

With just a little know-how and the desire to do something creative, you can add texture, colour, and interest to plain glassware or a simple item of white china, transforming it, as if by magic, into a unique and desirable object.

Give a new lease of life to a set of tired-looking tumblers with a simple but effective etching treatment: go with the designs on pp.198–99 or create your very own personalized designs. The same goes with plain, uninspiring tea light holders; these can be transformed with just a little paint into colourful objects to suit the scheme of your room.

Most high-street shops sell a basic range of white china at bargain prices, so once you've mastered the skills needed to paint a bowl or stencil a set of coasters, you can use your newly gained knowledge to decorate other plain white china – and perhaps, if you get totally engrossed in your new hobby, produce an entire hand-painted dinner service.

In order to complete the mosaic flowerpots on pp.216–17, you'll be breaking china instead of painting it! You'll learn two different mosaic techniques – direct and indirect – both of which produce really outstanding results.

By following the clear step-by step instructions given here, you'll have made your own unique hand-decorated items in no time at all: great for enhancing your own home or, if you're feeling generous, for giving away as presents.

Ceramics and glass

TOOLS AND MATERIALS

Working with glass, ceramics, and mosaics is a great way to create household items that are not only practical but can also be put on display. A number of specialist materials are required for these crafts, but the initial outlay is well worth the result.

FILM AND LEADWORK

A roll of self-adhesive lead These strips come on a roll and in different profiles (such as flat or oval). They have a peel-off backing. Even though they're metal they are quite soft and need careful handling. The narrower widths of lead come on a roll where they'll need cutting (along a guide line) to elicit the right width.

Sheets of coloured, self-adhesive film These sheets have a peel-off backing and are easy to cut using scissors or a craft knife. Smooth them down with a sponge or the side of your thumb nail.

Blu Tack This sticky stuff is great for positioning your paper design on the glass and holding in place.

A fine permanent pen Trace your design onto the coloured film with a fine permanent black pen.

Boning peg Available from the self-adhesive lead suppliers, this implement is perfect for the final pressing down and ensuring a good bond.

YOU WILL ALSO NEED...

Scissors Keep a pair of sharp paper scissors to hand; they're useful for cutting out the self-adhesive film and cutting lengths of lead strips.

Sponges Small scraps of sponge can be used for smoothing down self-adhesive film and easing out air bubbles caught underneath.

Sticky tape Useful for sticking film pieces to your duplicate design to keep track of your cutting out.

Scalpel and self-healing cutting mat For cutting self-adhesive lead or film for trickier or small shapes.

PAINTING GLASS

Glass to decorate Clear glass is the most versatile to paint on, but also consider coloured and frosted glass. Items to decorate could include tumblers, tea light holders, paperweights, bottles, and vases.

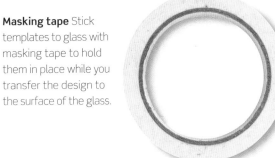

Methylated spirit Before embarking on a project, clean the glass inside and out with methylated spirit. This will degrease the surface so that masking tape and paint will adhere to it.

Scissors Keep a pair of sharp paper scissors to hand; they're useful for cutting out templates and snipping masking tape.

Tracing paper Use tracing paper to make templates to fit three-dimensional glassware. You can then create custom-made designs to trace onto the glass.

Masking tape Stick templates to glass with masking tape to hold them in place while you transfer the design to the surface of the glass.

Kitchen paper Rest the glass on a couple of sheets of kitchen paper for protection and to stop the glass rolling around. The paper is also useful to clean glass, wipe away mistakes, and mop up spills.

Glass paints These come in a range of vivid colours – water-based and oil-based versions are available. Some water-based glass paints can be fixed in a domestic oven; the results will be dishwasher-proof.

Craft knife Neaten any blobs of dried outliner with a craft knife. Don't neaten the line too much or it will lose its charming handcrafted appearance.

Old plate or white tile Mix paints on an old plate or white tile. You can mix water-based or oil-based paints together but do not mix the two.

Artist's paintbrushes Paint glass with good-quality medium and fine artist's paintbrushes. Clean the brushes immediately after use, washing off water-based paint with water. Follow the paint manufacturer's instructions to remove oil-based paint.

Glass outliner This is an acrylic paste piped from a tube. It creates a raised outline that contains the paint. Glass outliner is available in gold, silver, black, and pewter.

191

PAINTING CHINA/TILES

Scalpel and self-healing cutting mat For cutting card or paper stencils with intricate detail, use a scalpel or craft knife over a cutting mat to protect the work surface.

Card/thick paper Good for making stencils and sketching designs. For stencils, use thick paper or preferably card; anything too thin will get soggy.

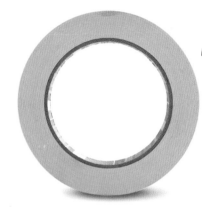

Masking tape Useful for sticking stencils to ceramics and keeping them in place. Also use it to mask off areas you do not want to paint over.

Ceramic paints These specialist paints come in an array of colours. Pens are also available. Read the manufacturer's instructions to see how durable they are once baked.

White bathroom tile This works like an artist's palette and is useful as a surface on which to pour small amounts of paint and for mixing colours.

Sponges Small scraps of sponge and even make-up wedges can be used for applying larger areas of colour and producing texture.

Paintbrushes A selection of shapes and sizes will give a variety of textures and brushstrokes. Experiment to see what effects can be achieved.

Small jar or pot Dip paintbrushes in a jar of clean water to rinse them and prevent them drying out.

Rag/cloth Use an old rag to clean paintbrushes and wipe off any unwanted paint or colour.

Cocktail sticks These are useful for drawing or making scratch marks in wet paint.

MOSAICS

Tiler's sponge These sponges are particularly dense. They are ideal for picking up surplus grout and make the job of cleaning the mosaic surface easier.

Small notched trowel This is used for applying cement-based adhesive to all backing materials when fixing paper-faced mosaic made using the indirect method. The small 3mm (⅛in) notches ensure that most of the surface is covered in adhesive, meaning that even small pieces will stick.

Plasterer's small tool This little trowel can be used to apply adhesive to flat and curved surfaces when using the direct method. The pointed end allows adhesive to be applied to awkward areas and can be used to scrape out excess adhesive.

Electrical screwdriver Useful for a multitude of tasks, from manoeuvring pieces into alignment to levering them off their backing.

Grouting float A good tool for spreading grout, particularly over large areas. It can also be used to press down on the mosaic to flatten out unevenness and ensure good contact with the adhesive.

Tile nippers This is the essential tool for mosaic cutting and can be used on all mosaic materials. The blades must be tungsten-tipped. It's worth paying a bit more to get a good pair that will cut accurately.

Double-wheel cutters These are primarily for cutting glass and give good, straight cuts. The blades can be turned when they get blunt so they last a long time. Replacement blades are also available.

Score and snap cutters These tools have a scoring wheel and a snapper for breaking the tiles. They are used when working with tiles larger than 2.5cm (1in) square to cut strips of the required size.

Found objects Popular found materials for mosaic include broken china and pebbles, but any small object can be used, including shells, marbles, beads, and buttons. Because found objects are usually irregular in shape, they are best used with the direct method and bedded directly into an adhesive bed.

Glazed ceramic Though small tiles only come in a limited colour range, you can get a much wider colour range in larger wall tiles then cut them down using a score and snap cutter. Glazed ceramic tiles are generally not frost-proof and only coloured on one side, so are best used with the direct method.

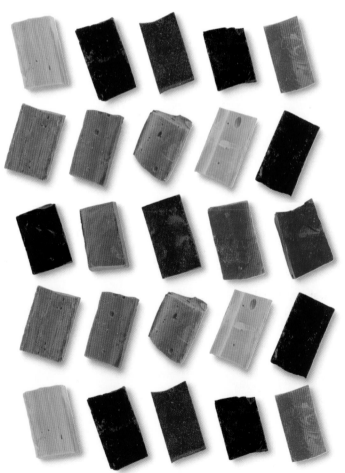

Washable PVA Polyvinyl acetate is a white liquid glue. The water-soluble variety, often sold as school glue, is used in a dilute form (50:50 with water) to stick tiles to paper in the indirect method.

Cement-based adhesive Tiling adhesives are based on traditional sand and cement but contain additives to improve adhesion and workability. Different types are available for different applications – always read the manufacturer's label to be sure you have the right product.

Smalti This beautiful enamelled glass has an uneven surface and a dense, often intense, colour. Usually available in 1.5 x 1cm (⅝ x ⅜in) pieces, which can be cut with tile nippers and double-wheel cutters.

Cement-based grout Mosaics for practical locations, such as splashbacks, floors, and walls are grouted to fill the gaps between the tiles. Ordinary tiling grout is used, which comes in a range of colours, as well as white, grey, and black.

Unglazed ceramic mosaic tiles Unglazed ceramic is a hard-wearing material that can be used on walls and floors. Tiles come in two sizes, 2 x 2cm ($\frac{3}{4}$ x $\frac{3}{4}$in) and 24 x 24mm (1 x 1in), and in an attractive range of muted colours.

Vitreous glass

A popular and readily available material in a wide range of vibrant and subtle colours. The tiles are of uniform 4mm ($\frac{3}{16}$in) thickness and 2cm ($\frac{3}{4}$in) square, and can be used both indoors and outdoors.

Gold, silver, and mirror Metallic leaf sandwiched between a coloured layer of glass and a much thinner clear layer creates a durable, glittering surface. Cheaper alternatives are ordinary mirror or more recently developed versions that are protected with primer instead of glass.

Marble This soft stone can be cut with tile nippers, especially long-handled ones. It is often cut down from polished tiles into rods and then hand cut into cubes that can be used either on the polished face or on the honed (back) face. The sparkling riven (inner) face can also be used by splitting the cubes in half.

Brown paper Used in the indirect method as a facing for the mosaic tiles. Use strong paper: 90g is recommended.

195

Film and leadwork TECHNIQUES

Using a combination of coloured, self-adhesive film and self-adhesive lead on clear glass panels – to hang in a window – or objects, this technique creates a beautiful stained-glass effect without the need for specialist equipment. The film comes in myriad colours and the lead strips in different widths and profiles so the possibilities are endless.

Cleaning the glass

Wipe the glass with methylated spirit to remove any grease, fingerprints, or smudges from the surface. Wash the glass in warm soapy water, rinse, and dry thoroughly.

Drawing and colouring the design

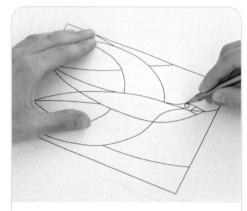

1 Mark the size of your glass panel on a piece of paper. Draw your design to comfortably fit within this size. Make a duplicate design to use later (see below).

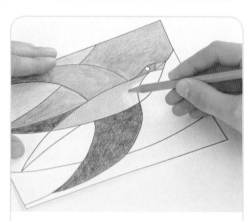

2 Colour up your design; you may want to try out several colourways before choosing the best one. Trim your paper to the size of the design.

Cutting out the pieces of film

1 Gather together the sheets of coloured film. Hold the design up to a window with the first sheet of film on top. Trace the area with a fine permanent pen.

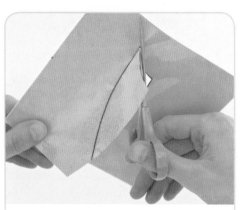

2 Put the design down and pick up some small sharp scissors. Cut out the film, following the drawn line. Now repeat for all the differently coloured areas of the design.

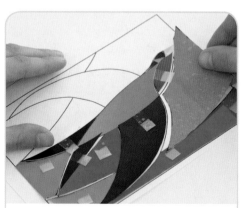

3 Arrange the pieces of film on a duplicate design to ensure you cut out every piece of film needed. Once all pieces are cut, you can start to apply them in turn.

Applying the coloured film

  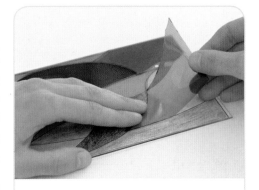

1 Fix the design to the back of the glass using Blu Tack, so that you see the design all the time. Take the first cut-out piece of film and carefully peel off the backing sheet.

2 Working from one edge, slowly position the film on the glass and, using a sponge, press the film down and ease out any air bubbles; the side of a thumb works well, too.

3 Now, repeat with the other pieces of coloured film until the design is completed.

Cutting and applying the lead strip

 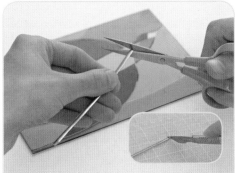 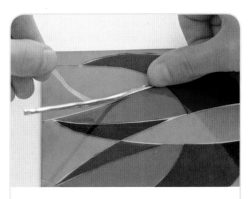

1 Cut the self-adhesive lead strip a bit longer than you need, using scissors. Lay it on the design and mark where to cut.

2 Cut the strip at the mark at the correct angle for the line on the design, using scissors or a craft knife and cutting board.

3 Peel the backing sheet from the lead strip, a little at a time. Then, stick down the strip along the line of the design.

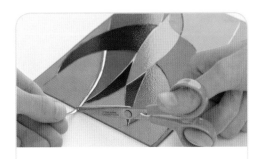 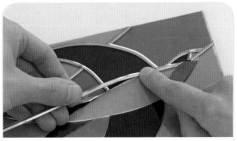 

4 Trim the lead strip at the edge of the glass panel. Continue laying down the lead strips until the design is complete.

5 When a strip of lead joins another, cut it at an angle. Ensure the final strips cover the joins and ends for a neat finish.

6 Press down firmly along all of the strips to ensure a firm bond between the glass and the lead. Wash your hands thoroughly.

Film and leadwork vase PROJECT

A plain vase has been transformed with the addition of a colourful, patterned band of film and leadwork. On a bright windowsill, the light will shine through the various square and rectangular panels of this Mondrian-esque design to bring whatever colours you choose to use to full effect. Such colourful bands would also work well on cylindrical vases or glass picture frames.

YOU WILL NEED

- 1 rectangular glass vase
- 2 sheets of paper
- a pencil and some coloured pencils
- a ruler
- scissors
- sticky tape
- sheets of self-adhesive coloured film
- Blu Tack
- a roll of 3mm (¹/₈in) oval profile self-adhesive lead

1 After cleaning the vase (see p.196), cut a piece of paper that fits all the way around the inside of the vase. Draw out and colour in your design and make a duplicate. Trace onto the sheets of coloured film, as necessary, using a fine permanent pen.

any pieces that wrap around a corner will need to be made longer than the paper design to account for the glass' thickness

2 Cut out the pieces of coloured film using small sharp scissors. And, as you go, start to stick these pieces down carefully onto one of the paper designs with sticky tape.

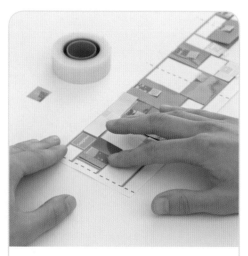

3 Once you've cut out all the coloured film pieces, finish sticking them to the duplicate design to check that you've got all the shapes you need.

4 Fix the paper design inside the vase with Blu Tack. Stick on the coloured film pieces one at a time, taking them from the paper design in turn.

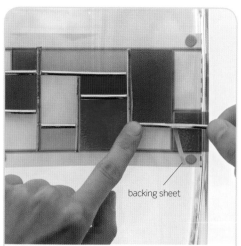

backing sheet

5 Cut small lead strips for the short lengths, peel off the backing sheet, and fix down to match the design. Work around the vase until all strips are done.

the top and
bottom strips
of lead are
added last

6 Cut two long lead strips to form the
borders of the band. Peel off the
backing, wrap around, and cut to length.
Press down firmly and wash your hands.

Painting glass TECHNIQUES

Glass painting is an inexpensive craft that requires minimal tools and materials. It is a great way to recycle old glassware and give it a new lease of life. Clear glass is the most versatile for painting on, but also consider coloured and frosted glass. Glass paint applied to frosted glass will make it transparent. Practise painting on acetate or an old piece of glass before starting on a project.

Making a template for a straight-sided or conical container

1 Slip a piece of tracing paper inside a straight-sided or conical container. Adjust the paper so that it rests against the glass, then tape it in place. Mark the position of the overlap and the upper edge with a pencil.

2 Remove the tracing paper and cut out the template along the overlap and upper edge. Transfer your design onto the tracing paper with a black pen. Stick the tracing under the glass with masking tape, butting the side edges of the template together.

Sticking a template under a double curvature

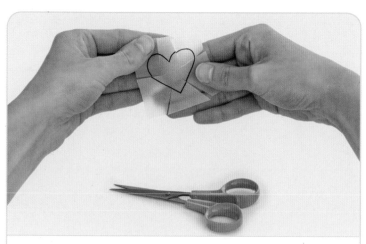

1 Templates to be used on rounded glassware need to be adapted to fit the shape. Make cuts into the template with a pair of scissors.

2 Tape the template under the glass at the top and bottom. The cuts will overlap or spread open to fit the curves of the glassware.

Transferring a design

1 If the aperture is too small to stick a template inside, the design can be transferred to the outer surface of the glass with a Chinagraph pencil. Turn the tracing over and redraw the lines with a Chinagraph pencil.

2 Tape the template, Chinagraph-pencil-side down, on the glass. Draw over the lines again with a sharp HB pencil to transfer the design onto the glass. Remove the template.

Applying outliner

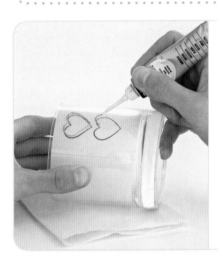

1 Resting the piece on kitchen paper and with the template in place, squeeze the tube of outliner, gently drawing it along the outline of the design. Leave to dry then turn the piece to continue.

2 Wipe away major mistakes immediately with kitchen paper. When dry, neaten any blobs with a craft knife. Once painted, the viewer's eye will be drawn to the painted areas and not the outliner, so don't overdo the neatening.

Painting on glass

1 Resting the piece on kitchen paper, apply the glass paint generously with a medium paintbrush. Use a fine paintbrush to push the paint into any corners. If working on a curve, keep the glass steady to avoid the paint running to one side.

2 To blend one colour into another, apply both colours to the glass, then mix them together where they meet, making sure that the paint reaches the edge of the outliner. Leave to dry, then turn the glass to continue painting.

Tea light holder PROJECT

Make a set of pretty painted tea light holders in warm shades of red and orange, outlined in gold. Candlelight will enhance the painted blossoms as it shines through the transparent glass paint. Use the simple motifs in different combinations to give individuality to a set of tea light holders. For a delicate finishing touch, decorate the motifs with tiny dots applied with outliner.

YOU WILL NEED

- straight-sided clear glass tea light holder
- tracing paper
- scissors
- pencil
- ruler
- black felt-tip pen
- masking tape
- kitchen paper
- gold outliner
- piece of white paper
- orange, red, and yellow transparent glass paints
- medium and fine artist's paintbrushes

1 Make a template and divide it into fifths. Trace the blossom and leaf motif on p.309 onto each section 6mm (¼in) below the upper edge with the felt-tip pen. Tape the template inside the tea light holder with masking tape.

2 Resting the tea light holder on its side on kitchen paper, trace the uppermost motif with gold outliner. Leave to dry. Turn the tea light holder and repeat to outline all the motifs. Remove the template when the outliner has dried.

3 Slip a piece of white paper inside the tea light holder to show up the area being painted. Apply orange paint to the outer edge of the petals with a medium paintbrush. Apply red paint to the inner edge with a fine paintbrush. Blend the colours at the centre. Leave to dry. Clean the paintbrushes.

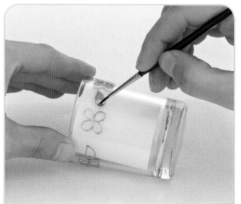

4 Apply yellow paint to the pointed end of a leaf with a clean fine paintbrush. Apply orange paint to the rounded end with a medium paintbrush. Blend the colours at the centre of the leaf. Leave to dry then turn the glass and continue painting.

5 When the last motif is dry, apply a dot of gold outliner at the centre of the flower to neaten it. Apply three tiny dots along the centre of the petals, then five dots along the leaf. Repeat on all the motifs. Leave the outliner to dry.

Painting china TECHNIQUES

Working with ceramic paints is as close as you can get to colour glazing ceramics without having to invest in expensive equipment, such as a kiln, to fire and set the colour. Ceramic paints come in a vast selection of colours and are easy and safe to use. Paint onto your chosen piece of china and bake in the oven to heat-fix.

Priming the surface

Use a cloth dipped in white spirit to clean the ceramic surface so that it is grease-free and ready to work on. Leave to dry.

Sketching and transferring your design

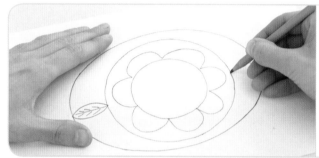

1 Sketch out your ideas on paper: it's a good idea to trace around the outline of your receptacle first to establish the frame within which your design must fit.

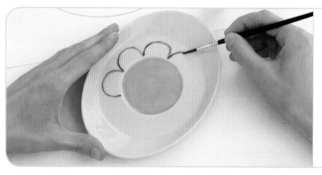

2 Once you are happy with your design, transfer it onto the ceramic. Since it is difficult to mark a glazed surface with pencil, transfer the design using a fine paintbrush and ceramic paints, then wash or wipe off any mistakes.

Experimenting with colour

Use a plain white tile for mixing different colour combinations and experimenting with paint effects (think of the tile as an artist's palette). Adding white to a colour makes it look more solid and less opaque.

Achieving different effects with paintbrushes

Different brushes give different results: a soft-haired brush produces soft, delicate paint marks, whereas a coarse paintbrush gives a streaky effect. Use different width brushes to produce thinner or thicker lines.

Rinsing paintbrushes

Rinse paintbrushes in cold water as soon as possible after use.

Sponging

1 Pour a little ceramic paint into a shallow dish or onto a tile (rather than dip the sponge directly into the paint pot).

dry make-up sponge

2 Dip a dry make-up sponge into the paint and dab it onto the surface. You can build up stronger colour by leaving the paint to dry then sponging on another layer of colour. Rinse the sponge in cold water after use.

Achieving a sgraffito effect

This is a painting technique where the colour is scratched off to reveal the surface underneath. The term comes from the Italian word "sgraffire", meaning "to scratch". Drag a cocktail stick or the end of a wooden paintbrush handle into wet paint to achieve a scratched effect.

FIXING CERAMIC PAINTS

Once the paint is dry, place the painted ceramic in a cold oven and then set the oven to the recommended temperature. Bake for the stated time, turn off the heat, and leave to cool in the oven. Do not be tempted to remove the ceramic from the oven when it is still hot as the sudden change in temperature may make it crack.

Fruit bowl PROJECT

This simple but effective project transforms a plain white ceramic bowl into a novel fruit bowl that will brighten up any kitchen. The inspiration here is a watermelon, but you could just as easily use an apple, with the outer surface of the bowl painted red or green, the inside cream, and the pips painted in the bottom of the bowl.

YOU WILL NEED

- white ceramic bowl
- cloth
- white spirit
- coarse 1–2cm (⅝in) wide paintbrush
- ceramic paints in peridot green, coral red, and dark brown
- cocktail stick
- shallow dish
- make-up sponge
- ceramic tile
- fine paintbrush

1 Clean the entire surface of the bowl, inside and out, using a cloth dipped in white spirit. Leave to dry before painting the outside of the bowl.

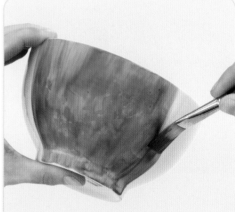

2 Using the coarse paintbrush, apply peridot green using swift, straight strokes. Start at the base of the bowl and work all the way to the rim. Try not to leave any gaps between strokes.

3 Work your way all around the bowl. Turn it upside down and, while the paint is still wet, brush it again with a dry brush to create texture. Work fast as the paint dries quickly but ensure the paint isn't too tacky as it may come off with the second brushing.

4 To create even more texture, add sgraffito work while the paint is still wet. Use a cocktail stick to scratch off lines of paint from the rim to the base of the bowl. Leave to dry for 24 hours.

5 Pour red paint into a dish and dip a dry make-up sponge in the colour. Dab the sponge on a tile to remove excess paint. Start in the centre of the bowl and work up the sides all the way to the rim to meet the green paint, dipping and dabbing the sponge as you go. Leave to dry for 15 minutes.

6 To paint the pips, dip a fine paintbrush in dark brown paint and paint pip-shaped dots inside the bowl. Don't overload the paintbrush or the paint will run. Leave to dry for 24 hours, then bake in the oven following the manufacturer's instructions. Leave to cool completely in the oven before removing.

Painting tiles TECHNIQUES

You can buy plain white bathroom or kitchen tiles quite cheaply from hardware stores. Transform them into colourful coasters, trivets, or even a kitchen or bathroom splashback with the help of ceramic paints, which come in a rainbow of delightful colours.

Designing and creating stencils

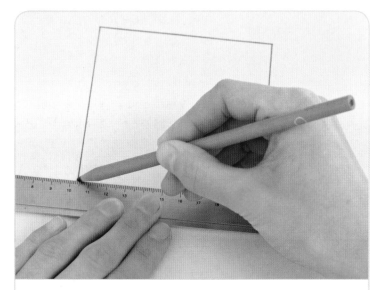

1 Using a pencil and ruler, mark onto card or thick paper the outline of the item you'll be painting onto (in this case, a tile). This outline is the frame within which your design must fit.

2 Draw your design onto the card. Centre the design within the frame and leave enough of an edge around it for the background.

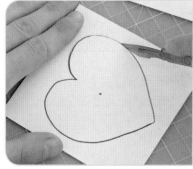

3 Once you're happy with the design, place the card on a cutting mat and use a scalpel to carefully cut around the drawn shape. You'll end up with two stencils: the solid shape you've cut out and its frame.

Fixing the stencil in place

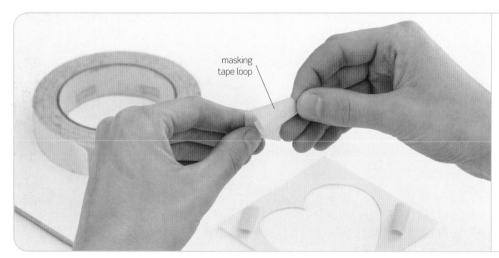

masking tape loop

Use a cloth dipped in white spirit to clean the surface of the tile. Cut a piece of masking tape and make it into a loop. On the reverse side of the frame stencil, stick a loop on each corner. Position the stencil in the centre of the tile and press it down to stick it in place.

Sponging

Using a dry make-up sponge dipped in ceramic paint, apply the colour to the tile. Press the inside edges of the stencil down with your fingers to ensure the paint doesn't seep underneath.

Removing the stencil

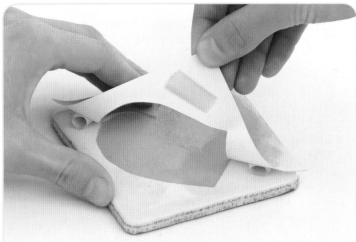

Leave to dry completely, for about 30 minutes. When the paint is dry to the touch, carefully lift the edge of the stencil and slowly peel it off, together with the masking tape.

Painting onto ceramics

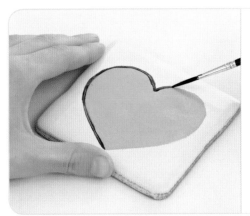

1 If you'd like to accentuate the shape, you could paint a thin line around the edge in a contrasting colour, using a fine paintbrush.

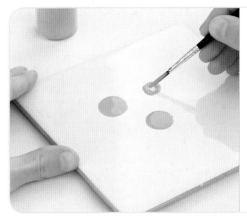

2 Achieving solid colour can be tricky with ceramic paints. Work with a loaded paintbrush and flood the area to be painted with colour.

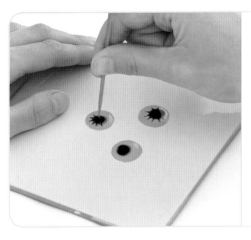

3 To achieve paint effects, you'll need to work quickly as ceramic paints become tacky soon after application. Experiment with dripping a second colour on wet paint and dragging with a cocktail stick.

FIXING CERAMIC PAINTS

Once the paints are dry, place the ceramic in a cold oven and set to the recommended temperature. Bake for the stated time, turn off the oven, and leave to cool in the oven. Do not be tempted to remove the ceramic from the oven when it is still hot as the sudden change in temperature may make it crack.

Set of coasters PROJECT

Make this fun set of four fruit-themed coasters using plain white ceramic bathroom or kitchen tiles. All four coasters require the same techniques – it's just the design that changes. Use the templates on p.312, or why not come up with your very own designs?

YOU WILL NEED

- 4 white ceramic tiles 10 x 10cm (4 x 4in)
- cloth
- white spirit
- card or thick paper
- pencil
- ruler
- scalpel and scissors
- cutting mat
- masking tape
- ceramic paints in turquoise, yellow, peridot green, and brown
- make-up sponge
- medium-size flat paintbrush
- fine paintbrush

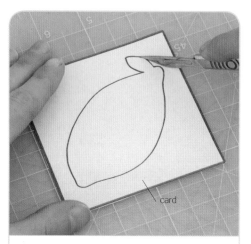

card

1 Clean the surface of the tile using a cloth dipped in white spirit. Leave to dry. Transfer the templates on p.312 onto card and cut out carefully using a scalpel, so that you have two stencils: a solid fruit shape and its frame.

ceramic tile

2 Stick the solid fruit stencil to the tile with masking tape loops stuck on the underside of the stencil. Pressing the edges of the stencil down to avoid seepage, sponge on the turquoise paint. Leave to dry for 30 minutes, then remove the stencil.

unpainted border

3 Using a medium-size flat paintbrush, paint the body of the lemon with a generous amount of yellow paint. Leave a thin, unpainted border around the shape for effect. Rinse the brush.

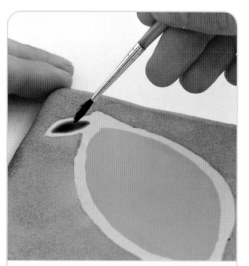

4 When the yellow paint is dry, paint the leaf in peridot green using a fine paintbrush. Rinse and dry the brush, then paint the stalk brown: try to paint it in just one or two even strokes.

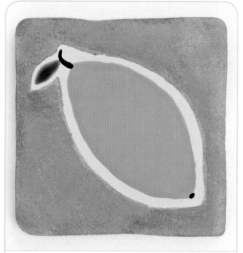

5 Leave the tile to dry for 24 hours. Repeat Steps 1 to 4 to apply the other designs to three more tiles so that you have a full set. Follow the paint manufacturer's instructions to set the colours.

Mosaics: the direct method

The direct method is a simple mosaic technique that is suitable for both flat and three-dimensional surfaces. One of its disadvantages, however, is that the adhesive is opaque and covers up the drawing as you work, so it's best to keep designs simple. The mosaic pieces are difficult to adjust once the adhesive has dried, so it pays to plan your piece out in advance.

Choosing your materials

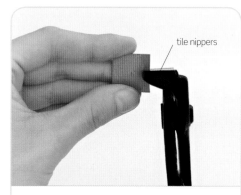

Vitreous glass and unglazed ceramic are easy to cut, while marble and smalti have a traditional look and appeal. Glazed ceramic and broken china are usually coloured on one side only, so these work well with the direct method of application.

Cutting and shaping the tiles

tile nippers

1 To achieve greater detail, quarter mosaic tiles before you begin. Place the tile nippers at the edge of the tile and squeeze gently while holding the tile with your other hand so that it does not fly away. Wear safety goggles to protect your eyes.

2 In order to create interesting patterns and representational designs, you can cut more defined shapes by placing the tile nippers at different angles and nibbling away at the edges of the tile.

Planning and transferring your design

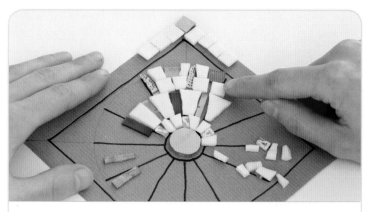

1 Draw your design on paper first. Lay out the cut tiles on your design, adjusting the colours and shapes until you are happy with the effect.

2 Copy or trace your design onto your chosen surface using a pencil or marker pen.

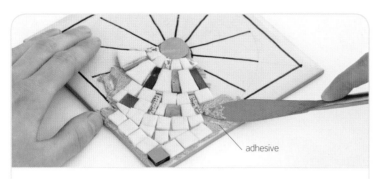

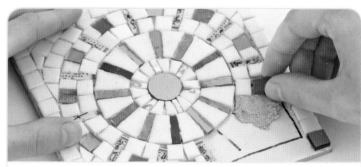

3 Mix cement-based adhesive with water to make a thick paste. Apply to the surface of the tile, using a plasterer's small tool or palette knife. Cover a small area at a time so that the adhesive does not skin over and the design is still visible.

adhesive

4 Carefully position the mosaic pieces in the adhesive bed. If you're not going to grout the tile, lay the pieces as close as possible, but if you are, leave even gaps between them. The size of gap can vary from 1 to 4mm ($\frac{1}{16}$ to $\frac{3}{16}$in) but it will look neater if the gaps are consistent.

Levelling the surface

Grouting the piece

If you're using mosaic pieces of slightly different thickness and want to achieve a flat final surface, add a little extra adhesive to the backs of the thinner pieces.

When the adhesive is dry, grout the piece. Mix the grout with water to form a thick paste and apply to the surface of the mosaic. You can use a grouting float to do this, but for small and 3D pieces it's easier to use your fingers protected by rubber gloves.

Removing excess grout

Clean off the excess grout with a damp sponge, turning the sponge over after every wipe so that you are always using a clean face. When the grout is almost dry, after about 20 minutes, clean off any surface residue with a dry cloth.

Mosaics: the indirect method

In this technique, the mosaic is made in reverse on paper before being fixed to its final position. This is a practical way of working, especially for larger projects. This method allows you to do all the cutting work while sitting comfortably at a work surface, and allows you to see the design you're following. It's also easy to make amendments as you go.

Transferring your design onto brown paper

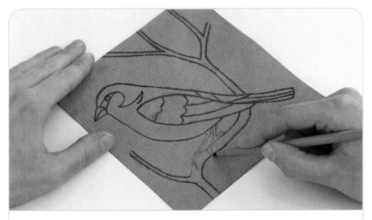

Draw the design onto brown paper, remembering to reverse it if it is not symmetrical or includes lettering. This can be done by turning over the original and tracing over it again on a lightbox or against a window.

Sticking the tiles onto the brown paper

tiles stuck face down

Apply a small amount of 50:50 washable PVA glue to water to the paper with a small brush, then apply a piece of mosaic, right side down. Repeat to complete the design. Leave to dry.

Fixing the tiles to your chosen surface

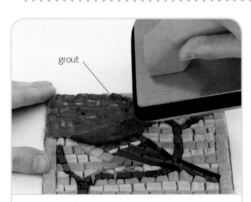

grout

1 The mosaic can now be fixed to any rigid surface such as a timber board, wall, or floor. Pre-grout the mosaic: mix the grout with water to form a thick paste and apply it to the mosaic to fill the joints. Wipe off excess grout with a damp sponge.

adhesive

2 Apply the cement-based adhesive to your chosen surface. Mix the adhesive with water to create a thick paste and comb it over the surface using a small-notched trowel to achieve a thin, even bed. Pay particular attention to the edges.

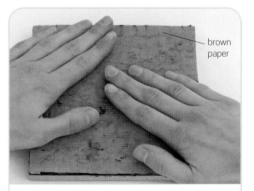

brown paper

3 Carefully pick up the mosaic and turn it over onto the adhesive. Make sure it's in place correctly, then apply gentle pressure all over to ensure that all the mosaic pieces are firmly bedded.

Removing the brown paper

1 Wet the paper with a sponge, keep the paper damp until the glue dissolves (about 15 minutes, depending on the strength of the glue and the air temperature). While waiting, apply a little more adhesive to the edges of the mosaic to strengthen them.

right side of mosaic

2 Lift a corner of the paper. If it comes up easily continue to peel, pulling it back parallel to the mosaic surface so as not to lift the tiles out of their bed of grout. If it's hard to peel the paper back, re-wet the surface with the sponge. Some grout will have bled through onto the surface of the tiles – wipe it off with a damp sponge before it dries. Keep turning the sponge so that you always use a clean face.

Grouting and finishing

1 Grout the front of the mosaic to fill any gaps either immediately or after the adhesive has dried. Moisten the surface of the mosaic with a damp sponge, then spread grout across the surface, working it into the gaps. Clean with a damp sponge, turning the sponge with every wipe.

2 After about 20 minutes, when the grout has begun to dry, pass a dry cloth over the surface of the mosaic to remove any residual grout.

Flowerpots PROJECT

These flowerpots are embellished with a simple but effective mosaic decoration, made up of fragments of broken china and unglazed ceramic tiles. The pots used here are the plain rimless terracotta ones, but the technique works equally well on terracotta pots with rims (plastic pots are not rigid enough). The designs on the two pots echo each other: one has a blue flower design on a blue and white patterned background, while the background of the other is white and the flowers are patterned. This project uses the direct method.

YOU WILL NEED

- blue and white china plates
- towel
- hammer
- tile nippers
- 2 terracotta pots approx 15cm (6in) high
- 70:30 solution of washable PVA glue and water
- medium-size paintbrush
- pencil
- blue glass mosaic tiles
- cement-based adhesive
- plasterer's small tool or palette knife
- white grout
- sponge

1 Wrap the china plates in a towel and smash them with a hammer. Cut the pieces into smaller, more regular shapes using tile nippers.

2 Seal the terracotta pot by painting it with the PVA solution and leave to dry.

3 Draw a simple design onto the pot in pencil and lay out the same motif on your work surface using the blue glass tiles. Cut these into strips to make the stem and into triangles for the flower and leaves.

adhesive

4 Apply cement-based adhesive to the pot's surface with a plasterer's small tool or palette knife, roughly following the design. Position the blue tile pieces on the adhesive, starting with the flower.

5 Fill in the background with pieces of broken plate. Choose pieces with a similar pattern to make a border around the rim. Apply adhesive to small areas at a time, turning the pot upside down to reach the base more easily. When the adhesive is dry, grout the piece and wipe away excess grout with a damp sponge.

Trivet PROJECT

Mosaic provides a practical wipe-clean surface and is ideal for functional pieces like this trivet. You can either use a ceramic floor tile or a wooden board base. Protect the underside with a felt backing. This project uses the indirect method.

YOU WILL NEED

- brown paper
- pencil or stick of charcoal
- approximately 270 (800g/1lb 12oz) vitreous glass tiles in orange, red, white, black, blue, and purple
- tile nippers
- 50:50 solution of washable PVA glue and water, plus extra undiluted glue
- small and medium paintbrushes
- 30 x 30cm (12 x 12in) MDF board, 12mm (1/2in) thick, or ceramic tile
- cement-based adhesive
- small-notched trowel
- sponge
- dark grey grout
- rubber gloves
- cloth
- 30 x 30cm (12 x 12in) piece of felt
- scissors

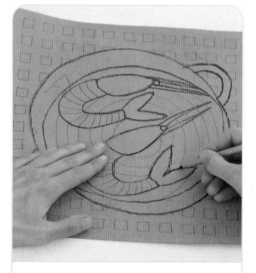

1 Transfer the template on p.313 onto brown paper using a pencil or charcoal.

2 Quarter the tiles using tile nippers. Cut thin strips for the antennae and more defined shapes for the tail. Using the small paintbrush, apply the PVA solution to a small area of the paper at a time. Start with the prawns, then work outwards to the pan, fixing the tiles right side down onto the paper.

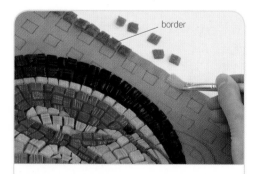

border

3 Before filling in the blue and purple checked tablecloth, lay a row of blue quartered tiles around the edge to create a neat border, then work inwards to fill in the tablecloth pattern. Once completed, leave the glue to dry. Pre-grout the mosaic.

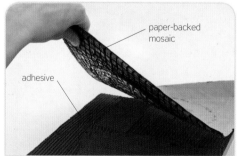

paper-backed mosaic

adhesive

4 Apply adhesive to the board or tile using the small-notched trowel. Turn the mosaic over and press onto the adhesive. Wet the paper with a damp sponge to dissolve the glue, then peel the paper off. Grout the piece and remove excess grout with a clean sponge. Wipe clean with a cloth.

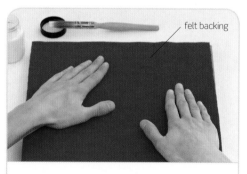

felt backing

5 Paint the underside of the board or tile with full-strength PVA and place the felt square onto it. Press down with your hands and wipe away any excess glue with a damp cloth. Allow to dry for one hour before turning over.

Candles and soap

Candles and soap

DIPPED TAPER CANDLES • THREE-LAYER CANDLE • ROLLED BEESWAX CANDLES

BOTANICAL SLAB • MOULDED ROSE SOAPS • CLEAR HEART SOAP

At the dawn of a new millennium, we are more aware than ever of the virtue of natural ingredients, and centuries-old crafts such as candle-making and soap-making are enjoying a revival. Homemade candles and soaps make delightful gifts for family and friends who will appreciate the effort you've put into making them – but only you will know how easy it really is.

If you've never made soap or candles before, you'll find this chapter a useful introduction. The creation of soaps involves a special kind of alchemy, but the simple methods shown here are within the reach of every crafter. They utilize basic equipment that you probably already own or can obtain easily and with the minimum of investment, such as electronic scales and a measuring jug for accurately measuring ingredients, a pestle and mortar or food processor for grinding dried herbs and flowers, and a microwave oven. You will, however, need to buy the specialist ingredients with which to make your soaps: goat's milk soap base or clear soap base, essential oils, colourants, and pigments.

Similarly, for making candles you'll almost certainly already have some of the basic equipment but you'll need to purchase items such as wax, dyes, wick pincers, and wicks. Fortunately, there are plenty of suppliers, while online shopping brings these items within the reach of everyone.

Before you embark on any of the projects in this chapter, read through the project instructions carefully, make a checklist of the items you need, and be sure to follow the safety guidelines.

Gather together all your equipment and ingredients, then banish children and pets from the room. Your kitchen is now your laboratory.

Of course, once you've tried and perfected the basic techniques, you can go on to create your own recipes, choosing fragrances and colours to suit your own taste. Before you know it, you'll be producing more candles and soaps than you have use for – in which case you can give away the surplus to appreciative friends and family.

Candles TOOLS AND MATERIALS

There are a number of tools required for making candles, most of which you probably already have in your home. Additionally, you'll need a handful of specialist tools, but most of these are fairly inexpensive and can be purchased from craft shops or specialist websites.

Candle moulds These are available in polycarbonate, plastic, latex, metal, and silicone, and can be sourced through specialist suppliers. Alternatively, you can make your own (see p.230).

Metal jug Used for pouring hot, melted wax into moulds. You can also use a glass or polycarbonate jug, but it's important that the jug can withstand the temperature of the wax and pours well.

Metal dipping pot A tall container used for making dipped candles (see pp.234–35).

Deep saucepan This (asparagus) saucepan is ideal for making dipped taper candles. First place the trivet in the saucepan, then put the dipping pot onto the trivet and two-thirds fill the saucepan with water.

Double-boiler You can buy a specialist one or use a large pan with a smaller pan on top. If you are heating large quantities of wax, you can buy purpose-made wax melters (see opposite).

Mini saucepan This little pan fits into the mini wax melter.

Mini wax melter This appliance is actually a chocolate fondue maker but is perfect for melting small quantities of soy wax, without the need for a double-boiler.

Craft thermometer This specialist thermometer is used to test the temperature of the wax. Some thermometers contain alcohol, others mercury, and some have numerical dials, which are easy to read and can clip to the side of the double-boiler.

Heat-resistant mat Used for resting hot pans and dipping pots.

Metal trivet This small stand is used to raise the dipping pot off the bottom of the pan.

Baking tray Used to protect the work surface from any spills. Alternatively, you could use foil.

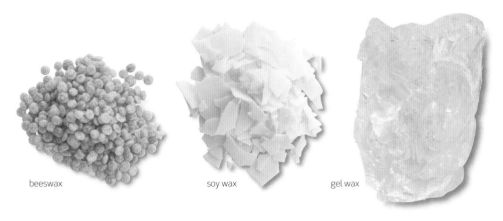

beeswax   soy wax   gel wax

Wax There are different types of wax: beeswax, soy wax, gel wax, and petroleum (paraffin) wax. Beeswax and soy wax are natural, clean-burning products. Soy wax is available in flakes and, as it is water-soluble, it is easy to remove from pans and utensils after use.

YOU WILL ALSO NEED...

Spoon/stirrer To stir the wax.

Measuring jug For measuring wax, fragrance, etc.

Electronic scales For weighing the wax, fragrance oil, and dye. Electronic scales are best as they are much more precise, especially when measuring small quantities of dye and fragrance oil.

Apron To protect your clothing.

Craft knife For cutting beeswax sheets.

Blu-tack or modelling clay To seal the holes in candle moulds to stop hot wax leaking out.

Oven gloves For holding hot pans.

Dyes These are available in flake and liquid forms. Flakes are easy to cut, measure, and handle, and produce no mess. Liquid dye is very concentrated and although you only need a few drops to colour your candles, it is more difficult to measure.

Palette knife Used for stirring wax and blending dye or fragrance oil into the wax.

Fragrance oils There are two types of fragrance oil: candle fragrance oil (a synthetic blend) and essential/aromatherapy oil (extracted from plants and flowers). Essential oils are more expensive than candle fragrance oils, but the fragrance is 100% pure.

Wicking pins/sticks Purpose-made pins or wicking sticks can be bought from specialist candle-making suppliers. Alternatively, you can make your own by joining together the ends of two 10cm (4in) long wooden skewers with small elastic bands.

Wicks There are many types and shapes of wick made from different types of material, ranging from flat-braided or square-braided cotton wicks to wooden or cored wicks. The size of wick you need depends on the diameter of the candle and type of wax.

Mini top-cutting pliers You can use sharp scissors, snip cutters, or mini top-cutting pliers (shown here) for cutting wicks.

Soap TOOLS AND MATERIALS

Besides the soap base itself, all the ingredients and equipment needed for soap-making can be found around the house or in a supermarket. A wide variety of soap bases is available online or from large craft suppliers, along with a huge range of fancy moulds, colourants, scents, and other additives.

Teaspoon or beaker For measuring out quantities of essential oil or fragrance.

Melt-and-pour soap base These clear or opaque glycerine bases are designed for melting and re-moulding into bars.

One or more heatproof bowls These are used for melting the soap, either on the hob or in the microwave.

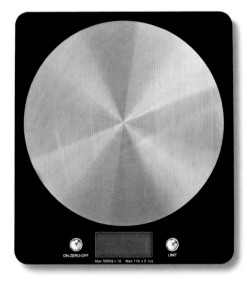

Kitchen scales Electronic or old-fashioned kitchen scales both work well. These are used for weighing out the soap and other ingredients.

Pans You can use any type of pan; just make sure the heatproof bowl fits neatly on top without touching the bottom of the pan.

227

Moulds These can be anything from fancy soap moulds to sturdy margarine tubs. Silicone bakeware and Tupperware are also ideal. Avoid anything that is liable to warp with heat.

Cocktail sticks These are handy for transferring dyes and pigments to the soap base in tiny increments.

Chopping board Chop the soap base into cubes on a plastic or wooden board.

Colourants Cosmetic pigments, dyes, and micas (powdered minerals) offer a safe and lasting way to colour soap. Food colours can also be used but are prone to fading so are best avoided.

Scents Essential oils are ideal for creating aromatherapy soaps, while synthetic fragrances offer a range of additional scent options. Only use essential oils or fragrances that are safe for cosmetic use.

poppy seeds

Texture enhancers Finely ground oatmeal, honey, powdered clays, and solid oils and butters can all be used to add exfoliating or skin-conditioning properties to soap.

honey

french green clay

shea butter

ground oatmeal

Metal scraper or knife Ideal for slicing soap into chunks and bars.

Botanical additives Dried flower petals or buds, herbs, and dried fruit slices can add decorative interest to soaps. (Note that some ingredients, such as rose petals, will fade when embedded within the soap and are best kept as surface decoration. Dried calendula petals, on the other hand, will retain their vibrant colour when stirred into the soap.)

YOU WILL ALSO NEED...

Microwave oven For melting small quantities of soap (as an alternative to melting on the hob).

Rubbing alcohol or surgical spirit A liquid used for removing surface bubbles and helping soap layers to adhere to each other. Pour into a small spray bottle for easy use.

Metal spoons For stirring the melted soap.

Clingfilm For storing finished soaps that are not for immediate use.

Candle-making TECHNIQUES

Once you have mastered these basic candle-making techniques, you'll be able to make a wide variety of candles, from coloured and fragranced candles to dipped and pillar candles. You may even want to experiment and make some novelty candles.

Choosing a mould

Candle moulds are receptacles into which wax is poured to create the shape of the candle. Professional moulds, made from materials including polycarbonate, plastic, latex, metal, and silicone can be purchased from specialist suppliers, but you can also use cake and chocolate-making moulds, as well as yoghurt pots and plastic soup containers.

Preparing your own mould

1 Wash out a container of your choice, such as a soup or yoghurt pot, and make a small hole in the bottom using a metal skewer. Secure a piece of wick, as explained in **securing the wick to the mould,** below.

2 If using a larger container, such as an ice-cream tub, you'll need more than one wick, so make two or three evenly spaced holes in the bottom of the container.

centre hole

Securing the wick to the mould

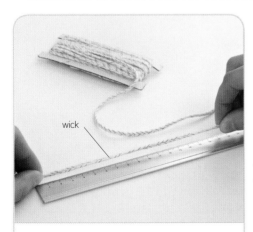

wick

1 Cut a piece of wick about 10cm (4in) longer than the depth of the mould and thread it through the hole in the base.

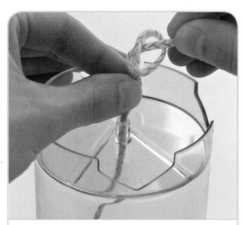

2 Tie a knot in the wick under the hole in the base to stop the wick from being pulled through.

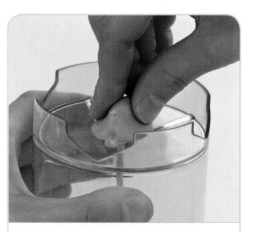

3 Seal the underside of the hole with Blu-tack or modelling clay. Make sure the wick is completely covered, with no gaps around it, otherwise the hot wax will leak out.

Making a wick holder

1 Wick holders keep the wick straight and taut in the mould. Secure the ends of two wooden skewers with elastic bands.

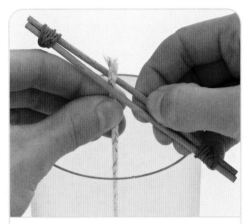

2 Insert the wick between the skewers and pull it gently so that it is fairly taut.

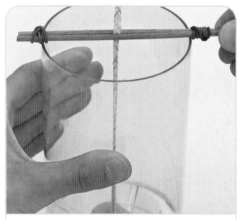

3 Rest the skewers on the rim of the mould, ensuring the wick is taut and centred in the mould.

Priming the wick

1 When making dipped taper candles (see pp.234–35) and rolled candles (see pp.240–41), the wick must be primed (coated in wax) first to ensure the candles light easily. To do this, melt a small amount of wax.

2 Submerge the entire wick in the melted wax: small bubbles will be released from the wick as it absorbs the wax.

wax-coated wick

3 After about a minute, or when there are no more bubbles, use a wicking pin or fork to remove the wick from the pan. Hold the wick over the pan so that any excess wax drips back into the pan.

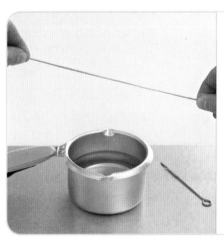

4 Allow the wick to dry for a few seconds, then, as it cools, pull it at both ends to straighten it.

Types of wax

beeswax

gel wax

soy wax

There are many types of wax. Most shop-bought candles use petroleum-based (paraffin) wax. However, there are some good alternatives, which are better for the environment and your home as they produce less soot. These are beeswax and soy wax, both of which are natural products and are cleaner burning. Soy wax comes in flakes, which are easy to measure out and melt. Soy wax is also soluble in water, making your pans and utensils easier to clean.

Measuring wax

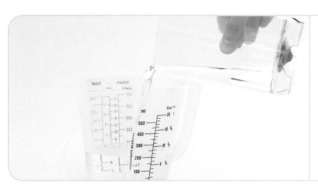

1 The easiest way to establish how much wax you need is to fill your mould with water after blocking the hole of the mould with Blu-tack. Pour the water into a measuring jug and make a note of the amount.

2 Convert the millilitres into grams (e.g. 100ml = 100g). Since melted wax weighs about 10% less than water, reduce the amount in grams by 10%: so for 100g of water you need 100g x 0.9 = 90g wax.

Grams of water	Grams of wax flakes
100	90
200	180
300	270
400	360
500	450
600	540
700	630
800	720
900	810
1000	900

Melting wax using a double-boiler

One-third fill the bottom part of a double-boiler with water and place the larger pan on top. Bring the water to simmering point, add the wax to the top saucepan, and melt, stirring occasionally with a metal spoon. As a rough guide, beeswax melts at 62°C (144°F) and soy wax melts at around 68°C (155°F). Refer to the manufacturer's guidelines for full instructions.

Melting wax using other appliances

Instead of a double-boiler, you can use a large saucepan partly filled with water, with a heatproof bowl on top. There are also purpose-made electric candle melters or, for small amounts of wax, you can use an electric chocolate fondue maker.

WARNING!

Never leave wax unattended when heating, and never let the temperature exceed 93°C (200°F).

Adding colour

1 The easiest way to colour candles is to use wax dye, available in liquid or flake form. The amount needed depends on the size of candle and the depth of colour required. As a rule of thumb, 1g ($^1/_{16}$oz) of dye will colour about 100g (3$^1/_2$oz) of wax, but do experiment first.

2 Once the wax flakes have fully melted, turn off the heat and add the dye. Stir it in thoroughly, particularly if you're using flakes rather than liquid. Bear in mind that the colour will look a lot paler once the wax sets.

3 If you're looking for a specific colour, test by dripping a small amount of dyed wax onto a plate and wait for it to set. If the colour is too pale add more dye; if it is too dark add more wax flakes.

Measuring fragrance oil

1 The amount of fragrance needed is usually specified by the supplier, but if using synthetic oil, you'll need between 5 and 10% of the weight of the wax. For essential oil, it's about 5%. You'll need to experiment and "burn test" your candles to make sure the fragrance "throw" (how well the fragrance is released into the room) is right.

2 Add the fragrance oil to the hot wax just before pouring. Stir it in thoroughly but carefully, and avoid adding air when stirring.

SAFETY FIRST

Place candles on a heat-resistant surface.

Burn candles in a well-ventilated room.

Extinguish candles when only 5mm ($^1/_4$in) of wax remains.

Never leave burning candles unattended.

Keep candles away from draughts and flammable materials.

Keep candles out of reach of children and pets.

Store candles away from sunlight and direct heat.

Dipped taper candles PROJECT

Dipped taper candles are traditional candles that have been made for many centuries. The concept is very simple (although it takes a little practice and patience) and involves building up thin layers of wax around a wick. This project makes a pair of candles.

YOU WILL NEED

- flat-braided wick
- scissors
- metal trivet
- deep saucepan
- tall metal dipping pot
- enough soy pillar wax flakes to fill the dipping pot
- craft thermometer
- wax dye
- metal spoon or stirrer
- oven gloves
- heat-resistant mat
- mini top-cutting pliers

wick

dipping pot

1 This project makes a pair of candles, so cut enough wick for the length of candle you want to produce (times two), plus 10cm (4in). So if your dipping pot is 20cm (8in) high, the total length of the wick should be 50cm (20in).

2 Place the trivet in the saucepan. Two-thirds fill the pan with water and bring to simmering point, then sit the dipping pot on the trivet. Three-quarters fill the dipping pot with wax flakes. As the wax melts, add more flakes so that the pot is 90% full. When the wax reaches 70°C (158°F), turn off the heat. Stir in the dye until dissolved.

3 Using oven gloves, lift the dipping pot out of the saucepan and place it on a heat-resistant mat. Alternatively, you can leave the pot in the pan, which helps maintain the temperature of the wax.

4 Fold the wick in half, hold it in the middle, and dip it into the wax for 30 seconds, then lift it out and allow the wax to drip back into the pot. Pull the wick taut with your fingers and let it cool for 3 minutes.

5 Dip the wick into the pot again for 15 seconds and lift out. Pull the wick taut while it's drying. When you have done this a few times, the wick will be more rigid and you won't need to hold it taut. When dipping, don't let the candles touch each other.

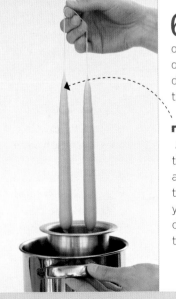

6 If you're making more than one pair of candles, leave one pair to dry while you dip the other. Continue dipping and drying until you reach the desired thickness (around 30 to 40 dips).

7 If the temperature drops below 55°C (131°F), return the dipping pot to the saucepan and bring the temperature back to 70°C (158°F). As you proceed, you'll need to add more wax and dye to the dipping pot to maintain the level of wax.

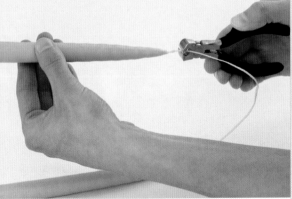

8 Hang the candles to dry. Then, using mini top-cutting pliers, cut the wick to about 1cm (³⁄₈in) above the top of the candles and leave for 24 hours before burning.

Three-layer candle PROJECT

You can make a pillar candle in a variety of colours and moulds; for this project we're using three shades of blue and a polycarbonate mould. Latex, metal, or silicone moulds are also available from suppliers – or you can make your own (see p.230).

YOU WILL NEED

- double-boiler
- soy pillar wax flakes
- craft thermometer
- metal spoon
- wick
- scissors
- candle mould
- blu-tack or modelling clay
- 2 wooden skewers
- 2 small elastic bands
- metal jug
- wax dye
- fragrance oil
- mini top-cutting pliers

1 One-third fill the bottom of a double-boiler with water and place the pan on top. Bring the water to simmering point and add the soy pillar wax flakes to the top saucepan. (To calculate the quantity of wax needed for your mould, see p.232, **measuring wax**.) Heat the wax to 70°C (158°F) and stir occasionally with a metal spoon.

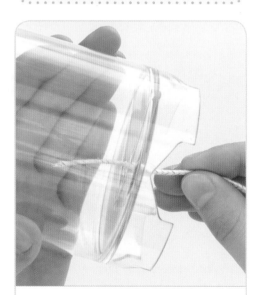

2 While the wax is heating, cut a piece of wick about 10cm (4in) longer than the length of the mould and thread it through the hole in the bottom of the mould.

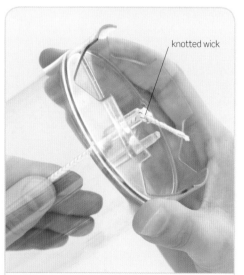

knotted wick

3 Tie a knot at one end of the wick to stop it pulling through the mould.

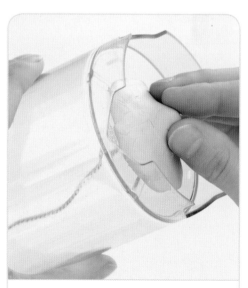

4 Seal the hole with Blu-tack or modelling clay, making sure there are no gaps around the wick, otherwise the melted wax will seep out through the hole.

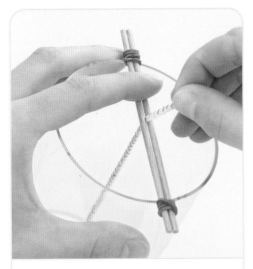

5 Secure the ends of two wooden skewers with elastic bands to make a wick holder. Insert the wick between the skewers and pull it gently so that it is fairly taut. Rest the skewers on the rim of the mould, ensuring the wick is centred in the mould.

6 Once the wax has reached 70°C (158°F) and has melted, pour it into a metal jug. This candle has three layers of colour; the top is the lightest in colour, the middle is slightly darker, and the bottom is darker still.

7 Start with the lightest colour. Determine how much dye you require for this colour (see **adding colour** on p.233). Stir the dye into the melted wax: this first layer will form the top of the candle.

8 Once the dye has fully dissolved, add the fragrance (see **measuring fragrance oil** on p.233) and stir again.

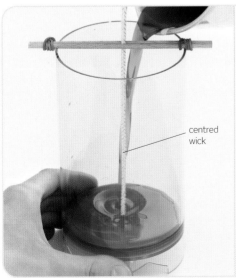

centred wick

9 Slowly pour the wax into the mould so that the mould is one-third full. Tap the mould with a spoon to release any air bubbles. Make sure the wick is centred. Pour the remaining wax back into the double-boiler.

10 Once the wax in the mould has set and is solid to the touch, reheat the second batch of wax in the double-boiler, transfer it to the jug, and stir in the amount of dye required for the next colour. Once the dye has fully dissolved, pour this second batch of wax into the mould so that it is about two-thirds full. Again, tap the mould to release air bubbles and ensure the wick is still centred. Pour the remaining wax into the double-boiler. Allow the candle to cool and set, for about 1 hour.

11 Heat up the last batch of wax in the double-boiler. Transfer the wax to the jug and stir in the dye for the darkest colour. Pour into the mould, leaving a 1cm (³⁄₈in) gap at the top. Save a tiny amount of wax in the jug. Tap the mould to release any air bubbles and check the wick is centred. Leave to cool overnight.

12 The next day, you'll notice that the top layer of wax has shrunk and is slightly concave. Heat up the saved wax and pour it into the small dip created by the shrinkage – don't fill the mould further or you'll end up with a wax line running around the candle. Leave the candle in the mould for 2 hours.

13 When the candle has fully set, turn the mould upside down so that the Blu-tack or modelling clay is at the top. Remove the Blu-tack.

14 Undo the knot in the wick, or cut it off using mini top-cutting pliers.

POLISHING OUT WAX LINES

old nylon tights

If you unintentionally let the stages of the candle solidify too much before pouring the next batch of wax, you'll end up with lines around the candle. This is caused by the candle shrinking very slightly in diameter as it cools, so that when you pour the next batch of wax, a small amount flows down the gap created by this shrinkage. This creates a line, which protrudes very slightly outwards. If this happens, rub the line with an old pair of nylon tights when the candle is fully cooled and the line will disappear. The tights will polish the candle at the same time!

15 Slide the candle out of the mould – it will have shrunk very slightly so will slide out easily.

Rolled beeswax candles PROJECT

Beeswax sheets are available in many colours, ranging from natural beeswax to all the colours of the rainbow. Before you start, make sure the wax is at room temperature so that it is pliable. If you need to warm the wax, use a hairdryer (taking care not to melt it) or place the wax close to a radiator for a few minutes.

YOU WILL NEED

- beeswax sheets
- cutting mat
- craft knife
- metal ruler
- primed square braided wick (see p.231)
- scissors

1 To make a straight rolled candle, place the beeswax sheet on the cutting mat and, using the craft knife and ruler, cut the sheet to 20 x 14cm (8 x 5½in).

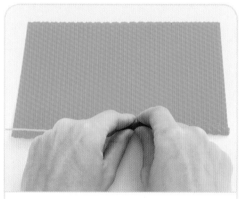

2 Cut a 22cm (9in) length of primed wick. Place the wick 5mm (¼in) from the long edge of the wax sheet and gently fold the edge of the sheet over to cover the wick.

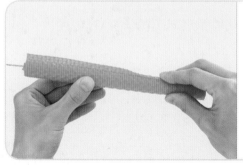

3 Start rolling the sheet, ensuring it is rolled evenly. Continue rolling to the end of the sheet. Press down the edge so that it doesn't unwind.

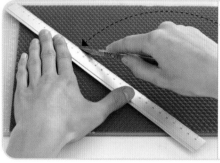

4 To make a slightly tapered candle, cut the sheet into a 20 x 20 x 28cm (8 x 8 x 11in) triangle, using the craft knife and ruler on the cutting mat.

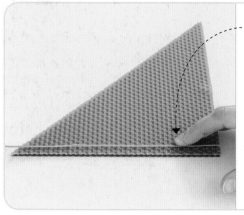

5 Place a 22cm (9in) length of primed wick 5mm (¼in) from one of the short edges and roll as in Steps 2 and 3. Press down the edge so that it doesn't unwind.

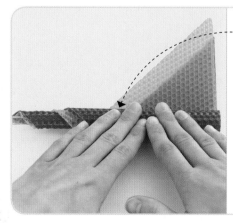

6 To make a double-layered tapered candle, cut two sheets into 20 x 20 x 28cm (8 x 8 x 11in) triangles, using the craft knife and ruler on the cutting mat. Place one triangle directly on top of the other, then follow Step 5.

Soap-making TECHNIQUES

The basic technique of soap-making involves melting a soap base and re-moulding it into bars or slabs filled with your own custom scents, colours, and additives. Once you have mastered these basics, you can branch out to create highly decorative soaps using techniques such as layering and embedding. The only limit is your imagination.

Preparing the soap base

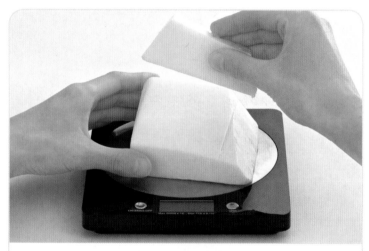

1 Weigh out enough soap base to fill your moulds, allowing a little extra for wastage. Average-sized bars usually require 80 to 100g (3 to 3½oz) of soap. If you're not sure how much soap your mould requires, try cutting a slab to fit it.

2 Use a sharp knife to slice the soap into 2.5cm (1in) chunks. As a rule, the smaller and more regular the pieces, the more quickly and evenly the soap will melt.

Melting the soap base

1 To melt soap on the hob, place it in a heatproof bowl over a pan of simmering water until the soap becomes fully liquid. Stir occasionally but try to avoid generating air bubbles.

2 Small batches of soap can be melted in the microwave. Place the soap in a microwave-proof bowl and heat on full power for a series of 10-second bursts until the soap becomes fully liquid. Never overheat or boil the soap. It only needs to be warm enough to melt.

Colouring the soap

liquid dye

1 Liquid dyes and pigments should be added in tiny increments to the melted soap. Use the tip of a cocktail stick to add colour, one drop at a time.

2 If the colour isn't quite strong enough, add a little more dye and stir until it is fully incorporated into the melted soap.

powdered pigment

3 Add powdered pigment to a small batch of the melted soap and stir to dissolve it. Then incorporate this with the rest of the melted soap, little by little.

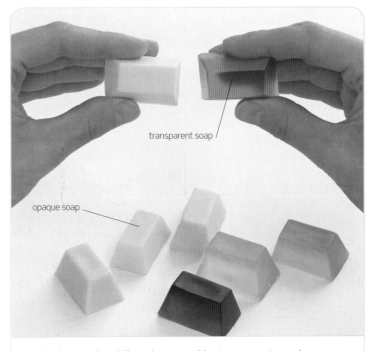

transparent soap

opaque soap

4 For intense, jewel-like colours, combine transparent soap base with liquid dyes or pigment. For flatter, paler shades, use opaque soap base with liquid or powdered colourants.

Scenting the soap

fragrance

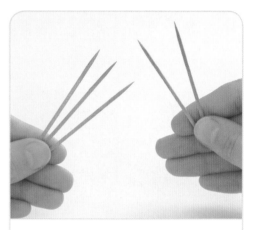

1 Add essential oils and fragrances to the soap just before moulding to minimize evaporation from heat. For small batches, add the oil drop by drop until the aroma is as desired.

2 For larger batches, measure out the fragrance into a beaker. Aim for 2 to 3% of the total weight of the soap, or 10 to 15ml (2 to 3tsp) per 500g (1lb 2oz) of soap.

3 When blending scents, experiment with top, middle, and base notes. Putting different combinations of dipped cocktail sticks in a ziplock bag is a good way to play with scent blends.

Enhancing soaps with natural ingredients

1 To add a luxurious, creamy texture to opaque soap, stir in a small portion of a solid moisturising oil such as shea butter while the soap is melting. Do not exceed 5g (⅕oz) per 100g (3½oz) of soap.

shea butter

2 For an exfoliating soap, stir in a handful of finely ground oatmeal into the melted soap before moulding. Dried calendula or safflower petals can also be used to create a colourful, mottled texture.

melted soap

3 For a decorative flourish, place slices of dried citrus fruit in the bottom of the mould and make them adhere by pouring a very thin layer of soap on top. After a minute or two, spritz with rubbing alcohol or surgical spirit then pour in the rest of the soap.

Moulding and storing soap

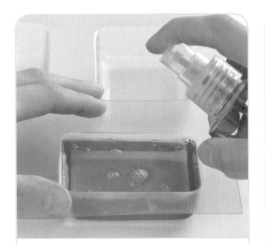

1 Once all the additives are in place, carefully pour the soap into the moulds. It is common for surface bubbles to appear after pouring; these can be dissolved by spritzing immediately with rubbing alcohol or surgical spirit. Leave to set.

2 After several hours, turn the mould upside down and flex each edge gently to release the soap. If the soap is stubborn, place it in the freezer for 15 minutes and try again. Once unmoulded, slabs can be sliced into bars using a knife or metal scraper.

3 If the soap is not for immediate use, store it in clingfilm to prevent its high glycerine content from attracting humidity in the atmosphere and "sweating".

Layering and embedding

centrepiece

1 It is possible to create bars with multiple colours or scents by pouring in separate layers. Spritz the surface of the soap with rubbing alcohol or surgical spirit immediately after pouring, then leave to set. Spritz again before pouring the next layer.

2 Another popular technique is to embed small pieces of contrasting soap into the centre of the soap bars. These may be anything from simple, hand-cut shapes to decorative centrepieces, created with chocolate moulds or cookie cutters.

3 To create the finished bar, chill the centrepieces in the freezer for at least 30 minutes and then work as you would to layer the soap, placing the centrepieces in the middle layer of the soap. Spritz each layer with rubbing alcohol or surgical spirit before pouring the next.

Botanical slab PROJECT

Have you ever wandered around a craft market and admired the array of rough-cut, rustic-looking, natural soaps that are on offer? You too can produce your very own slab of soothing lavender soap that can be cut up into bars and shared with friends. The same approach can be used with a wide range of dried herbs, flower petals, and essential oils.

YOU WILL NEED

- 1 cup of dried lavender buds
- pestle and mortar or food processor
- 650g (1lb 7oz) goat's milk soap base, chopped into small pieces
- heatproof bowl
- saucepan
- metal spoon
- small measuring beaker
- 15ml (3tsp) lavender essential oil
- Tupperware container (approx 12.5 x 18cm/5 x 7in)
- metal scraper or knife

1 Divide the lavender buds into two equal portions. Finely grind one of the portions using a pestle and mortar or a food processor. Set aside.

2 Place the soap pieces in a heatproof bowl over a saucepan of simmering water and heat gently, stirring occasionally with a metal spoon until the soap has melted. Remove from the heat.

3 Add the lavender essential oil and the ground lavender and stir constantly for 1 to 2 minutes. This will help the lavender to remain evenly suspended within the soap. Allow the soap to cool slightly without setting.

4 Pour the mixture into the container. Before the soap starts to form a skin, immediately sprinkle over the unground lavender buds and press gently with your fingers to help them adhere to the surface.

5 Allow to set for several hours before unmoulding and slicing into smaller blocks using a metal scraper or knife.

Moulded rose soaps PROJECT

Here is a bouquet of soaps that will infuse your bathroom with the scent of summer flowers. Rose absolute essential oil is one of the most expensive aromas that money can buy and is rarely used in soaps. However, it is still possible to treat yourself to the gorgeous scent of roses by using it in its diluted form and combining it with the complementary scent of geranium.

YOU WILL NEED

- 840g (1lb 14oz) goat's milk soap base, chopped into small pieces
- electronic scales
- microwave-proof container
- microwave oven
- cocktail sticks
- selection of liquid soap colourants (this project uses crimson red, salmon pink, orange, and purple)
- 5ml (1tsp) each of diluted rose absolute essential oil and geranium essential oil
- silicone tray with six rose-shaped cake moulds
- small spray bottle containing rubbing alcohol or surgical spirit

1 Divide the soap base into six equal portions of 140g (5oz). Place one portion in a small, microwave-proof container and heat on full power, using a series of 10-second bursts, until the soap is evenly melted.

2 Once the soap is fully liquid, work quickly to add colour by dipping a cocktail stick into your chosen colourant and swirling it into the soap. Repeat as often as you wish, mixing and matching the colours until you achieve a shade and intensity that you desire. (If the soap starts to form a skin, place it back in the microwave for another 10 seconds.)

essential oil

3 Immediately before pouring, add 12 to 15 drops each of the rose and geranium essential oils and stir well.

4 Pour the soap into one of the six moulds and spritz immediately with rubbing alcohol or surgical spirit to remove any surface bubbles. Repeat these steps for the remaining five soaps, varying the colours each time.

5 Allow to set for several hours or until firm and cool. Once all six soaps are set, peel back the moulds to reveal your bouquet of roses.

Clear heart soap PROJECT

This project uses the technique of embedding to capture a heart within a crystal-clear bar of soap. The soap contains a hidden secret as the outer bar is scented with sweet, spicy rosewood essential oil while the heart at the centre is infused with warm vanilla. The heart centrepiece is created using a chocolate mould but you could just as well use a heart-shaped cookie cutter.

YOU WILL NEED

- 4 x 25g (1oz) portions of clear soap base, chopped into small pieces
- electronic scales
- microwave-proof container
- microwave oven
- teaspoon
- 1/8 tsp bleed-proof powdered soap pigment (this project uses Red Lake)
- 1ml (approx 20 drops) pure vanilla extract
- 4cm (1½in) heart-shaped chocolate mould
- small spray bottle containing rubbing alcohol or surgical spirit
- 2ml (approx 40 drops) rosewood essential oil
- 7.5cm (3in) square soap mould

1 Place one portion of soap in a microwave-proof container and heat on full power using a series of 10-second bursts until melted. Add the pigment and stir until fully dissolved. (If the soap starts to set, put it back in the microwave for 10 seconds.)

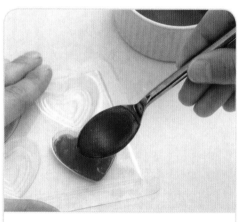

2 Now stir in the vanilla extract and pour into the heart-shaped mould. Spritz the surface immediately with rubbing alcohol or surgical spirit to remove any bubbles and place in the freezer for at least 30 minutes to set.

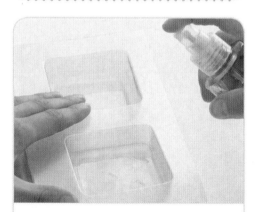

3 Meanwhile, melt a second portion of soap. When it is liquid, add 10 to 15 drops of rosewood oil and stir gently to avoid introducing bubbles. Pour into the square mould, spritzing with alcohol to dissolve any bubbles. The soap should fill one-third of the mould. Leave to set for at least 30 minutes.

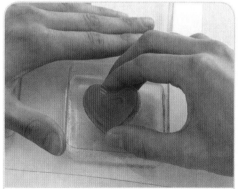

4 Melt another portion of soap and scent with 10 to 15 drops of rosewood. Set aside for 1 to 2 minutes. Pop the heart out of its mould, spritz with alcohol, and place it on the first soap layer. Spritz the entire layer liberally with alcohol then spoon the melted soap around the heart to trap it in place. Leave to set for at least 30 minutes.

5 Repeat Step 3 with the remaining soap. Once it is scented, spritz the previous layer of soap liberally with alcohol to help the final layer to adhere. Pour the melted soap into the mould and spritz one last time to remove any bubbles. Allow to set for several hours before unmoulding.

Eco crafts

Eco crafts

BASKETRY • RAG RUGGING • NATURE CRAFTS • PRESSED FLOWER WORK • RECYCLING

PAINTING FURNITURE • TINWORK • WIREWORK

Crafting can be really good for the soul – and it can also be extremely good for the planet. A project that uses materials that would otherwise be consigned to the bin means that there is less to dump in landfill sites and more to decorate your home. It's all about turning trash into treasures – so join the eco-craft revolution!

This chapter includes a range of crafts which make the most of natural or recycled materials. This is crafting with a conscience, the emphasis being on utilizing materials that might otherwise be thrown away.

Celebrating nature's bounty, by making baskets from stems of willow, a wreath from fresh and dried foliage, or a greetings card from pressed flowers could not be simpler. You may well be able to collect all the materials you need from a walk in the woods or from your own garden.

City dwellers who may not enjoy such easy access to nature may prefer to try the crafts that involve recycling. You'll be amazed what you can make with rubbish. For instance, tin cans become candleholders and coat hanger wire is manipulated into a decorative, button-bedecked

heart or a quirky chandelier. Even eggshells can be transformed into mini mosaics that breathe new life into an old picture frame.

An unloved piece of furniture, destined for the scrapheap, can be revived and revitalized with a lick of paint and a couple of new knobs, or with a little hooking and prodding, a rag bag of scraps can be turned into a comfy rug.

Most of us can tackle these eco-craft projects with ease or you may like to get together with some like-minded friends and try making one or more of these projects as a group. A basket-making, rag-rugging, or wreath-making workshop is fun for the participants and passing on these techniques and skills to others will no doubt appeal to the committed eco-warrior.

Eco crafts TOOLS AND MATERIALS

The great thing about crafting using old, recycled, or found materials is that they're free! You'll only need to invest in a handful of specialist tools, depending on which projects you make. A rummage in old storage boxes can unearth all sorts of treasures that can be turned into beautiful home decorations.

Basketry

Brown willow This type of willow is dried with its bark on. It needs to be soaked for several days so that it is flexible enough to use.

Bodkin This metal tapered spike is useful for making spaces in weaving. If you don't have one, use a metal skewer or screwdriver instead.

Compass This will help draw circles and semicircles to make a cardboard former. Measure the required radius on a ruler. For instance, a 15cm (6in) diameter circle will need a radius of 7.5cm (3in).

String Use this to tie the ends of a basket while you weave and to hold the shape of a basket after removing it from the former.

Buff willow Buff willow has been boiled and stripped. It becomes pliable after much less soaking than brown willow, so is handier if you don't have much time.

Side cutters These are needed to trim the willow accurately and closely. Garden secateurs can also be used, so long as they are sharp.

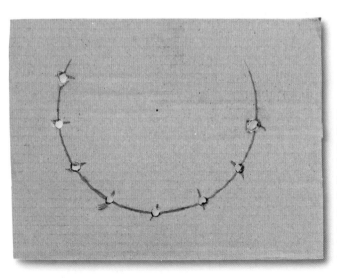

Former A former holds the willow stakes in shape while you weave. It can be made to suit whatever size structure you are making. Punch holes in a piece of cardboard then feed the willow through the holes.

Rag rugging

Recycled textiles In true keeping with rag rugging, textiles should be recycled: old T-shirts, fine-knit woollens, cotton sweatshirts, wool blankets, and old cotton sheets are all good. Heavy curtain material and fabrics that fray are unsuitable.

Hessian 10oz common hessian forms the base of the rug. It has an open weave and is easy to work on. You could also use jute grain sacks or coffee sacks.

Cutting gauge Used for cutting even tabs of fabric from a long strip.

Felt-tip pen Chalk out your design on the hessian and when you are happy with it, go over it with a felt-tip pen to make the lines clear.

Rug hook This brass rug hook with a bulbous yew handle is used for creating a hooked, looped pile.

Bodger With a pointed end and sprung jaws, this tool can grab short tabs of fabric so they can be pulled through hessian to create a proddy, clipped pile.

Embroidery hoop Used to stretch hessian taut to make rug hooking easier. Alternatively, you could use a tapestry frame.

Strong thread Use jute thread and strong button or carpet threads to securely stitch worked pieces of hessian together.

257

Nature crafts

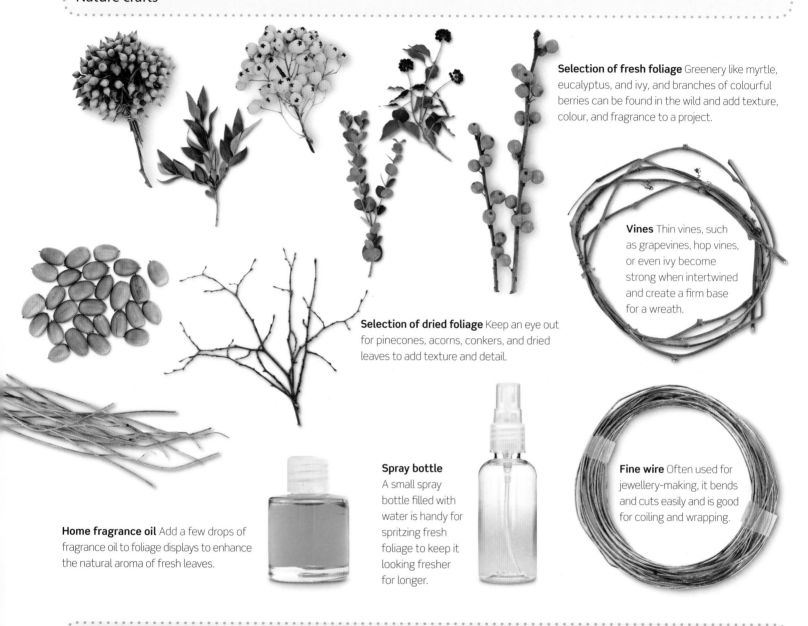

Selection of fresh foliage Greenery like myrtle, eucalyptus, and ivy, and branches of colourful berries can be found in the wild and add texture, colour, and fragrance to a project.

Vines Thin vines, such as grapevines, hop vines, or even ivy become strong when intertwined and create a firm base for a wreath.

Selection of dried foliage Keep an eye out for pinecones, acorns, conkers, and dried leaves to add texture and detail.

Spray bottle A small spray bottle filled with water is handy for spritzing fresh foliage to keep it looking fresher for longer.

Fine wire Often used for jewellery-making, it bends and cuts easily and is good for coiling and wrapping.

Home fragrance oil Add a few drops of fragrance oil to foliage displays to enhance the natural aroma of fresh leaves.

Pressed flower work

Air-dry press Made of open-density foam with cotton layers onto which the flowers are placed, this press is held together with plastic mesh and Velcro straps. Warm air must be allowed to pass through the press in order for the flowers to dry in a day or two.

Traditional press This is made of sheets of newspaper separated by layers of smooth cardboard and held together by plywood boards secured with wing nuts. The flowers are placed between paper tissues or blotting paper, which are then placed between the newspaper layers. Left in a warm place, the flowers should be dry within a week or two.

Microwave press Two layers of felt with two cotton layers in between are held together with two microwavable plastic boards and clips. (The flowers are placed between the cotton layers and microwaved). They are pressed and ready to use in seconds. There are two sizes: 12.5cm (5in) and 27.5cm (11in) square.

Desiccant pads press Consists of a number of desiccant pads between which the flowers are placed on paper tissues. The pads lie between polystyrene boards held together with elastic bands. The flowers will be dry in a few days. After removing the flowers, the pads should be dried before reuse.

Card Obtain the best-quality card for optimal results. The card should be 225 to 260gsm to ensure it stands up when the flowers are attached.

Rubber-based glue Use a rubber-based glue; water-based glues will reintroduce moisture into the pressed and dried-out flowers. This will cause discolouration over time.

Furniture painting

Primer undercoat This seals the wood and forms an opaque base coat in preparation for painting with satinwood or eggshell.

Matt emulsion paint This is applied over primer undercoat on areas to be painted or stencilled. It provides a better surface for painting than primer undercoat alone. Finish with two coats of varnish.

Satinwood/eggshell Satinwood or eggshell is a top coat applied to furniture and interior woodwork. It has a contemporary, mid-sheen finish. Two coats are usually required.

Quick-dry water-based varnish This varnish is transparent and colourless. It is painted over the parts of furniture that have been stencilled or painted to protect against spills and knocks. Two coats are recommended.

Scalpel This knife is very sharp and must be used with care. It is the easiest and most accurate way to cut designs from stencil card. Alternatively, you can use a craft knife.

Wood filler Used for filling small dents and gaps in wood. It can be sanded flat when dry.

Acrylic paints and/or sample pots of emulsion These are used to apply designs to furniture using stencils or paintbrushes. They can be mixed together to produce more colours.

Stencil brushes A stencil brush is short and stubby with firmly packed bristles. The stiff bristles reduce the chance of paint seeping under the stencil.

Stencil card Stencil card is oiled, heavyweight, and water-resistant. Designs are cut out of the card to create images which can be applied with a stencil brush to furniture, walls, and accessories.

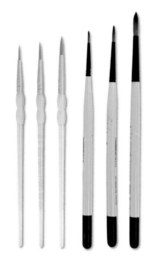

Small artist's paintbrushes Brushes intended for use with watercolour and gouache paints are most suitable. Choose round brushes with sable or synthetic hairs. They are used for painting designs onto furniture and adding detail to stencilled designs.

Woodcare paintbrushes These brushes are used for painting and varnishing the body or the shell of furniture. The smaller sizes are useful for hard-to-reach areas.

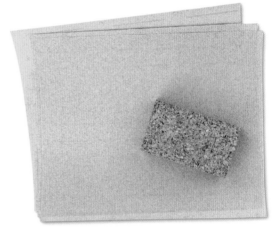

Medium-grade sandpaper and sanding block Sandpaper is used for smoothing bare wood, removing varnish or old paint, and for sanding between coats of paint. When sanding a flat surface, it is more efficient to use the paper wrapped around a sanding block.

Tinwork

Tin cans These are actually not made of tin – they are sheet steel with a thin tin plating. Cans with a ring pull are ideal as they leave the rim intact and smooth.

Masonry nails These nails are hardened so they are an ideal choice for punching through a tin can.

Sandbag If you don't have a suitable fabric bag, a piece of heavy fabric will suffice – place sand in the centre, draw up the sides, and close with a cable tie.

Hammer Find a hammer that is comfortable to hold, but not too light. The weight of the hammer should do the work, rather than your arm.

Wirework

Small bolt cutters These are ideal for cutting through heavy wire – if you don't have bolt cutters, the built-in wire cutters on general-purpose pliers will do the same job.

Wire coat hangers These are made from relatively thick wire, which can be uncoiled and used for any craft project requiring wire.

Wire cutters Basic side-cutting wire cutters snip through thin- and medium-gauge wire.

Gardening gloves Wear gardening or thick fabric gloves when using wire to help you shape it more easily and protect your hands from sharp ends.

Cable cutters These are more robust than wire cutters and can cut through thicker wire, such as the type used for coat hangers.

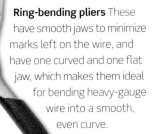

Ring-bending pliers These have smooth jaws to minimize marks left on the wire, and have one curved and one flat jaw, which makes them ideal for bending heavy-gauge wire into a smooth, even curve.

Small mole grips Also known as vice grips, these are ideal for bending wire into straight lines or sharp angles. They can be adjusted so that they lock onto the item that you are gripping.

Medium-gauge wire A thinnish wire that bends and cuts easily and is good for coiling, wrapping, and joining wire ends together.

Basketry TECHNIQUES

Willow is a beautiful material to use in basketry, but you need to follow some simple guidelines for its preparation and handling. Once you've learned the basics, you can experiment with making different-sized baskets and work with more complicated weaves.

Selecting materials

The stakes and weavers should be even in length and thickness. The stakes form the framework for the basket and the weavers weave around them. The stakes should be selected from a 5ft bundle of willow; the weavers from a 3ft bundle of willow. The thick end of the willow is called the butt; the thin end is called the tip.

Soaking and mellowing the willow

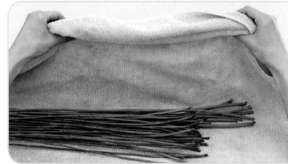

Willow is brittle when dry, so must be soaked by totally submerging it in cold water to make it pliable. After soaking, mellow the willow by wrapping it in a damp towel and leaving it overnight in a cool place to rest.

CALCULATING WILLOW SOAKING TIME

Buff willow has been boiled and stripped, so takes less time to soak than brown willow. Soak buff willow for 1 to 2 hours in cold water. Soak brown willow in cold water for one day per foot of willow (so 3ft willow will need to be soaked for three days). If you need to speed up the soaking time, use hot tap water and soak for a shorter time.

Making a cardboard former and framework

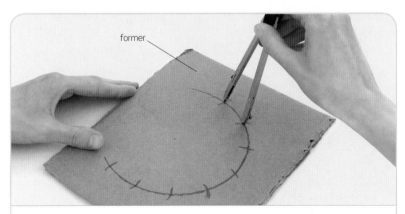

1 A former is used to hold the willow frame in the desired shape. Using a compass, draw an extended semicircle 15cm (6in) in diameter on a piece of cardboard, or draw around a plate of a similar size. Mark eight equally spaced points around the circumference. The points should be 3.5cm (1⅜in) apart.

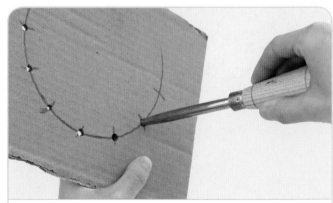

2 Make a hole through each point on the cardboard using a bodkin or skewer.

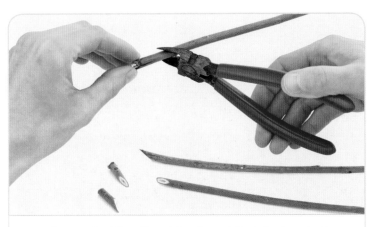

3 Before you feed the willow stakes through the holes to make the framework, cut a sharp angle across the butt end of the stakes using side cutters to help feed them through more easily.

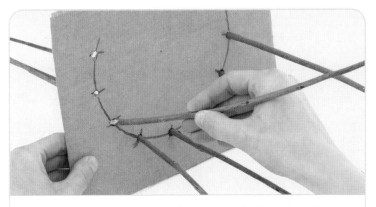

4 Push the first stake, butt end first, through the first hole until it is one-third of the way through. Push the next stake, butt end first, through the next hole from the other side of the cardboard until two-thirds of the stake is through. Continue pushing the stakes in alternately until they are all in place and the frame is completed. The ends should line up as a butt then tip, a butt then tip, and so on.

5 Tie one end of the stakes securely with string to hold them in place.

Basic weaving

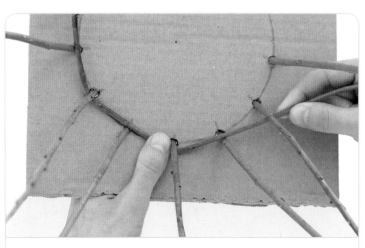

The weaving is worked by threading a weaver in front of one stake and behind the next. Each row of weaving should sit in the opposite place to the previous row. Use thicker weavers where the spaces between the stakes are big, and finer weavers as the spaces between the stakes become smaller.

Weaving around the edges

1 You can weave around the end stake by simply twisting the weaver around the stake and then weaving it back in the opposite direction.

2 To make a more secure edge, wrap the weaver tightly around the end stake twice before weaving it back in the opposite direction. This ensures the weaver holds the stakes tightly.

Joining weavers

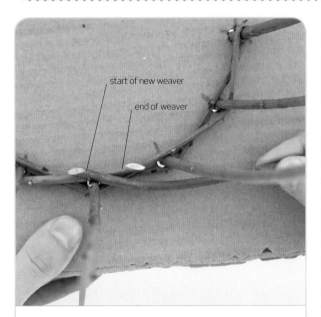

start of new weaver

end of weaver

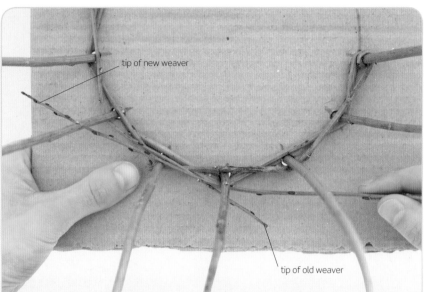

tip of new weaver

tip of old weaver

1 When you finish with a butt end, join in a new weaver by placing a new butt in the next space. Continue weaving with the new weaver. Leave the butt ends inside; they will be trimmed at a later stage.

2 When you finish with a tip, lay the tip of the new weaver over the old weaver so that they overlap and run together for a short distance. Continue weaving with the new weaver.

Finishing off

1 Always finish weaving a basket with a tip, tucking its end away under the previous row of weaving.

2 Trim away any ends using side cutters, making sure that each weaver rests on a stake. When the willow dries out it shrinks a little, so ensure you leave the weaver a little on the long side. You can trim it back further when it has completely dried.

Binding stakes

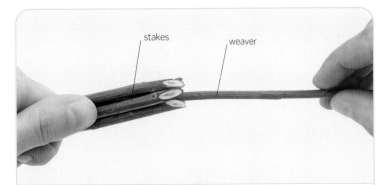

1 Binding is a method of tying the stakes of a basket together to make the framework secure. This is done after the weaving is complete. Trap the butt end of a weaver between the ends of the bunch of stakes, with the tip of the weaver pointing outwards.

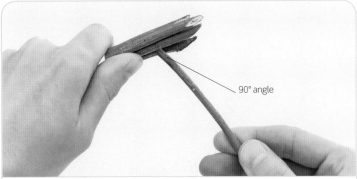

2 Bend the weaver at a 90° angle, making sure that the butt end of the weaver is held firmly between the stakes.

3 Wrap the weaver around the bundle of stakes, keeping plenty of tension.

4 Continue wrapping the weaver until there are five rows of binding, each sitting alongside the next.

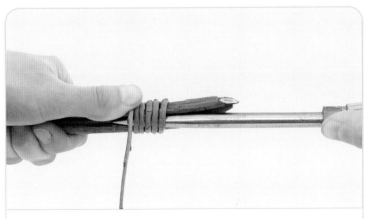

5 Holding the binding securely in place, use the bodkin to make a small space under the binding.

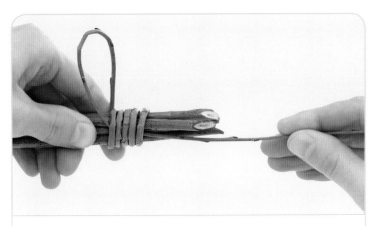

6 Remove the bodkin and feed the tip of the weaver underneath the rows of binding and back out in the direction it was originally pointing. Pull tightly to secure.

Willow fruit basket PROJECT

This quick and simple project uses brown willow to make a frame basket. The basket is woven around a cardboard former which holds the basket in shape while you concentrate on the weaving. Once you've mastered the basic weave you can enjoy watching the piece take shape. This basket makes a great fruit basket or looks good as a sculptural piece hung on a wall.

YOU WILL NEED

- stakes: 8 thick rods of 5ft brown willow
- weavers: 60 rods of 3ft brown willow
- towel
- side cutters
- cardboard former (see pp.262–63)
- compass
- string
- scissors
- ruler
- bodkin

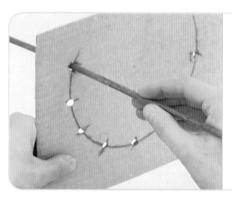

1 Soak and mellow the stakes and weavers, as shown on p.262. Push a stake through the first hole of the former, butt end first, until one-third of the stake is through. Push the butt end of the next stake through the next hole from the other side of the cardboard until two-thirds of it is through. Continue pushing the stakes in alternately until all eight are in place and the frame is completed. Tie the stakes together at one end with string.

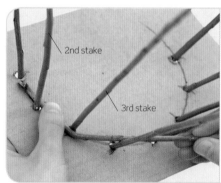

2 Begin weaving the untied side: place the butt of a weaver between the second and third stakes. Weave it in front of one stake, then behind the next. Wrap the weaver tightly around the last stake twice, then continue weaving in the opposite direction.

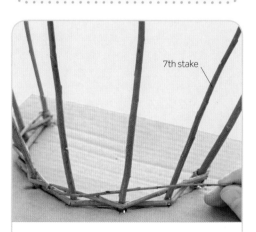

3 Repeat until the weaver has travelled back and forth three times across the stakes, finishing on the opposite side to where it started. The tip of the weaver should sit on the outside of the seventh stake.

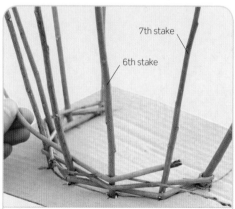

4 Place the butt of the next weaver between the seventh and sixth stakes and weave it across in the same way.

5 Continue weaving. Join in a new weaver at the opposite side of the basket to the last one. After weaving in six weavers, tie the ends of the stakes together with string to form a tapered end.

6 Continue weaving until there is about 15cm (6in) of weaving. Untie the ends of the stakes when they are too close to weave between.

7 Remove the cardboard former and tie string across the centre of the basket to hold the shape. Weave the second half of the basket in the same way as the first.

8 Bind the ends as shown in **binding stakes** on p.265. Trim any ends using the side cutters. Remove the string.

Rag rugging TECHNIQUES

This traditional craft is a great way to recycle fabrics. Use long strips of fabric worked onto a backing of hessian with a rug hook to create a dense, looped pile. To create a shaggy, clipped pile, pull shorter tabs of fabric through the hessian using a bodger.

The hooking technique

Preparing the fabric

Using a rug hook

2-3cm (³⁄₄-1¹⁄₄in) wide strips

Cut strips as long as the fabric allows. For speed, fold the fabric over and cut through the layers. The strips should be 2 to 3cm (³⁄₄ to 1¹⁄₄in) wide, depending on the thickness of the fabric. Generally, the thicker the fabric, the narrower the width of the strip.

1 Secure a piece of hessian in an embroidery hoop, ensuring the hessian is taut. Mark out your design, first in chalk and then, when you're happy with it, go over the lines with a felt-tip pen.

2 Hold the hook in one hand and the fabric strip in the other, under the frame. Following the design, push the hook into the hessian and catch the end of the strip in the hook.

3 Pull the end up through the hessian to about 2.5cm (1in) above the surface. It will be snipped off later to the height of the loops. Release the strip from the hook.

first loop

end of strip

4 Push the hook down into the hessian again three threads forwards, and pull a loop of fabric up to about 2cm (³⁄₄in) above the surface. Repeat, creating even loops, until you reach the end of the strip of fabric.

5 To start a new strip, push the hook down into the hessian where the end of the last strip came out. Pull up the end of the new strip. Allow about three threads of hessian between each row.

6 Carefully snip off the strip ends so that they are level with the loops.

The proddy technique

Preparing the fabric

1 Cut your chosen fabric into 2cm (¾in) wide strips. For speed, you can fold the fabric over several times and cut through the layers.

2 For this technique, you need tabs of fabric about 7.5cm (3in) long. To make these, wind a long strip of fabric around a cutting gauge, then cut along the groove using scissors.

Using a bodger

1 Mark your design on a piece of hessian using a felt-tip pen.

2 Following the design, push the pointed end of the bodger down into the hessian and back up two or three threads forwards, to create a "double hole".

3 Open the jaws of the bodger, grab a tab of fabric by its end, and pull it halfway though the two holes. Release the tab.

4 Push the bodger into the last hole made, bring it out two or three threads forwards, and grab the next tab of fabric.

5 Repeat, leaving two or three threads between each adjacent row of fabric. Set the stitches slightly further apart if you're using fluffy fabric as this will splay out, covering a greater area.

Rag rug mat PROJECT

The shaggy pile of this rag rug was made using the proddy technique, with wool and cotton recycled fabrics. Six small squares are made and then joined together, creating a wonderfully tactile and functional rug that would be ideal for the bedside, doorway, or in front of a fireplace.

YOU WILL NEED

- six 26cm (10¼in) squares of 10oz common hessian
- ruler
- felt-tip pen
- cardboard templates: 20cm (8in) square, with circle, heart, and flower shapes to fit within the square
- fine-knit recycled woollens and cottons in reds, greens, blues, and purple
- cutting gauge
- scissors
- bodger
- glass-headed pins
- strong thread or jute thread
- sack needle

1 Using a felt-tip pen, mark each piece of hessian with a 20cm (8in) square. Within each square, draw either a circle, heart, or flower, using the cardboard templates. You can make two squares of each design or vary the design according to your own taste.

2 Prepare the fabrics, cutting them into tabs 2cm (¾in) wide and 7.5cm (3in) long. Following the **proddy technique** on p.269, use the bodger to create a proddy pile on each hessian square.

3 Continue in this way, working on one square at a time and using different coloured strips to make a pleasing design, until you have completed all six squares, right to the marked edges.

4 When you have worked all the squares, turn each square to the wrong side and turn a double-hem in the unworked hessian along all four sides. Fold the hem into neat mitres at the corners. Pin and handstitch using strong thread or jute thread.

5 Lay out the squares face down in a three-by-two rectangle and pin the hemmed edges together. Using strong thread or jute thread, sew the squares together to create the complete rug.

Nature crafts TECHNIQUES

Working with natural foliage provides the perfect excuse to go for a walk in your local park, woodland, or forest – or you may even find suitable greenery in your garden. Look out for items that have fallen off trees, such as pine cones and acorns. Using fresh cuttings of berries and firs creates a lovely seasonal aroma, or you can enhance the natural fragrance with a few drops of an appropriate fragrance oil.

Making a wreath frame

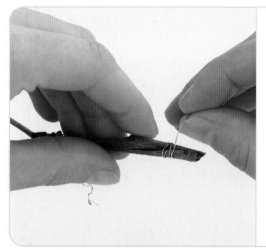

1 Strip two equal lengths of vine of their leaves. Secure them together by binding with a short length of fine wire.

twisted vines

2 Twist the vines together to make one strong length. Secure the other end with wire.

3 Bring the two ends together to create a circle. Twist the ends around each other and tie them together with a short length of wire. If the vines are too long, overlap the ends; if they're too short, introduce an additional length.

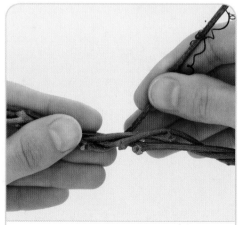

4 To strengthen the frame, add more lengths of stripped vine. Tie one end to the frame with wire and wind the vine around the frame, securing the other end with wire. Repeat until you have a strong, firm frame.

5 To keep the shape even and strengthen the frame more, tie small pieces of wire at regular intervals around the frame.

Working with fresh foliage

1 Ensure each stem of foliage is fresh, clean, and dry, and check it looks healthy. Avoid using materials that are mouldy as the mould may spread.

2 Use a sharp pair of scissors to trim foliage to the required size. For thick stems, use a pair of secateurs. These specialist gardening scissors can cut through branches up to 2cm (³⁄₄in) thick.

Making fir bunches

Use a sharp pair of scissors to trim the sprigs of fir to 4cm (1½in) lengths. Take small bunches of fir (about five sprigs) and wind a length of wire around the bottom of their stems to hold them together.

Securing foliage to the frame

1 To secure fresh foliage such as fir bunches to the frame, use a short length of wire to wrap the base of the bunch to the frame.

2 Use superglue to attach dried foliage, cones, and other material. Apply a dot of glue to the base of the item and then press in place, making sure not to glue any other foliage together.

Keeping foliage fresh

Fresh foliage should last throughout the winter season, though will wilt more quickly if it is left outdoors without shelter from the wind. Spritz it regularly with a fine mist of water to keep it fresh.

Enhancing the fragrance

Add a few drops of fragrance oil to fresh or dried foliage to enhance the natural fragrance.

Winter wreath PROJECT

Wreaths are a great introduction to floristry, giving you a chance to work with both fresh and dried foliage. Here, bunches of fir create the base for the frame, and pine cones, acorns, and colourful berries are dotted around to add texture and colour. You could also add leaves, dried fruits, and nuts to create a design that is unique and smells gorgeous.

YOU WILL NEED

- stripped vine stems
- scissors or secateurs
- fine wire
- selection of fresh foliage (fir sprigs, myrtle, berries, eucalyptus leaves)
- measuring tape
- selection of dried foliage (pine cones, acorns)
- superglue
- hook or ribbon
- fragrance oil (optional)
- spray bottle

1 Follow **making a wreath frame** on p.272 to make a 30cm (12in) diameter circular frame. Around six rounds of vine will make a thick, sturdy frame.

2 Follow **making fir bunches** on p.273 to make 15 to 20 bunches. Attach each one to the frame with wire so that they face the same direction. Overlap one bunch with the next to cover the entire frame.

measuring tape

3 Trim the remaining fresh foliage to size and arrange it around the wreath. Play with the design until you are happy with it before securing the foliage in place. Use a measuring tape to check that the spacing between the foliage is even.

4 Tuck individual sprigs of fresh foliage into the frame between the fir bunches. Attach other bunches of foliage with short lengths of wire, tucking the ends of the wire into the fir to hide them.

5 Arrange the dried foliage on top of the wreath to get an idea of the finished look, then glue in position.

6 Hang the wreath on a hook, or if you prefer, attach a ribbon at the top to hang it. You can scent it with a few drops of fragrance oil or leave it as it is. Spritz regularly with water to keep it fresh.

Pressed flower work TECHNIQUES

Follow a few basic principles and you'll find that pressed flower work can be most enjoyable. Flowers that press well and keep their colour include roses, buttercups, forget-me-nots, daisies, hydrangeas, and larkspur. Once you have more experience, you'll be able to press almost any plant material and achieve good results, though pressing fleshy flowers such as hyacinths and sedums may be more challenging.

Making a flower press

YOU WILL NEED

- 2 (5-ply) 15 x 20cm (6 x 8in) plywood boards
- 50 sheets newspaper cut into 15 x 20cm (6 x 8in) pieces
- 4 pieces 15 x 20cm (6 x 8in) smooth cardboard, 1.5mm (1/14in) thick
- 3 elastic bands, or 2 clamps, or 4 wing nuts and bolts

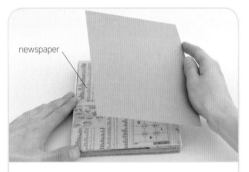

newspaper

1 To assemble the press, place one plywood board on the work surface and top with 10 sheets of newspaper. Place a thick piece of cardboard on top. Repeat the newspaper/cardboard layers until you have sufficient layers for the flowers you wish to press.

plywood board

2 Position the other plywood board on top to finish the sandwich. Hold the press together with elastic bands, clamps, or wing nuts and bolts. (If using bolts, you'll need to drill two holes either side of the plywood boards to accommodate the bolts.)

Pressing using other devices

paper tissue

Flowers may also be pressed between paper tissues in the pages of a heavy book. Place the book in a warm place to ensure the flowers will dry in one to two weeks. Other flower presses are available (see pp.258–59).

Choosing flowers and leaves

Only press perfect specimens and make sure you press more than you'll need as some petals and leaves will inevitably get damaged when you handle them.

CONSERVING FLOWERS AND LEAVES

To ensure flowers remain in excellent condition, pick them on a dry day and put into the press straight away.

Warmth and low humidity are essential when pressing flowers. These conditions help to remove the moisture content quickly from the plant material and keep the colours vibrant.

Pressing flowers and leaves

1 Place the flowers and leaves in the press between layers of paper tissues or other smooth, white absorbent paper, such as blotting paper. Don't use kitchen paper (you'll end up with dimpled petals) or newsprint (the ink will mark the petals and leaves). Put flowers of a similar thickness on the same page in the press. This will produce an even pressure when drying.

2 Small flowers may be pressed whole but larger ones, such as some roses, gerberas, and peonies must be taken apart and pressed petal by petal. Reassemble them when dry.

3 Large flowers, such as freesias, may be cut through the middle before pressing to produce two flowers from one.

4 As soon as the flowers are dry, remove them from the press using tweezers. If they are not being used straight away, store them flat, in a dry place, in clearly labelled envelopes.

Glueing flowers and leaves to card

dot of glue

Dip the tip of a cocktail stick into a rubber-based glue and dot onto the back of a flower or leaf before placing onto card. Use just enough glue to hold the flower in position.

Sealing the work

1 If you're framing your work, seal it under a sheet of glass or acrylic; if you're making jewellery, resin may be used.

2 For a greetings card or bookmark, use heat-seal film for best results. This film can be removed many times to replace straying flowers and when perfect, it is heated with an iron to seal the card. You can also use a normal self-adhesive film, but once applied it cannot be removed.

Greetings card PROJECT

Friends and family love receiving homemade gifts, and this pressed flower card depicting a vase of flowers will be no exception. The flowers, leaves, and stems are sealed in place so that they will not spoil when the card is taken out of the envelope.

YOU WILL NEED

- thick white card or blank greetings card measuring 30 x 40cm (12 x 16in)
- pressed tendrils (sweet pea, bryony, or passion flower)
- milk bottle top or jar lid to hold the glue
- rubber-based glue
- cocktail stick
- 3 or 4 different types of pressed flowers, such as larkspur, buttercups, potentilla (cinquefoil), and melilot (sweet clover)
- tweezers
- 2 different types of pressed leaves, such as alchemilla conjuncta (silver lady's mantle) and potentilla
- small scissors
- pressed grass stems
- self-adhesive or heat-seal film

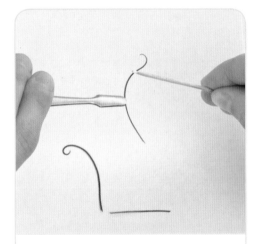

1 Fold the card in half then open it up. Work on the right-hand side of the card. Use the tendrils to create the sides and base of the vase. Apply a very small amount of glue on the back of each tendril using the tip of a cocktail stick and secure in place.

2 Arrange the flowers above the vase using tweezers so that the largest flower is level with the top of the vase. Arrange the flowers until you're happy with the design. Use some half flowers or buds to add interest, then glue the flowers onto the card.

3 Dot leaves in the gaps. If they are thin enough, tuck them under the flowers. Otherwise, cut the leaves and butt them up against the flowers.

4 Cut some pieces of grass to make stems of different lengths. Add the curly tendrils so that the straighter ends appear to go into the vase.

5 Use a piece of grass to create the water line and a few more to suggest a table. Scatter a few damaged or cut petals on the table to represent fallen petals.

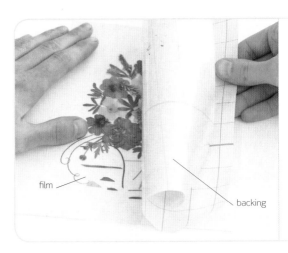

film

backing

6 Cut a piece of film slightly larger all round than the front of the card. Remove the backing and place the film over the flowers. If using self-adhesive film, ensure good contact is made around all the edges of the plant material.

7 If using heat-seal film, place a few layers of cotton fabric on top of the film and press using a warm iron for about 5 seconds: the small air holes will close when sufficient heat has been applied. Do not move the iron during this process. Trim the overlapping edge of the film.

Recycling TECHNIQUES

Natural materials are inexpensive (and often free) and can transform household accessories and ornaments into beautiful objets d'art. You can decorate a box with pine cones, make a pretty picture with shells and driftwood, or create a mosaic with small items such as cloves, seed heads, or even eggshell. Remember to prepare the natural materials carefully before use so that they don't smell or go mouldy over time.

Preparing natural materials

1 Wash out eggshells and boil in a pan of water for a few minutes to sterilize. When cool, peel away the membrane from inside the shell.

2 Soak non-porous items like shells and pebbles in a weak solution of bleach or boil in water to sterilize and kill any bacteria that may cause mould and odours.

3 Dry out pine cones and other porous objects by spreading them on baking parchment on a metal tray. Bake on a low heat for about 30 minutes.

Embossing recycled metal

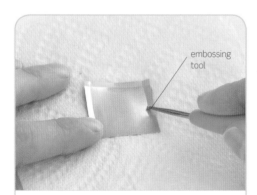  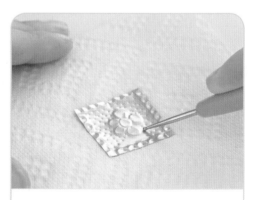

embossing tool

nylon-tipped embossing tool

1 Lay a piece of aluminium cut from a drinks can on a pad of folded kitchen paper. Use a fine embossing tool to draw lines on the silver side of the metal. Rub the tip of the tool in a beeswax block to make it easier to draw with.

2 To create a contrast in texture and also to keep the metal flat, turn the panel over and draw on the reverse side. For thicker lines, draw the motif freehand using a nylon-tipped embossing tool.

3 Turn the panel over to the right side and finish filling in texture. Use a fine or medium tip to add dots around the motif. You can also add dots or additional lines in a border for a more decorative effect.

Making eggshell mosaic

1 Slightly watered-down PVA glue has a longer drying time: use it to attach pieces of prepared eggshell. Position the pieces using a bamboo skewer, leaving even gaps between them. Attractive eggshells can be stuck face up; stick plain brown hens' eggs face down.

2 Paint the pieces of eggshell with acrylic or watercolour paint for solid colour, or water down the paint for a mottled effect. Leave to dry for 1 hour before grouting.

Grouting the eggshell mosaic

1 Fill the gaps between the pieces of eggshell with grout to create a smooth surface. Mix the grout with a little water to the consistency of thick cream (about 1 part water to 2¾ parts grout). Spoon the grout onto the surface of the mosaic.

2 Using a flat-edged spatula or palette knife, gently smooth the grout over the mosaic. Work the grout into the crevices, allow to dry for a few minutes, then carefully remove as much of the excess grout as possible with the spatula.

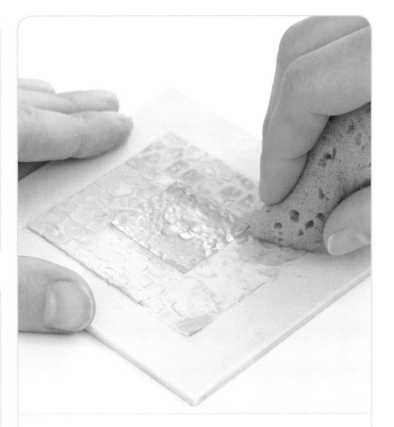

3 Leave to dry for a few more minutes, then wipe clean with a barely damp sponge. Keep rinsing the sponge out in water as you go until the surface is clean but the crevices are still filled with grout. Leave to dry completely, then gently polish the surface with a soft cloth.

Eggshell picture frame PROJECT

This pretty mosaic frame looks so stunning that not many people will guess it's made from ordinary hens' eggs. You can use speckled eggs or even pale blue duck eggs if you can find them, but it's quite easy to colour plain eggshell with watercolour paint. This project is the perfect way to transform that charity shop find. Paint the frame white before you start to give it a neutral finish.

YOU WILL NEED

- pointed craft scissors
- aluminium drinks can
- scrap of paper
- pencil
- flat picture frame, painted white
- kitchen paper
- embossing tools
- strong PVA glue or epoxy resin
- fine and medium paintbrushes
- masking tape
- eggshells
- bamboo skewer
- black watercolour paint
- mosaic grout
- flat-edged spatula or palette knife
- sponge
- soft cloth
- matt acrylic varnish

1 Using pointed craft scissors, carefully pierce an aluminium can and cut around the top and bottom. Cut along the length to create a rectangle. Make a paper template to fit the corners of your frame and use it to cut four squares from the aluminium rectangle.

2 Draw a border on the silver side of the metal squares. Refer to the template on p.315 to draw a heart shape and embellish it with dots. Draw some lines around the border on the reverse side both for decoration and to keep the metal flat.

3 Use a strong PVA glue or epoxy resin to stick the aluminium squares onto the corners of the frame. Wrap masking tape across the corners to hold the squares in place until dry.

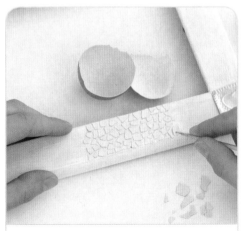

4 Prepare enough eggshells for the size of the frame, following **preparing natural materials** on p.280. Break the eggshells into small pieces and stick to the frame with PVA glue diluted with a little water.

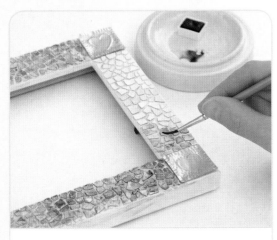

5 Once the glue has dried, mix black watercolour paint with water to make a wash and paint the pieces of eggshell to create a mottled effect. Leave to dry for about 1 hour.

6 Mix some mosaic grout with a little water to make a thick cream. Following the directions for **grouting** on p.281, apply the grout to the mosaic. Leave to dry completely, then buff with a soft cloth. Apply matt acrylic varnish over the mosaic to finish.

Painting furniture TECHNIQUES

Painting furniture is an excellent way to give an old piece a new lease of life, as well as a personal and individual touch. If you're a novice, it's sensible to choose a plain, uncomplicated piece of furniture to start with, and to paint it with a simple design. Once you've mastered the techniques, you can progress to more intricate decoration.

Preparing the furniture

If the furniture is varnished, sand all outer surfaces lightly with medium-grade sandpaper. This roughens the surface so the paint will adhere. Wipe off any dust with a damp cloth.

Priming and painting the furniture

1 Working in the direction of the wood grain and using a large brush, apply two coats of primer undercoat to the outside of the furniture. Use a small brush for hard-to-reach areas. Leave to dry for six hours, then apply two coats of satinwood or eggshell paint to areas that are not to be stencilled.

2 On parts of the furniture that will be stencilled, such as drawers or doors, paint two coats of matt emulsion over the primer undercoat. This provides a good surface for the decoration and will be protected by two coats of clear varnish once the design has been added.

Making a stencil

1 For inspiration, look through interior design magazines and look at wallpaper and fabric designs. Additionally, there is a wide range of copyright-free design books available, which provide a variety of exciting images.

2 Transfer your chosen design to a piece of stencil card. Working on a cutting mat, cut around the design with a scalpel. It's easier to move the stencil around rather than the scalpel. The frame left is the stencil.

Stencilling a two-colour design

1 Fix the stencil firmly in place with masking tape on the item of furniture you are stencilling. Make sure it is properly centred.

areas for first colour

2 Mask off the areas of the stencil which will be painted in the second colour.

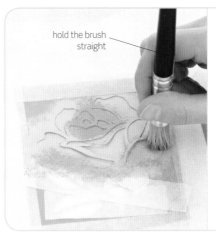

hold the brush straight

3 Artists' acrylic paints work well on wood and can be mixed to create any colour. Dip the tip of a stencil brush in the paint so the brush is fairly dry. Do a test stipple first, then stipple straight up and down through the stencil to prevent the paint seeping underneath. Leave to dry.

areas for second colour

4 When the first colour is dry, remove the masking tape. Mask off the area that has been stencilled and apply the second colour in the same way, using a clean brush. Remove the masking tape.

Creating stripes and checks

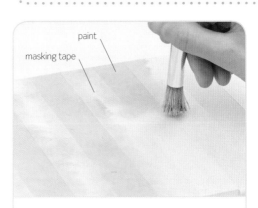

paint

masking tape

1 Masking with tape is a simple way to create crisp stripes. Using a pencil and ruler, mark out the stripes, then apply strips of masking tape within the pencil guidelines. Smooth down the tape to prevent the paint seeping, then stencil as above. Leave to dry.

2 To create checks, remove the tape and apply a second set of tape strips at right angles to the stencilled lines. Stencil in between the tape using a different colour for greater effect.

3 Allow the paint to dry, then peel off the masking tape to reveal the checked design.

Bedside cabinet PROJECT

Transform a plain piece of wooden furniture into an eye-catching focal point. A lick of paint and an attractive design give it a personal and individual look. For a smart, contemporary effect, choose a pale, neutral colour for the background, and a darker neutral for the design. Add new drawer knobs to complement the piece.

YOU WILL NEED

- cabinet
- screwdriver
- medium-grade sandpaper
- cloth
- masking tape
- primer undercoat
- large and medium decorating brushes
- quick-dry satinwood or eggshell paint
- matt emulsion to match the satinwood
- tracing paper
- pencil
- artists' brushes in various sizes
- artists' acrylics or sample pots of paint
- quick-dry clear varnish

1 Remove the knobs and pull out the drawers. Lightly sand all surfaces, including the drawers, then wipe off any dust. Stick masking tape on the sides of the drawers to prevent marking them with paint.

2 Apply primer with a large decorating brush to the body and drawers, painting evenly in the direction of the wood grain. If the paint looks patchy, apply a second coat, allowing two hours' drying time between each coat.

3 Apply two coats of satinwood or eggshell paint to the body of the piece (but not the drawers), allowing six hours between coats. Paint one coat of matching matt emulsion on the drawer fronts.

4 Use a photocopier to enlarge or reduce the template on p.316 (or use your own design) so that it fits the size of the drawers. Transfer onto tracing paper then pencil over the reverse. Secure the tracing paper with masking tape to the drawer fronts with the design the right way round, then pencil over the lines to transfer the design onto the drawers and body. Remove the tracing paper.

5 Use artists' brushes to paint the design on the drawer fronts, not forgetting the stems that continue onto the body of the piece. Use artists' acrylics or sample pots of emulsion.

6 With a medium-size brush, apply two coats of varnish to the drawer fronts to protect them from damage. Use an artists' brush to varnish the painted stems. Fit the drawer knobs.

Tinwork TECHNIQUES

Tin plate is a versatile medium: it's strong, long lasting and can be decorated with a variety of finishes. Large, flat sheets of tin can be acquired by cutting open cooking oil cans and flattening out the metal. If you're painting metal, avoid water-based paints as they tend to flake off. If you prefer a natural finish, a coat of lacquer or Danish oil will protect the surface.

Choosing and cleaning the can

Choose a suitable can. Cans with a ring pull – and in particular sweetcorn cans – are ideal because they have a white lining that helps to reflect the light – perfect if you're **making lanterns** (see pp.290–91). Alternatively, you can use any tin can. Tear off the label and remove any blobs of glue with white spirit.

Packing the can

Before punching holes, you'll need to pack the can to prevent it from denting. Fill it with sand, press the sand down firmly with your fingers, then pour water on top until you can add no more. Place the can in the freezer overnight.

Punching holes in the can

1 Masonry nails are hardened, so they are ideal for punching holes in tin cans. Place the can on a sandbag. To make large holes, punch with a small nail first, then punch in the same place with one or more larger nails to enlarge the hole.

2 If the nail sticks in a hole, use mole grips and a twisting action to remove it.

Making wire handles

1 To add handles, punch a pair of holes opposite each other 1cm (³/₈in) below the top of the can. Once you've emptied the can (see below), cut a piece of coat hanger wire slightly longer than the final handle size.

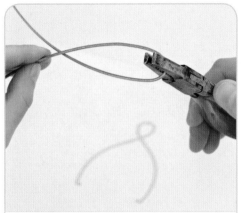

2 Use ring-bending pliers to make a tight curve in the middle of the length of coat hanger wire. Use your hands to bend the ends into gentle downward curves, using the template on p.315 as a reference.

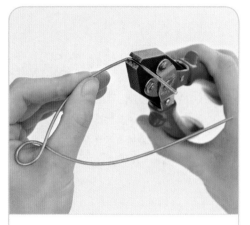

3 Bend the wire ends at right angles and trim these to about 3mm (¹/₈in) with a small pair of bolt cutters. Squeeze the handle to compress it slightly, then fit the ends into the holes in the can – the handle should hold in place by natural spring action.

Emptying the can

When you've finished punching holes, empty the can by placing it in a container and pouring on boiling water. Leave for 10 minutes to allow the ice to melt, then pour out the sand and water. Rinse and dry the can.

Painting the can

1 Fill the can with newspaper to protect the inside and lay sheets of newspaper over your work surface to protect it.

2 Spray the outside of the can evenly with the colour of your choice, then leave to dry for 24 hours. Alternatively, you can brush on an appropriate metal paint or apply a thin coat of oil-based paint.

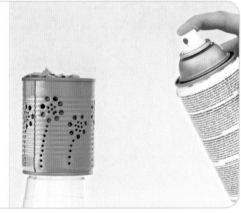

Tin can lanterns PROJECT

It's remarkable what you can make with rubbish! Here's an attractive way to recycle tin cans into simple lanterns. This project uses small cans, but if you use larger ones, you might find glass jars that fit inside them to protect the candles from the wind. If you don't have any wire coat hangers, 2mm (¹⁄₁₀in) diameter galvanized fencing wire is a good substitute.

YOU WILL NEED

- tin cans
- cloth
- white spirit
- sand
- paper and pencil
- sticky tape
- fabric bag filled with sand
- masonry nails
- hammer
- small mole grips
- wire coat hangers
- small bolt cutters
- ring-bending pliers
- newspaper
- spray paint

1 Remove the label and any blobs of glue from the can. Pack the can with sand, top up with water, and freeze overnight.

2 Draw your design on a piece of paper to fit the size of the can or photocopy one of the templates on pp.314-15. Tape in place. If you're drawing your own design, ensure that the gap between holes is at least as large as the diameter of each hole.

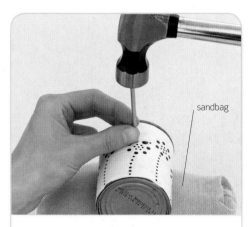

3 Place the can on the sandbag. Punch holes in the can. Place the can in the freezer for about 30 minutes after each 10 minutes of work to ensure the can remains solid. If you're making several lanterns, work on them in rotation.

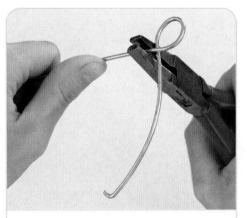

4 Once your design is complete, punch a pair of holes opposite each other 1cm (³⁄₈in) below the top of the can for fitting the handle. Remove the sand. Make a handle out of a 25cm (10in) length of wire, following **making wire handles** on p.289.

5 Fill the can with newspaper and spray-paint it evenly. Make sure you work in a well-ventilated area or outside. Once the can is dry, attach the handle.

Wirework TECHNIQUES

Wire comes in a myriad of types. If you are a beginner, copper wire is very good to work with as it is malleable. Many craft stores stock wire in a range of coloured finishes, and coat hanger wire is ideal when a strong structure is required. Household pliers can be used for wirework, but the serrated jaws can mark soft metals such as copper or aluminium.

Straightening a wire hanger

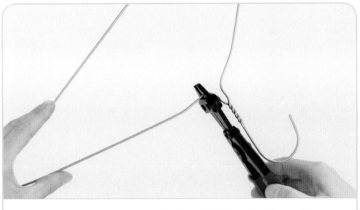

1 Cut the hanging loop and twisted section from the wire coat hanger using small bolt cutters.

2 Straighten the length you are left with – it may help to use mole grips to straighten the corners.

Straightening lengths of wire

Binding wire together

Shaping wire

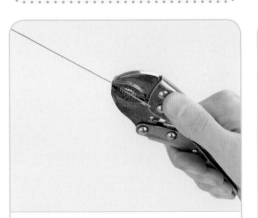

Pulling soft metal wire such as copper or aluminium to straighten it works well. Attach one end to a strong fixing point (a door handle for instance) and hold the other end in mole grips. Pull until the wire is straight.

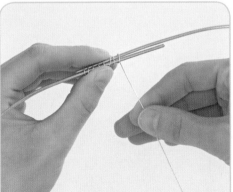

To bind two lengths of coat hanger wire together, overlap the ends by at least 5cm (2in) and wrap medium-gauge wire around the overlap until the ends are held firmly together.

Gentle curves can be bent by hand, but for tighter curves in heavy-gauge wire, use a pair of ring-bending pliers – their smooth jaws do not mark the wire. If you're following a template, have it nearby for reference.

Twisting wires

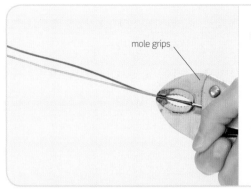

1 If you need a long length of twisted wire, bend a length of wire in half, attach it to a strong fixing point (a door handle works well) and lock the two ends in a pair of mole grips.

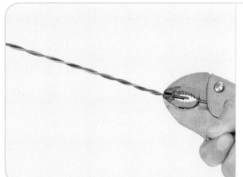

2 Pull the wire taut and turn the mole grips until you have an even twist along the whole length. Cut the wire to remove it from the fixing point.

Joining wires

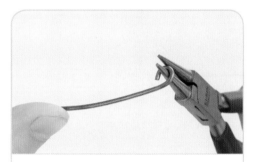

If you're working with wire and it breaks or runs out, attach another length by making a tiny loop in the end of each wire using round-nose pliers. Link the loops together, and press them closed with mole grips.

Wrapping wire

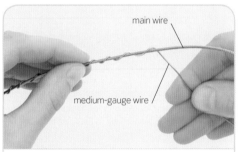

Cut a length of medium-gauge wire one and a half times the length of the main wire. Curl the end of the medium wire around one end of the main wire, then wrap it around the main wire. Maintain tension so it is wrapped tightly and keep the spacing even.

Making a circular base

Bend a length of wire to form a circle. Overlap the ends by 4cm (1½in). Wrap a short length of medium-gauge wire around the overlap to hold the structure together.

Making a hanging jar

1 Cut a length of medium-gauge wire about 55cm (21½in) long and wrap it once around the jar, just below the lip. Twist the end around the wire to secure.

2 Pull the free end of the wire over to form a handle, then thread it under the loop around the jar. Twist the end to secure it onto the ring. Trim any excess wire.

Making an "S" hook

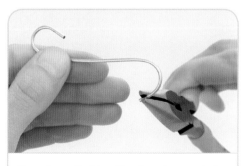

To make an S-shaped hook, curl one end of a 10cm (4in) piece of coat hanger wire using pliers to create a curve and the other end inwards to create a small loop.

Wire heart decoration PROJECT

This wire heart makes a perfect Mother's Day gift or a gift for a close friend. It's fashioned from a wire coat hanger and a handful of mother-of-pearl buttons. If you can't find any suitable buttons, use beads instead.

YOU WILL NEED

- wire coat hanger
- small bolt cutters
- mole grips
- ring-bending pliers
- fine 0.4mm silver-plated wire
- wire cutters
- superglue
- mother-of-pearl buttons

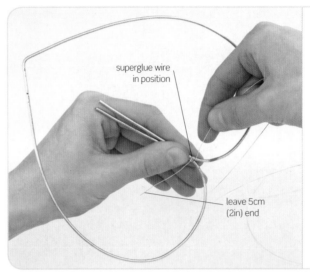

superglue wire in position

leave 5cm (2in) end

1 Cut the hanging loop off the hanger and straighten the hanger. Bend it following the template on p.317, using your hands and ring-bending pliers. Cut a 2.5m (8ft 2in) length of fine wire with wire cutters. At the top of the heart, where the curves meet, join the ends of the coat hanger wire with four of five turns of fine wire. Pull the wire tight, leaving a 5cm (2in) tail. Add a drop of superglue to fix the wire in position and leave to dry.

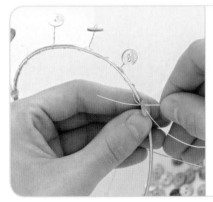

2 With the long end of the fine wire, make two loose turns along about 2cm (³⁄₄in) of the heart, then pull the end of the wire up through one hole in a button and back down through the other hole. Take care not to kink the wire as you pull it through.

rotate button

3 Hold the button 1.5cm (⁵⁄₈in) from the heart and grip the two pieces of fine wire where they meet the heart. Rotate the button to twist the wire. Make two more turns of the fine wire around the heart, add another button, then repeat all the way round.

4 After the last button, make a couple of turns of the fine wire to return to the starting point. Take the wire through three buttons, adding a turn around the heart each time, then twist the 5cm (2in) tail of wire to finish off. Trim the twisted wire to 5mm (¹⁄₄in) and fix in place with a drop of superglue.

5 Cut a 30cm (12in) length of fine wire, bend it in half, and twist, following **twisting wires** on p.293. Form it into a loop. Tuck one end of the loop under the point where the first button was attached to the heart and bend the ends back on themselves. Trim the excess wire and cut off the ends of the wire hanger with small bolt cutters.

6 Fix the other end of the loop to the last button attached to the heart, as in Step 5. Add a button at the mid-point of the loop by threading a short length of thin wire through the button and fix in place by twisting the ends at the back. Trim the ends. Adjust the buttons so that they are arranged neatly around the heart. Add a dab of superglue to the back of each button to fix it in place.

Wire chandelier PROJECT

It's amazing to think that a few wire coat hangers and glass jars can be transformed into something so spectacular! Wrapped wire hangers form a stable structure for this chandelier, while the curled ends add a touch of elegance. Save small glass yoghurt or baby food jars and fill them with tea lights. Hang the chandelier above a dining table to create a romantic ambience.

YOU WILL NEED

- 10 wire coat hangers
- small bolt cutters
- mole grips
- medium-gauge wire
- wire cutters
- long-nose pliers
- 8 small glass yoghurt or baby food jars with a lip
- 8 tea lights
- wire or ribbon

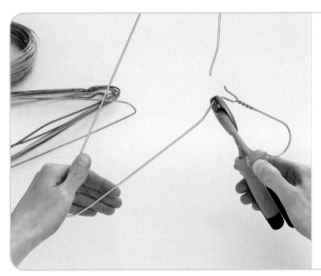

1 Cut off the hanging loops and straighten all 10 hangers, following **straightening a wire hanger** on p.292. Cut lengths of medium-gauge wire one and a half times longer than the length of the straightened hangers. Wrap this wire evenly around nine of the hanger wires. These will be used to construct the frame of the chandelier, while the plain wire will be cut into lengths and used to hang the jars.

2 Use one of the wrapped wires to make a circle 27.5cm (11in) in diameter. This is the top tier. Overlap the ends of the wire and wrap a short length of wire around the overlap to secure.

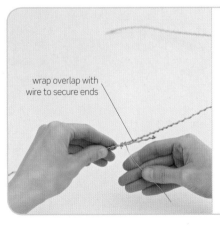

wrap overlap with wire to secure ends

3 Make the bottom tier by joining two lengths of wrapped wire together to make one long length, overlapping the ends by 12.5cm (5in). Wrap the overlap with a short length of wire. Bend the wire into a circle 36cm (14in) in diameter and secure the ends.

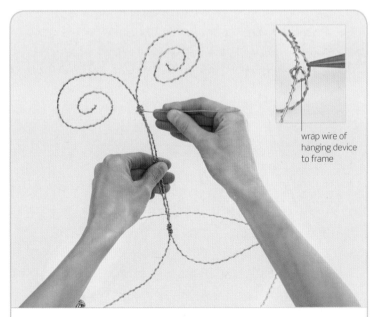

wrap wire of hanging device to frame

4 To make the hanging device, shape the ends of two lengths of wrapped wire into decorative curls, as shown. Wrap the other ends at opposite sides of the top tier using long-nose pliers. Cover the joins where they meet the tier by wrapping with wire. Wrap a short length of wire just below the two curls and again a little further down to keep the two wrapped wires together.

5 To attach the pillars that link the tiers, curl a wrapped wire around the top tier using long-nose pliers, then wrap the other end around the bottom tier, 30cm (12in) along its length. Shape the end of the wire to create a decorative curl. Wire-wrap the joins on both tiers and repeat to make the three other pillars, spacing them out evenly.

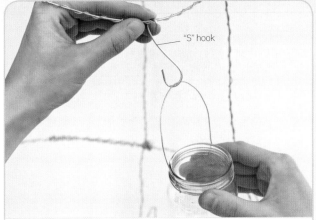

"S" hook

6 Make eight hanging jars, following **making a hanging jar** on p.293. Suspend the jars from "S" hooks made from 10cm (4in) lengths of the remaining non-wrapped wire. Drop a tea light in each jar and hang four jars on each tier. Finally, tie a wire or ribbon through the central stem at the top of the chandelier to hang it.

The authors

A talented and dedicated team of crafters, all experts in their field, contributed towards the making of this book. If you like what you see, visit the websites or subscribe to the blogs listed here to discover more inspirational projects for your home.

Michael Ball
info@btnw.co.uk

| film and leadwork | tinwork | wirework |

Momtaz Begum-Hossain
www.thecraftcafe.co.uk / contact@momtazbh.co.uk

| fabric marbling | fabric painting | nature crafts | wirework |

Jane Cameron
www.janecameron.co.uk / jane@janecameron.co.uk

| silk painting | batik | screen printing |

Angie Corbet
www.vintagecraftstuff.co.uk / angie@vintagecraftstuff.co.uk

| papermaking | paper marbling |

Sarah Ditchfield
www.candlebynight.co.uk / contact@candlebynight.co.uk

| dipped taper candles | three-layer candle | rolled candles |

Susan Flockhart
http://susiefhandmade.blogspot.com / susan@susanflockhart.com

| botanical slab | moulded rose soaps | clear heart soap |

Fiona Goble
fkgoble@btinternet.com

| silkscreening | stencilling | appliqué | bead embroidery |

Tessa Hunkin
tessahunkin@blueyonder.co.uk

| mosaics (direct) | mosaics (indirect) |

Helen Johannessen
www.yoyoceramics.co.uk / helen@yoyoceramics.co.uk

| painting china | painting tiles |

Susie Johns

www.susieatthecircus.typepad.com / susiejohns@colourful.co.uk

dip-dyeing

tie-dyeing

block printing

papier-mâché

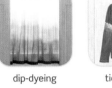

scrapbooking

lino printing

paper decorations

découpage

quilling

card-making

box-making

Annemarie O'Sullivan

www.annemarieosullivan.co.uk

basketry

Cheryl Owen

cherylowencrafts@aol.com

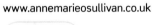

beading

silver wirework

cold enamelling

loom weaving

polymer clay

air-dry clay

metal clay

painting glass

Wendy Shorter

www.wendyshorterinteriors.co.uk / wendy@wendyshorterinteriors.co.uk

upholstery

Debbie Siniska

www.debbiesiniska.co.uk / info@debbiesiniska.co.uk

wet felting

needle felting

rag rugging

Denise Stirrup

www.realpressedflowers.co.uk / www.pressedflowerguild.org.uk

pressed flower
work

Anne Taylor

www.anne-taylor.co.uk / contact @anne-taylor.co.uk

furniture painting

Dorothy Wood

www.dorothywood.co.uk / info@dorothywood.co.uk

patchwork

ribbon weaving

paper punching

recycling

Useful resources

Basketry
Musgrove Willows (selection of basket-making willow)
www.musgrovewillows.co.uk
+44 (0)1278 691105

Somerset Willow Growers Ltd (willow, bamboo, cane, rattan, and seagrass)
www.willowgrowers.co.uk
+44 (0)1278 691540

Batik
Candle-makers Supplies (batik and silk painting materials, and candle-making supplies and moulds)
www.candlemakers.co.uk
+44 (0)20 7602 4031

Handprinted (textile decoration supplies, including dyes, brushes, and wax)
www.handprinted.co.uk
+44 (0)1243 697606

Textile Techniques (wax, waxpots, batik fabrics, and dyes)
www.textiletechniques.co.uk
+44 (0)1588 638712

Candle-making
The Norfolk Candle Company (candle-making materials and candle accessories)
www.norfolkcandleco.co.uk
+44 (0)1502 677313

Whicksnwhacks (fragrance oils, wicks, thermometers, wax, and dyes)
www.whicksnwhacks.com
+44 (0)7512 686102

Felting
Blooming Felt (needle and wet felting supplies, felting needles, and wool tops)
www.bloomingfelt.co.uk
+44 (0)1245 471690

The Knit Shop (felting kits and accessories, and wool tops)
www.knitshop.co.uk
+44 (0)20 8144 4523

World of Wool (natural and dyed wool tops, and specialty fibres)
www.worldofwool.co.uk
+44 (0)1484 846878

General craft supplies
Baker Ross (papercrafts, beading, and felt supplies)
www.bakerross.co.uk
+44 (0)844 576 8933

Hobbycraft (materials for more than 250 different arts and crafts activities)
www.hobbycraft.co.uk
+44 (0)845 051 6599

Jewellery-making
The Bead Shop (jewellery findings, stringing materials, tools, and pendants)
www.the-beadshop.co.uk
+44 (0)161 2744040

Sanctuary Beads (beads, jewellery findings, needles, and polymer clay)
www.sanctuarybeads.co.uk
+44 (0)1493 601213

Spoilt Rotten (beads, jewellery-making tools and supplies)
www.spoiltrottenbeads.co.uk
+44 (0)1353 749853

Mosaics
Hobby Island (ceramic and glass mosaic tiles, kits, tools, glues, and grouts)
www.hobby-island.co.uk
+44 (0)843 2896764

Mosaic Supplies Ltd (ceramic and glass mosaic tiles, millefiori, smalti, and tools)
www.mosaicsupplies.co.uk
+44 (0)1299 828374

Mosaic Workshop (ceramic, glass, and mirror mosaic tiles, smalti, adhesives and grouts, frames, and tools)
www.mosaic-workshop.co.uk
+44 (0)20 8670 4466

Papercrafts
Grafton Crafts (papercraft materials, including punches, dies, stencils, and stamps)
www.graftoncrafts.co.uk
+44 (0)1480 862850

Mad About Cards (quilling strips, paper punches, and scrapbooking materials)
www.madaboutcards.com

RU Craft (découpage papers, paper punches, rubber stamps,
and quilling materials)
www.rucraft.co.uk
+44 (0)844 880 5852

Patchwork
The Cotton Patch (patchwork fabrics, waddings, haberdashery, and notions)
www.cottonpatch.co.uk
+44 (0)121 702 2840

Patchwork Direct (patchwork fabrics, quilting accessories, and haberdashery)
www.patchworkdirect.com
+44 (0)1629 734100

Scrapbooking
Craft Superstore (scrapbooking, card-making, and papercraft supplies)
www.craftsuperstore.co.uk
+44 (0)845 409 7595

Memory Keepsakes (scrapbook albums and refills, and general
papercraft supplies)
www.memorykeepsakes.co.uk
+44 (0)1630 638342

Soap-making
Just a Soap (fragrance oils, melt-and-pour soap bases, moulds, and also
candle-making supplies)
www.justasoap.co.uk
+44 (0)1842 855975

The Green Range (soap ingredients, fragrance oils, soap and candle kits,
and also candle-making supplies)
www.thegreenrange.co.uk
+44 (0)1908 821235

The Soap Kitchen (soap ingredients, kits, fragrance oils, and also
candle-making supplies)
www.thesoapkitchen.co.uk
+44 (0)1805 622944

Upholstery
J A Milton (upholstery supplies, including tacks, barrier cloth, and tools)
http://jamiltonupholstery.co.uk
+44 (0)1691 624023

Upholstery Warehouse (nails, webbing, foam, trimmings, fillings, and tools)
www.upholsterywarehouse.co.uk
+44 (0)1903 201081

ACKNOWLEDGEMENTS

Dorling Kindersley would like to thank Fiona Corbridge for her invaluable input in the early stages of development, Ira Sharma and Era Chawla for design assistance, Jane Ewart for photography art direction, Ruth Jenkinson for photography, Carly Churchill for hand-modelling and photographic assistance, Meryl Davies for photographic assistance, Hilary Mandleberg for sense-checking, Katie Hardwicke for proofreading, and Anna Bennett for indexing.

PICTURE CREDITS

Running head banner on pp.88–145: Orhan Çam, Dreamstime (dreamstime_xxl_13293911)

Templates

Shoe bag (pp.32-33)

302

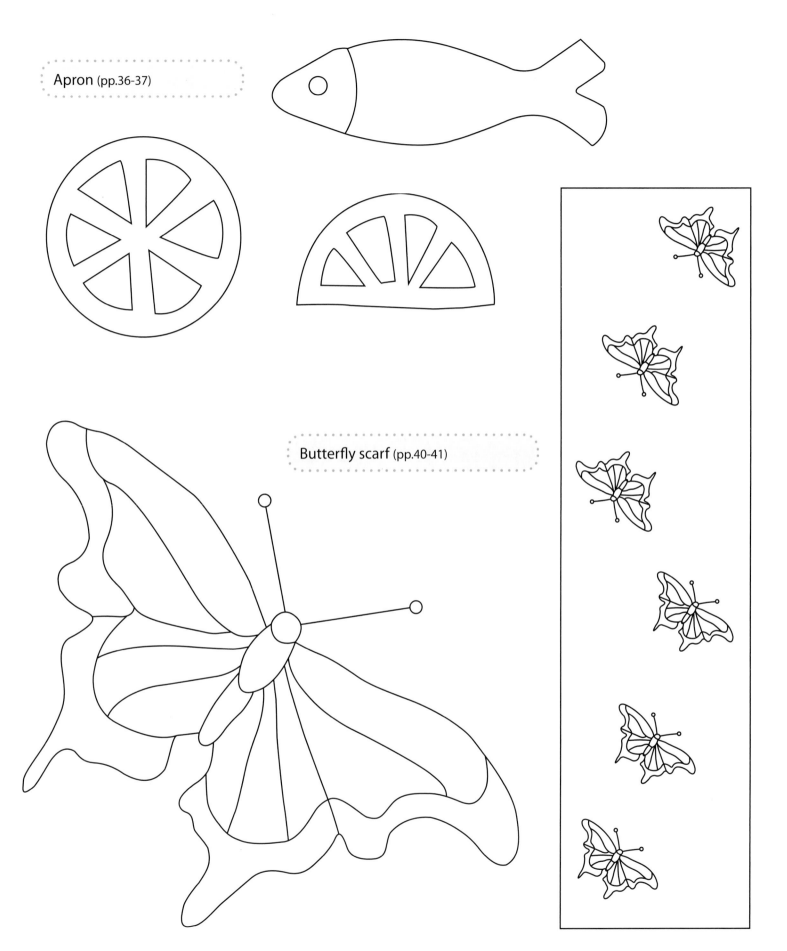

Apron (pp.36-37)

Butterfly scarf (pp.40-41)

Sarong (pp.44-45)

Tea towel (pp.48-49)

Cushion cover (pp.52-53)

Enlarge by 110% on a photocopier

305

Throw (pp.60-61)

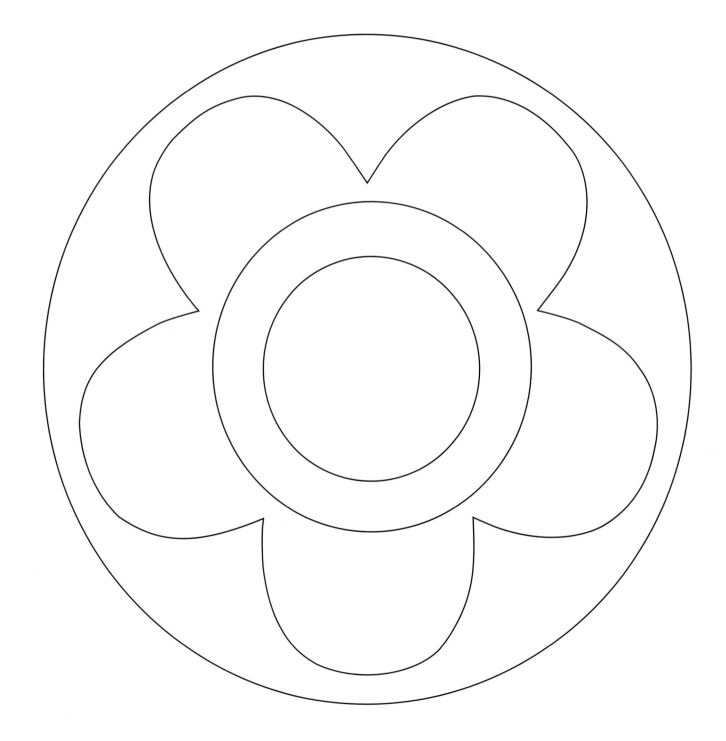

Throw (pp.60-61)

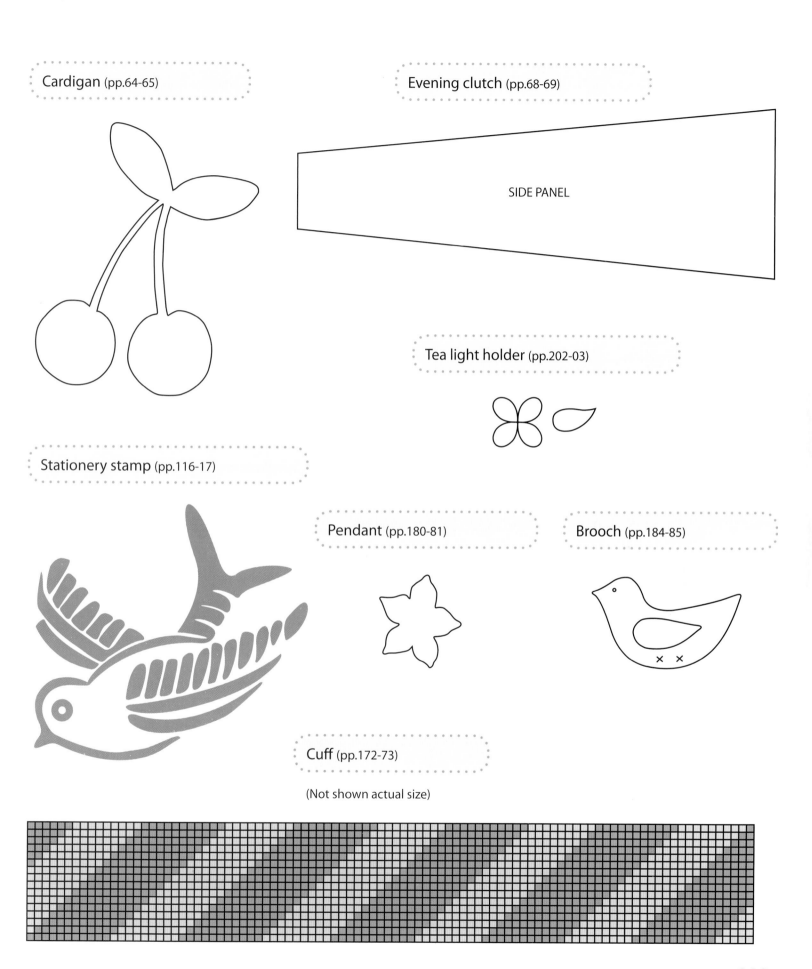

Cardigan (pp.64-65)

Evening clutch (pp.68-69)

SIDE PANEL

Tea light holder (pp.202-03)

Stationery stamp (pp.116-17)

Pendant (pp.180-81)

Brooch (pp.184-85)

Cuff (pp.172-73)

(Not shown actual size)

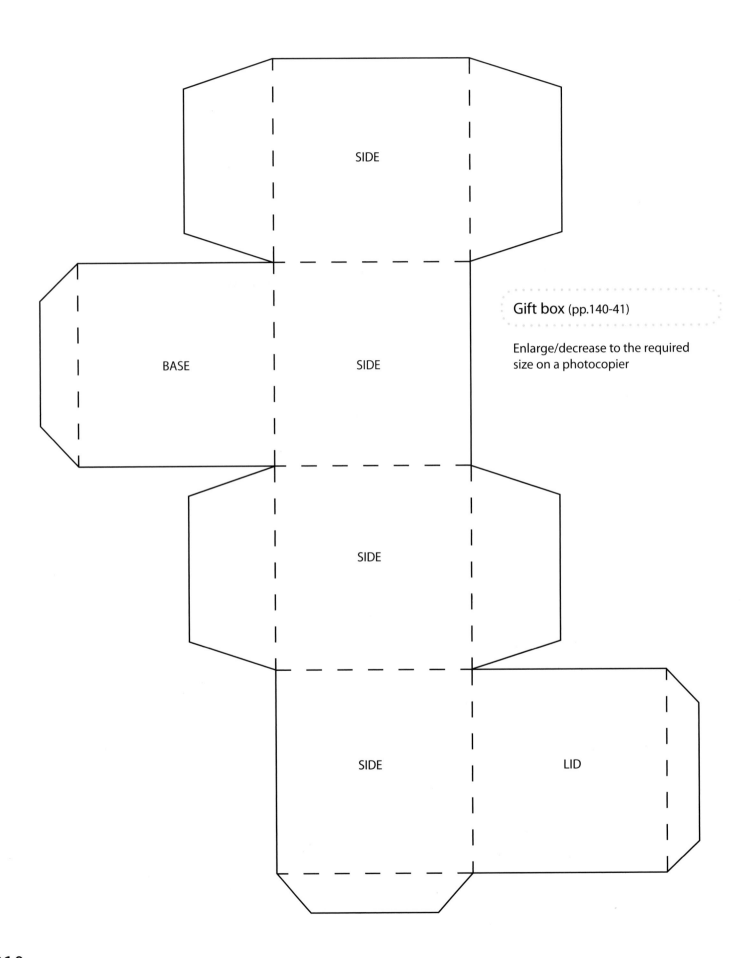

SIDE

BASE

SIDE

Gift box (pp.140-41)

Enlarge/decrease to the required
size on a photocopier

SIDE

SIDE

LID

Postcard (pp.144-45)

Coasters (pp.210-11)

Trivet (pp.218-19)

Enlarge by 150% on a photocopier

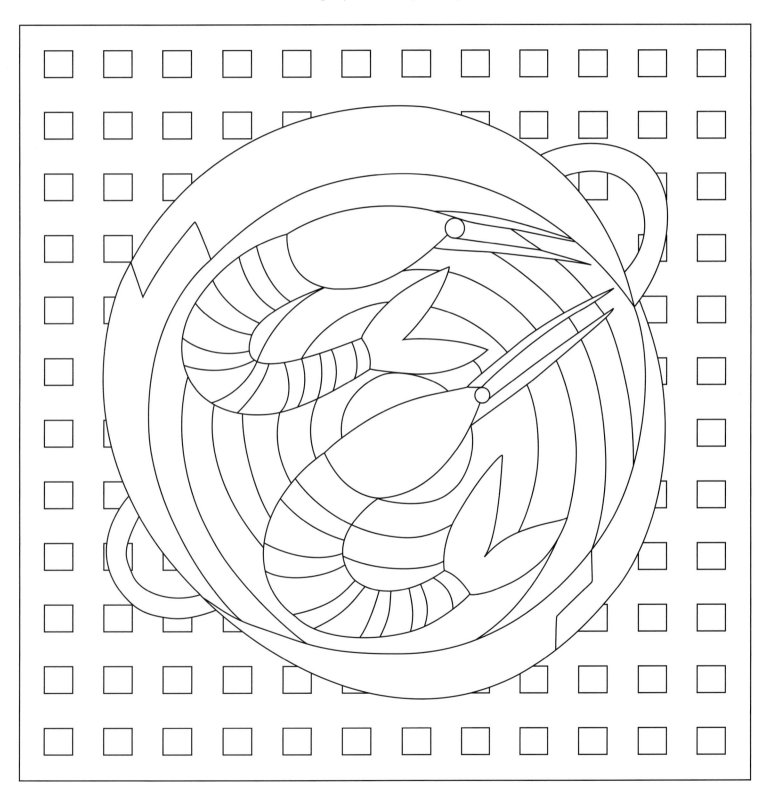

Tin can lanterns (pp.290-91)

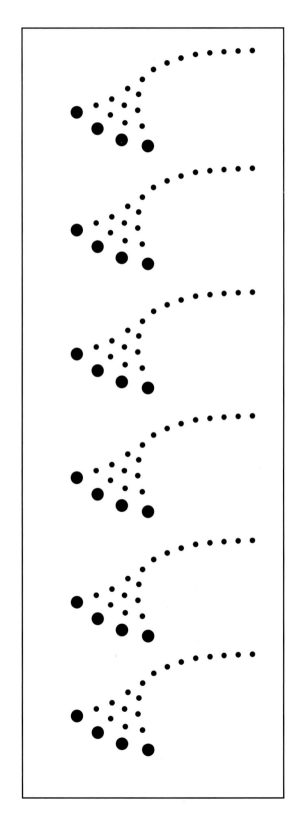

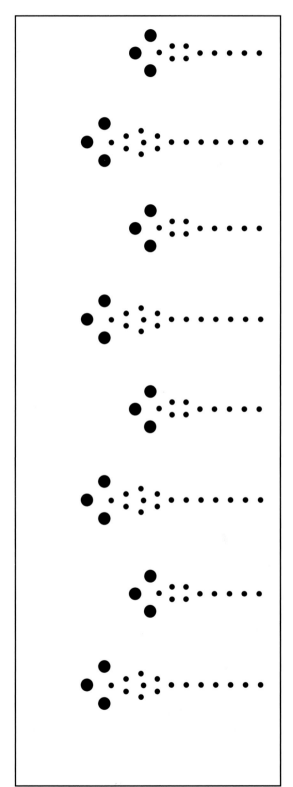

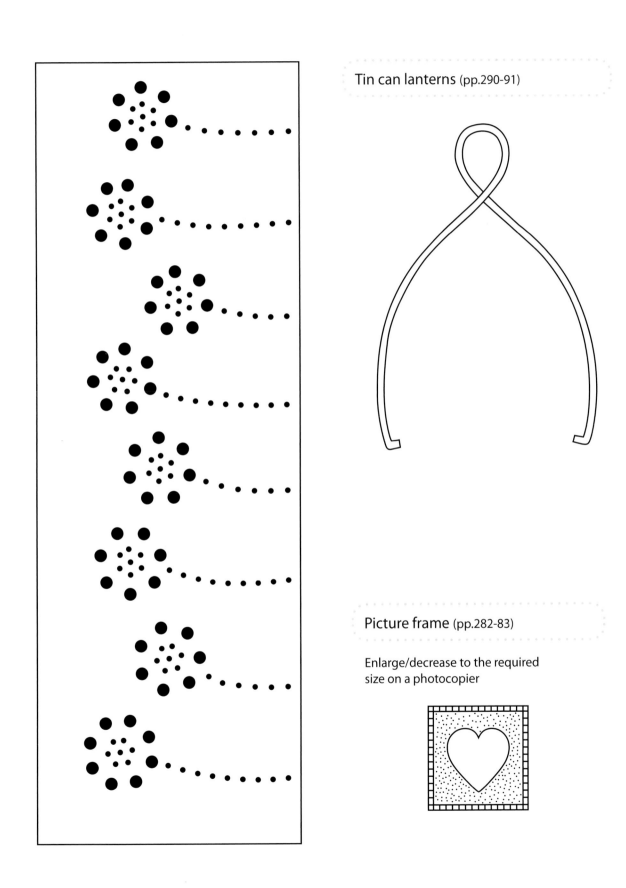

Tin can lanterns (pp.290-91)

Picture frame (pp.282-83)

Enlarge/decrease to the required
size on a photocopier

Bedside cabinet (pp.286-87)

Enlarge/decrease to the required
size on a photocopier

Wire heart decoration (pp.294-95)

Index